TUGS, TOWBOATS
AND TOWING

Tug *Holland* of The Baker-Whiteley Towing Co., Baltimore, docking U.S. Lines Company's S.S. *American Challenger* —maiden voyage, August 23, 1962.

TUGS, TOWBOATS AND TOWING

By

EDWARD M. BRADY

CORNELL MARITIME PRESS, INC.

CAMBRIDGE   MARYLAND

1967

Library of Congress Catalog Card Number: 67–17537

Manufactured in the United States of America

CONTENTS

ACKNOWLEDGMENTS

Preparation of a work of this nature requires some assistance from many persons and organizations. I should like to express appreciation for photographs and other material provided by the following: American Chain & Cable Co.; American Manufacturing Co.; Bay-Houston Towing Co.; Curtis Bay Towing Co.; Dravo Corp.; Baker-Whiteley Towing Co.; Federal Barge Line; Goodyear Tire & Rubber Co.; Harbor Towing Corp.; L. Smit & Co., Sleepindeinst, Holland; Loveridge, Ltd., U.K.; Merritt-Chapman & Scott Corp.; Mississippi Valley Barge Line Co.; Moran Towing & Transportation Co., Inc.; Plymouth Cordage Co.; Port of London Authority; United Rope Co., Ltd., Holland; Wall Rope Co.; The United States Coast Guard and The United States Navy.

The photographs in Figs. 3, 5, 7, 8, 16, 41, 42, 43, 62, 88, 103, 104, 120, 127 and 143 are from the collection of Mr. John S. Blank III.

Of the many individuals the following have been singled out for the number and value of their opinions expressed over a period of years (opinions, it might be added, that do not necessarily endorse those of the author): Mr. Russell Brierly, Marine Surveyor, Houston, Texas; Mr. Johan J. Schoo, Marine Surveyor, Willemstad, Curacao, N.A.; Mr. John R. Lindgren, President, United States Salvage Association, Inc.; Mr. Joseph K. Tynan, Principal Surveyor, Gulf Coast U.S.A., United States Salvage Association, Inc.

Sincere thanks to Mr. Frank Braynard of Moran Towing & Transportation Co., Inc., for providing the splendid photographs of Mr. Jeff Blinn, Chief Photographer of *Towline*, the official magazine of the same company.

Much of the research was conducted in the Engineering Societies Library and in the New York Public Library whose staff relieved a considerable burden by extending to me the use of Room 315-S and the facilities of the Wertheimer Study.

E.M.B.

PREFACE

A major problem in compiling a book on this subject is limiting the enormous scope of the related fields and confining the contents to pertinent information concerning practical towing. A work of this nature has a tendency to branch out in many directions because of the complexity of the subject. A definitive treatment of the material covered would probably take a score or more years and the result possibly would sell better by the pound than by the word. Obviously, there is need for compromise; therefore, this work is directed to operating personnel in the towing trade. Sophisticated details of design and development have been avoided in the main and only those design features that affect tug and towboat maneuverability have been touched upon with the thought in mind to acquaint operating personnel with some of the more important aspects affecting maneuverability rather than to presume to inform or instruct naval architects and marine engineers.

Another important point needs clarification. Except for safety practices there are few static rules applicable to all vessels in the towing trade. Some common practices are described and general guidelines established, but they are neither complete nor definitive. Rather, they should be considered composites to which experienced towboatmen and surveyors may apply any variables that would affect changes in the total tow hook-up.

There is an infinite variety of tow hook-ups, as much affected by locale as local "know-how." Obviously, to explain all towing methods employed by all tugs would result in an unwieldy, voluminous book that would tend to confuse the reader and defeat the purpose of a general reference manual.

Edward M. Brady

TUGS, TOWBOATS

AND TOWING

CHAPTER I

TYPES OF TUGS AND TOWBOATS

There are a multiplicity of needs in marine transportation for an auxiliary propulsion force that can be applied in a variety of ways. Tugs and towboats were evolved to fill those needs.

Large ships require the assistance of tugs for docking operations, maneuvering in confined waters and narrow channels, and escorting to clear water.

Barges, cranes, "A" frames, derricks, lighters, tank barges, railroad floats and diverse other floating equipment require tugs to tow them on innumerable occasions for countless reasons.

The economic lifeblood of a nation is enriched by an increase in the marine traffic that courses through its arterial waterway systems, propelled by tugs and towboats. Figure 1 illustrates this point. Here is a scene of some of New York's harbor traffic in the Upper Bay and North River, a segment of the total local waterborne transportation picture during any given period of time. To get some idea of the volume of national waterborne traffic, the marine traffic of all continental American ports, lakes, rivers, and coastal, intracoastal and intercoastal waterway systems must be added to this picture; a concept of staggering proportion to the imagination.

The economic health of a nation depends to a great extent on the continuous flow of material products carried through its physical geography by tugs and barges in the circulatory system of its rivers, canals and waterways.

Ocean towing may involve the transport of a vital nonself-propelled piece of floating equipment from one geographical point to another on the surface of the globe. In addition, mining equipment, drill rigs, dredges, barges, floating towers, "dead" ships, scrap hulls, damaged marine equipment—in fact, any structure that can float—may be towed on an ocean.

From all the foregoing we can get some idea of the magnitude of the problems and scope of the specialization necessary to effect tows of all types.

1

Because all tows are not alike, some attempt will be made to classify the principal types of tows in this chapter and to describe them in greater detail later on.

One rather simple classification system is worthy of mention:

1. Small harbor and utility tugs—approximately 40′–65′ in length.
2. Large harbor and coastwise tugs—70′–120′ in length.
3. Ocean-going and salvage tugs—over 125′ in length (note 1).

In this book tugs are separated into further categories to include Western Rivers towboat and other special purpose tugs.

Fig. 1. New York Harbor traffic. Upper Bay at top right; North River extends from bottom center diagonally toward Upper Bay; East River runs from the left under the Manhattan and Brooklyn Bridges toward Governor's Island. Moran

HARBOR AND DOCKING TUGS

Harbor and docking tugs are classed together here because in a harbor trade the docking and undocking of large ocean-going ships is no small part of the potential revenue of any tug. At various times during slack periods when the need for docking tugs is curtailed as a result of sporadic, intermittent ship sailing schedules, the tug may be employed in other harbor work and made available to perform an extensive range of miscellaneous duties at a moment's notice. Here we see the need not only for power, but also for speed where, in a harbor, the ability of a tug to arrive quickly on the scene of a job may mean the difference between activity and lay-up.

The general harbor tug employed in ship handling may be seen in Fig. 2. A tug of this type is usually limited to about 100 feet in length or less, simply to make it accessible to confined areas and to facilitate maneuvering in tight spots and narrow channels.

Truly, it may be said that the harbor tug is a multi-purpose vessel, and it must be in order to provide service in ship handling, to tow

Fig. 2. The *Dana L. Moran* easily towing the *Christian Radick* safely through crowded New York Harbor. The sail ship will dock on schedule regardless of adverse wind, tide or current. Moran

barges and railroad car floats on bays and sounds, for marine construction assistance and small salvage work.

Probably the chief areas for improvement in harbor tug design, to be discussed in Chapter II, lie in the investigation of hydroconic hull designs and in controllable pitch propellers.

One of the earliest functions of the New York harbor tug (and for other harbors' tugs, as well) and a primary reason for its beginning was the practice of towing into and out of harbor and assisting in berthing the numerous sailing ships of earlier days. This function is adequately illustrated in a later day scene depicted in Fig. 2.

From that early practice the tug found other similar uses upon the introduction of slow ponderous steam vessels. And while these vessels were capable of entering and leaving a harbor unassisted without waiting for tides, still they proved cumbersome and unmanageable during docking operations.

As vessels improved in maneuverability and their power increased, the assist rendered by tugs in berthing (docking and undocking) operations was not outmoded, because the size and tonnage of most vessels also increased.

The earlier tugs were steam-engine powered and, except for a few remaining similar to the one shown in Fig. 3, most tugs built today are diesel-engine driven.

American harbor tugs are designed for pushing, butting or towing abreast and, therefore, the earlier tugs had long deckhouses as shown in Fig. 3, but houses of later tugs have been shortened considerably in order to improve maneuverability while towing.

The average American harbor tug is distinctive in its proportionately long deckhouse that covers approximately two-thirds of the main deck. The house is rounded forward for streamlining and square to allow for a larger deck working area at the stern. The mean

Fig. 3. The steam tug *John L. Sullivan* in 1949, off the Battery on the Hudson River.

height of the deckhouse above normal waterline is approximately eight or nine feet. A pilothouse, rounded forward for greater visibility and square at the rear, rests atop the forward end of the deckhouse. The stack is located amidship on the centerline directly above the machinery space. Lifeboats in chocks are along the deck edge and adjacent the stack. Exposed steering and control stations are at the after end of the boat deck and in the bridge wings for improved visibility and control through outside conning of the tug.

The usual practice for American harbor tugs is to tow tied up alongside as illustrated in Fig. 4, which is not generally the case in Great Britain and Europe.

Harbor and docking tugs are rarely over 120 feet in length with engines that, until recently, seldom developed over 800 brake horsepower. The trend, however, is to build tugs of greater brake horse-power to facilitate handling large ocean-going passenger ships, super-tankers and heavy sea tows using fewer tugs in order to reduce costs.

During recent times New York harbor has seen the introduction of 3600 hp giants for docking purposes as well as for heavy ocean towing.

The general harbor tug usually operates with three crews of five men each on a 24-hour-day basis, seven days a week. One crew is ashore while two crews are aboard at all times.

Small harbor tugs are manned by a single day crew and they usually tie up at night.

Fig. 4. A general harbor and docking tug assisting the S/T *National Defender* to berth. Note the fenders and recessed superstructure to facilitate operating under the flair of the bow. Bay-Houston

A docking tug usually works one crew and a cook on a day shift. The tug ties up at night and all hands go home. Some tugs work two crews for a 24-hour operation.

RIVER TOWBOATS

A major study in itself in the waterborne transportation field is the river towboat. Note: Do not call a riverman's towboat a tugboat even though it neither tows nor tugs, but rather, it pushes. And although it pushes, it still is a towboat . . . you figure that one!

Towboats operate on rivers from New Orleans, La., to Lockport, Ill., St. Paul, Minn., and Pittsburgh, Pa. Other towboats of special design work into Chicago and Calumet (special design with removable or retractable pilothouses to enable passage under low bridges).

Among marine people the riverboatman seems to be a specially skilled breed, as much at home with his towboat in midstream as he is bow onto a shallow bank. More of a rugged country boy than a seaman, he often thinks of the river with its numerous small river towns and "honky-tonks" more in the nature of a marine highway than as a body of navigable water. Special tribute is his for making seem easy what to an offshore seaman usually is difficult work . . . river navigation.

There are probably over 2,000 towboats of various sizes in use on the Mississippi River alone. When we take into consideration the

Fig. 5.   The coal tug, *Steel City*, about to pick up several barges of coal on the Monongahela River a few hundred yards below the Point Bridge, Pittsburgh, Pa., on August 3, 1951. R. M. Cady

number of other waterways both large and small in the inland river systems, the job of estimating the number of towboats in operation becomes a problem as elusive to solution as it is to the imagination.

The appearance of towboats, sometimes rather more correctly referred to as pushboats (note 2), presents a picture of fairly basic pattern: a squared-off house on a squared flush deck with vertical push-knees forward on a shaped bow.

The screw-propelled river boat inherited its general topside squat design from the earlier extinct paddle-wheel towboat. An amazing story in itself concerns the rapid disappearance of the stern paddle-wheel towboat, illustrated in Fig. 5, from a position of prominence on the river scene until World War II. With the olden paddle-wheel towboats went the unlamented steam engine propulsion. Steam propulsion, although in use for years, did not prove economical or safe on the rivers. Boiler explosions were not uncommon occurrences.

Tugs and barges are the ideal set-up for river trade for the following reasons:

1. They are of shallow draft to easily navigate the upper reaches of the Mississippi, Missouri, Ohio and Columbia Rivers.

2. They are adaptable to changing needs.

3. There is a minimum delay in the operation of the towing plant in that the tug, unlike a ship, need not wait until cargo is discharged before engaging in another job.

The river tug is usually between 75 and 100 feet in length except for giants in excess of 200 feet operating on the Ohio and Mississippi Rivers. Figure 6 shows a typical large river towboat.

Fig. 6. Towboat giant of the Mississippi Valley Barge Line Co. river fleet is the *W. S. Rhea*, a 176-foot twin-screw towboat powered by two 16-cylinder diesel engines having a total of 3,200 horsepower. It was built by Dravo. Miss. Barge

As an illustration of the size of giant river tows, consider the following. The M.V. *United States* develops 8,500 hp on four (4) propellers, can push 40 barges loaded with 40,000 tons, which is four times a normal freighter capacity, or three times the size of a normal tow 15 years ago; or it equals ten freight trains of 100 cars each. Fitted with four steering rudders and six flanking rudders, the helm can be put hard over in 14 seconds while towing. The towboat was built by St. Louis Shipbuilding & Steel Company for Federal Barge Lines, Inc., at a cost of $1,700,000 (note 3) to serve the lower Mississippi between St. Louis and New Orleans.

CANAL TUGS

As the name implies, a canal tug operates on canals of inland waterway and intracoastal systems and is designed to pass under the innumerable low bridges built over most waterways.

Figure 7 illustrates the silhouettes presented by typical canal tugs. Note their low appearance. Recently specially designed tugs have been put into service that feature telescoping pilothouses, some hydraulically controlled and automatically operated, that can be lowered in a matter of seconds. Some tugs have been fitted with hydraulic telescoping radar masts, counterweighted masts and similar devices installed to speed up and facilitate passage under bridges.

Ballasting is another method in common use to enable tugs to pass easily beneath low bridges. Fore and aft peak ballast tanks are installed that can be readily ballasted in order to increase draft during high water conditions, thereby reducing the head clearance of a tug.

Erie Barge Canal Tugs. Bridges along the Erie Barge Canal require a 15′ 6″ minimum clearance; consequently all tugs designed for

Fig. 7. Canal tugs cluster at the river wall above Albany's deepwater port. Note the low silhouette necessary so that the tugs can pass under fixed bridges of 18-foot clearance on New York State canals. Maritime Information Co.

operating on the Erie Canal have a low silhouette. In the obsolete older wood-hulled steam tugs, the smokestack usually was hinged to enable lowering quickly for passage under bridges. The newer diesel tugs of steel or wood have low stacks, hence they can pass under bridges easily.

Because of freezing weather the trade is restricted to the period from April 15 through December 15; at other times the tugs may operate in open harbor areas if equipped for winter weather.

A tug and tow of five 110-foot canal barges can lock through the New York State Canal locks at one time and a passage takes from 5 to 15 days.

RAILROAD TUGS

The railroad tug tows car floats that transport railroad freight cars. The railroads own and operate much of the harbor craft, i.e., tugs, barges, ferries, excursion steamers, derricks and workboats. Besides local towing around the harbor, railroad tugs tow empty car floats up the Hudson River to Albany and Troy and return with loaded railroad cars.

Because a railroad tug must maintain tight schedules with no time losses, dependability is the principal consideration in its design— a factor that brought into early use diesel engines for propulsive power. Maneuverability, power and visibility are the next most important factors in design.

A high pilothouse is a must for visibility. Railroad car floats when loaded present a considerable interference to visibility because of

Fig. 8.   The Reading Lines railroad tug *Tamaqua* under full power. Note long deckhouse, flush deck and watertight doors on the long main deckhouse.
MacGramlich

the height of trains on a loaded float and the usual position of the tug while towing.

Improved maneuverability has been gained by the use of a semi-balanced rudder that provides good all-around steering control.

The crew work in three daily shifts and live ashore, thereby eliminating the need for crew quarters. A tug can see a lot of service with three crews working around the clock, hence the need for dependability—a most important factor.

Radar should be installed to enable the tug to operate in all conditions of weather in order to maintain schedules. A typical railroad tug is shown in Fig. 8.

There are approximately 19 freight cars on an average car float. When loaded the car float and trains present a large sail area to the force of any winds which in turn requires great power in order to control the tow. In many instances, the tug takes up a tow position aft between two floats that weigh up to 2,000 tons. Hence, the need for special highly maneuverable tugs of great power.

The trend here is toward controllable pitch propellers because of two factors important to the trade; first, the engine need not be reversed, consequently maintenance costs are reduced and second, the propeller pitch and engine's horsepower may be automatically controlled in order to obtain maximum performance under any condition of engine loading.

COASTAL TUGS

A tug in the coastwise trade is generally heavier than a harbor tug, has greater horsepower, larger all-around dimensions and increased fuel capacity.

A capstan or towing engine is installed to handle heavy tow hawsers.

In appearance the tug usually has two masts that support navigation equipment, radio, radar and radio direction finder. The house contains sleeping quarters for a crew and it is fitted with watertight doors and ports.

The use of tugs and barges is one of the cheapest methods of transporting coal, lumber, ore, oil and bulk cargoes in the river and coastal trades. The tug can be utilized in both directions by disconnecting and leaving the barge upon delivery and connecting up to another tow for the return trip, thereby keeping the tug in constant and continuous use.

Coastwise tugs are engaged in a variety of trades in addition to those above listed, including railroad freight car float transport and chemical shipment. An unusual coastal tow is illustrated in Fig. 9.

Coal. Vast quantities of coal are moved from Norfolk and Baltimore to New York and Boston in three and four barge tows. The tugs tow barges in ballast on the return leg of the trip.

Lumber. In the past coastwise barge towing was usually restricted to the East and Gulf Coasts. Recently, however, huge lumber barges fitted with self-unloading cranes have been put into service on the West Coast. The West Coast lumber trade extending from Columbia River and Puget Sound to Alaska and San Diego was carried on in earlier days by *steam schooners*.

Ore. The earlier tugs and barges formerly in operation on the Great Lakes have been replaced by the Great Lakes bulk freighter developed to transport great quantities of coal and ores quickly and efficiently. Ice conditions tend to restrict the trade during winter months so that the bulk of ores are moved during more favorable seasons.

Railroad Car Floats. Railroad car floats are towed between Cape Charles and Norfolk, Va., on the East Coast and from the mainland to Vancouver Island on the West Coast. The tug is generally 100'–115' in length utilizing approximately 750–900 hp.

Oil. Oil is transported by barge to coastal areas not easily accessible by other means; i.e., rail, truck, pipeline.

Chemicals. There are many barges towed in the coastwise trade that transport a variety of chemicals.

AMERICAN OCEAN TUGS

The ocean tug is one of the largest towing plants afloat and is second only to giant river towboats. It may undertake towing of any ship or floating marine structure any distance, anywhere, at anytime.

The tug is basically a small ship in itself with a large fuel capacity, quarters for a crew, and stores and provisions for extended operations. Great Britain and Holland have firms that specialize in ocean towing and they have proven records of greatest continuous success. The United States and France have firms that provide ocean towing facilities, but they do not specialize in the trade.

Fig. 9. An unusual coastal tow consisting of salvage vessel *Curb* towing a section of the Chesapeake Bay Bridge-Tunnel, 300-foot length, 37-foot beam and approximately 2,600 tons displacement. A total of 37 tunnel tube sections were towed during 1961 and 1962 from the builders' yard in Orange, Texas to Norfolk, Virginia by the salvage vessels *Curb* and *Cable*. Merritt-Chapman & Scott

Ocean towing being a drastic change from river, harbor and even coastwise towing requires the utmost skills in preparation and seamanship. Even experienced tugboatmen have a tendency to become deceived after a few consecutive relatively easy successful tows. The basic code of ocean towing is that "no two tows are alike" and the rule of thumb, if such there be, is to prepare a tow for the maximum weather that can be encountered during the course of the tow. This last involves total effort in the preparation of all tows. As an example, a fast tow progressing on a short hawser in good weather from New York to Rio may suddenly result in disaster, after rounding Recife along the eastern coast of Brazil, before the tow hawser can be paid out because of rapidly changing sea conditions due to local adverse weather.

The ocean tug is approximately 125–250 feet in length with 1200–4200 hp and capable of extended operating radius.

Figure 10 shows a typical ocean tug.

It is common practice for ocean tugs to tow anywhere in the world, far from home port. As a result the fitting out is generally of a more complete and extensive nature than for other tugs. Among such items as salvage pumps, oxyacetylene cutting torches, welding

Fig. 10.   Ocean tug *Foundation Lillian*. Note towing span across the after deck. Foundation Maritime, Ltd., Canada.

machines and heavy duty wire cutters, a well equipped machine shop is considered necessary.

The ocean tug is designed with a high forecastle and enclosed foredeck with all sections of the vessel accessible from inside. A heavy automatic towing winch is installed. The after hold contains spare hawsers, wire and gear necessary for replacement due to attrition.

RESCUE AND SALVAGE TUGS

The rescue and salvage tug is the same size as, and in many cases larger than, the ocean tug. A rescue and salvage tug contains extensive equipment for diving and salvage work and it is equipped and ready to operate on very short notice.

The R & S tug guards the 500 KC radio band to intercept immediately any SOS that may be sent by a distressed vessel.

In rescue and salvage work the tug generally operates under a *Lloyd's Open Form of Salvage Agreement* (No cure–No pay).

Tugs from England, Holland and France work fairly regularly because of the nature of prevailing weather and sea conditions adjacent to their shores; however, where a rescue and salvage tug is stationed in a locale of only seasonal sporadic storms, some form of subsidy is needed to maintain the vessel on station. It is to the credit of maritime nations that they station some rescue and salvage tugs strategically around the globe in consideration of the lives of seamen as well as the value of ships and their cargoes.

A typical R & S tug operating out of North America is illustrated in Fig. 11.

Fig. 11. The 213'-6" ocean-going rescue and salvage vessel *Cable* is especially designed, equipped and manned for offshore ship salvage work of any scope.
Merritt-Chapman & Scott

U. S. NAVY TUGS

The following five (5) types of tugs designed for special uses are employed in the U. S. Navy:

ATF. Known as a fleet type tug, the *ATF* is designed for operating under the most arduous ocean conditions. The tug, over 200 feet in length, is capable of towing the largest naval vessels afloat. Four diesel engines, powering twin screws through diesel-electric drive, develop approximately 3,000 hp. Towing gear includes an Almon-Johnson, 3-drum towing engine and more than 2,000 feet of over two-inch diameter HGPS wire rope.

Referring to Fig. 12, a look at the after deck shows a large working area. The towing engine is just discernible forward of the main towing "H" bitts located on the centerline. A large capstan is also located on the forward end of the after deck at starboard side. Note the absence of large tow spans, or Dutch bars usually fitted across the stern deck of many civilian tugs. The towline is prevented from snagging on various deck obstructions by the installation of individual bars placed just forward of each projection. Note also the stern roller, side Norman pins, protected location for towing winch, main deck bulwark lifelines (portable), raised tank vents along deckhouse, foundation plate doublers for bitts, and heavy ten-ton cargo boom.

ATA. The *ATA* is a fleet auxiliary tug approximately 149 feet in length and capable of developing approximately 1,500 hp through diesel-electric drive. Equipped with a single drum towing winch, it is employed in general towing and servicing of the fleet, towing barges and vessels. The *ATA* is a versatile tug readily adaptable to general inland towing as well as ocean towing.

Figure 13 shows a compact seagoing tug with raised foredeck—a popular design for British and European ocean tugs. Note the stern horizontal roller and two vertical rollers in the raised position. A towing cleat and closed chock are also fitted at the stern on the centerline.

Fig. 12.   U.S.S. *Seneca*, ATF-91, starboard quarter view. U.S. Navy photo.

YTB. The Yard Tug Boat (*YTB*) is assigned to a Naval District or Navy Yard. Diesel powered in a range from 1,000 to 1,200 hp they are employed for general local towing and equipped with fire-fighting apparatus.

Figure 14 illustrates the usual design of a *YTB*. Note the capstan on forward deck as well as the capstan on starboard side of the after deck. The tug is fitted with numerous rope fenders for docking work. Note also the additional fenders along the bridge deck, probably required because of the exaggerated flair and curvature of the sides apparent in most high-speed naval vessels. Two fire monitors and a wide assortment of fire-fighting gear are also visible.

YT. This smaller edition of the Yard Tug is diesel powered in a range from 400 to 800 hp and it is equipped for fire-fighting duties. Diesel powered, it is a handy tug for limited towing operations within a harbor.

ARS. Although not primarily employed as a tug in the strictest sense of the word, the rescue salvage ship is designed to undertake heavy long-range ocean towing jobs. Heavily powered, diesel-electric, twin-screw drive, she is easily handled in all towing conditions of fair weather or foul, and she is equipped with an automatic towing engine in addition to a complete allowance of salvage and diving gear sufficient to sustain prolonged offshore salvage ventures.

From Fig. 15, it will be noted that the main deck is enclosed from forward to a point aft approximately adjacent to the forward limit of the towing winch. This main deck enclosure permits access to all parts of the vessel without going outside on a weather deck.

The location of the towing winch so far aft may impede maneuverability of the tug at times, but this is overcome by the added advantage

Fig. 13. U.S.S. *Pinola*, ATA-206, port quarter view. Official U.S. Navy photo

of twin screws that greatly improve maneuverability. In addition, the use of a Liverpool bridle is recommended to maintain course under the most arduous towing conditions. The possibility of tripping or girding this vessel is minimized by locating the towing connection far aft, an important consideration that loses some of its significance because of the size and weight of the vessel.

OTHER TUGS

In addition to the foregoing general classification of tugs designed and built for specific purposes there are numerous tugs and towboats in operation that are designed and built for particular special needs. The following is a brief list of some of these special needs: ice breaking; towing logs in the river lumbertrade; furnishing steam;

fire fighting; towing floating equipment such as derricks, cranes, mining equipment, floating pipe lines, pipe-laying barges, and off-shore drilling barges.

Small utility tugs are used on the rivers feeding the lumber trade and for towing rafts of lumber to sawmills. The range of a lumber tug is increased through shallow draft. The shallower the draft, the closer to the headwaters of a river the tug can operate, thus mini-mizing the distance that logs must be transported overland to places with depths where tugs can operate. Aluminum tugs, because of

Fig. 14.   U.S.S. *Tensaw*, YTB-418, passing close aboard to U.S.S. *Shangri-La*, CVA-38, leaving the Port of Yokosuka, Japan. Official U.S. Navy photograph

their light weight and resulting reduced draft, prove quite satisfac-tory for this type of service. Copper base fittings are not used in the construction of aluminum tugs.

The hulls of ice-breaking tugs are reinforced and stiffened. Bal-last and trim tanks are installed to rock the tug and change the trim for breaking ice.

Barges and lighters are usually towed by small utility tugs of shallow draft to facilitate access to and operation in creeks and inlets. The tugs, being small for their trade, develop considerably less hp than docking tugs. When manned by a single day crew, they tie up at night.

Crew.   The sizes of tugboat crews vary depending on the service in which the tug is employed. A brief look at the following will give a general idea of the manning scales:

1. *Small harbor tugs.* Manned by a single day crew, the tugs generally tie up at night and the crews go home. Living quarters do not exist or are limited.

2. *Construction contractor's tugs.* Usually very small, they serve only to transfer or shift the contractor's floating equipment, such as derricks, cranes, barges, stiff-legs, pipe-laying barges, concrete mixer barges, pile drivers, divers' barges and, in fact, any piece of floating equipment used by a contractor to perform his services. The tugs employ a two- or three-man crew during working hours only.

Fig. 15. U.S.S. *Deliver*, ARS-23, broadside view. Official U.S. Navy photograph

Fireboats. A fireboat in reality is a tug with special features added to enable the tug to provide fire-fighting services. The fireboat essentially houses pumps and the propulsive power to deliver the pumping plant to the scene of a fire at maximum speed.

Basically, a fireboat should be capable of providing approximately 15,000–20,000 gallons of water per minute.

Four crews man a tug 24 hours a day for a 7-day week.

Diesel electric propulsion appears to be the most effective power for a tug of this type. Electrical energy can be used to drive the propeller or to pump water, the source of the energy being the same for both needs.

Some consideration should be given to the installation of a Pleuger active-rudder in the design of fireboats, since the rudder can be used not only to steer the tug, but also to counteract the thrust of the monitors, thereby holding the tug in position and resulting in a minimal use of the main engines for that purpose. The Pleuger active-rudder can propel the tug by itself when necessary, although at a very slow speed.

Some fire-fighting apparatus, monitors and pumps are installed on all harbor tugs built for private operators. A tug so equipped becomes available to a local fire department for use during disaster with trained fire department personnel directing operations. As a supplement to existing fireboats, tugs so equipped and manned markedly increase the fire combativeness at the scene.

A fireboat has one or more batteries of fire-fighting monitors installed topside. Formerly some fireboats were designed without towing "H" bitts; however, it is perhaps the better practice to provide towing bitts so that, without undue difficulties, a fireboat can tow a burning vessel to clear water or remove it from the vicinity of berthing areas and other vessels to prevent spreading of fire.

BRITISH AND EUROPEAN TUGS

Unlike their American cousins, British and European tugs are generally separated under the following classifications (note 4):

River   Coastal
Harbor   Ocean-going

The basic requirements for these tugs are:

Stability under all conditions   Adequate towing power
Maneuverability   Strength of hull fittings

Inland—River and Canal Tugs. The towing practice on the Thames is a result of past practice, design of barges, and to some extent tug design. The practice is in a real sense towing and not push-towing as practiced on our Western rivers.

Local regulations play an important part in the make-up of tows as can be seen by the Port of London River Bye-Laws which restrict the size of tows to within 320 feet between London Bridge and Charlton, or 400 feet elsewhere. The length of the tow is measured from the stern of the tug to the stern of the last barge in tow. The size of the tow can be limited by the distance of the tug from the lead barge. As a result swim-ended barges are towed behind the tug at very close quarters. (note 5)

In general, British tugs designed to limited drafts are required to operate under low bridges and in canal locks. They must also jockey barges in congested and narrow waterways.

The tow hook is placed amidship to increase maneuverability and tow-bows are fitted over the engine-room skylight. The midship house does not extend aft to cover the engine room as in most American practice and therefore the engine-room skylight is mounted within a coaming on the main deck. The tow-bows are transverse bars extending from port gunwale to starboard gunwale. The tow-bows keep the tow howser off the main deck clear of the skylight and prevent snagging deck fittings.

A tow-bow is similar to a tow span. Light tow ropes are employed so that a capstan is not required. Samson posts are installed port and starboard forward and amidship, to facilitate towing alongside or breasted and to provide connections for backing (astern) control.

The trend on European canals is toward self-propelled cargo barges rather than tugs and barges, whereas on the Rhine River the trend is toward American-type, integrated, pusher-type tows.

Harbor and Docking Tugs. The harbor and docking tugs used in England through the 1930's were paddle-wheeled. The paddle wheel was once employed in the main because of its great turning force, an important factor in docking tugs. In addition, it proved exceptionally good for shallow water operations. However, in recent years with increased hp, improved rudder, propeller and hull form design, etc.,

Fig. 16.   1000 HP ocean tug *Noordzee*, owned and operated by L. Smit, Ltd., specially built for long-distance towing. Teunissen

the propeller tug has replaced those classic work-horses to a great extent.

The European docking tug is generally under 500 hp, and it is customary to use a towing hook with steel spiral spring similar to the British method.

Docking tugs in Great Britain range from small to large. A medium sized harbor tug may have 1400 to 1700 bhp and a static bollard pull of from 15 to 25 tons and more. The harbor and docking tug is built to serve a function best described by R. Munro-Smith, "A tug is fundamentally a floating powerhouse and its function is to assist other vessels to maneuver in restricted waters or to tow ships to their destination." (note 6) As a result the British and European harbor tug is designed so that most of the engine power is absorbed on a towline and a relatively small percentage propels the tug itself.

Coastal Tugs. The British and European coastal tug has good sheer forward and ofttimes a forecastle. Large freeing ports (washports) and numerous scuppers are installed since the tugs are required to operate in coastal waters that are considerably rougher than the sheltered waters of harbors. The tugs are also designed for good free running speed and equipped with fire and salvage pumps necessary to provide salvage services. All crew, berth and mess areas should be accessible from within the hull because of the rough weather frequently encountered.

Ocean-going, Salvage and Rescue Tugs. Displacement, power, range and stability are the important factors. Deep draft and large dimensions are desirable to enable the tug to keep and maintain a steady course by throwing a large wheel.

A high covered forecastle extends aft to approximately above the after bulkhead of the machinery space. A weighty vessel broad of beam is advantageous.

Although the American preference is for a multiengined twin-screw vessel, the British and Europeans often prefer a multiengined single-screw tug.

One particular design features four engines connected to the shaft through electromagnetic slip couplings. Two of the four drive directly-coupled generators and are not reversible although they may be uncoupled. The after two engines are reversible.

European ocean-going tugs powered up to 1200 hp customarily employ a towing winch, and for greater hp and larger tugs a Dutch towing beam (tow-bow) is incorporated for ease in clearing fantail obstructions. Figure 16 illustrates a typical Dutch tug.

Fairleads are used in line with bollards to provide a straight line direction of pull.

Towing "on the hook" is commonly used as a means of quickly connecting up and releasing the tow. The arrangement is explained in Chapter II.

NOTES: CHAPTER I

1. D. A. Argyriadis, "Modern Tug Design with Particular Emphasis on Propeller Design, Maneuverability and Endurance," *Society of Naval Architects and Marine Engineers*, Paper n. 7 for meeting Nov. 14–15, 1957, 48 p.

2. "Push Boats and Integrated Tows," A. C. Hardy, *Shipbuilding & Shipping Record*, v. 90—17, Oct. 24, 1957, p. 541–543.

3. E. Renshaw, "World's Most Powerful Towboat," *Marine Engineering and Log*, v. 64, n. 1, Jan. 1959, p. 42–47.

4. R. Munro-Smith, "Tug Design," *Shipbuilder and Marine Engine Builder*, v. 69, n. 650, January 1962, p. 47–53.

5. J. B. Griffith, "Tug Power in Relation to Towage of Swim Ended Barges," *Shipbuilding & Shipping Record*, v. 90, n. 4, July 25, 1957, p. 110–113.

6. R. Munro-Smith, *op. cit.*, p. 49.

CHAPTER II

CONSTRUCTION AND DESIGN

DESIGN OF TUGS AND TOWBOATS

The tug and towboat are vessels that provide propulsive power as an auxiliary motive force for a specific purpose or for a combination of uses in waterborne transportation systems.

Some uses of tugs are: to assist other larger, less maneuverable vessels in docking and escorting to and from the open sea through crowded hazardous inland waters; to provide detachable propulsive power for nonself-propelled vessels; to push massive integrated river tows; to pull large ocean tows.

When designed for a combination of uses the earning power of a tug is greatly increased through versatility and adaptability. For instance, a harbor docking tug designed with sea-keeping characteristics for use as a coastal and ocean tug, or an ocean tug designed to perform salvage and rescue services.

The tug or towboat is basically a housing for a main propulsive unit. If it were only required to provide a housing for the main engine, the construction would be rather simple; however, there are many additional design considerations that must be met before the final vessel is completed, which is termed a tug or towboat. The basic housing must also contain other functional equipment to support some primary needs for towing and secondary needs of the plant. Thus the tug gradually becomes more sophisticated as successive needs are considered and problems resolved until a final form evolves. Some considerations that affect the design of a tug are based on the need for the following: a watertight underwater buoyant body; restrictions and modifications due to trade, such as operating draft and fuel capacity; a maximum height of superstructure above the waterline; shape of the forebody; superstructure limitations, e.g., length of deckhouse; any auxiliary deck power needed; stowage for consumable and expendable gear; living accommodations and any hotel services provided.

The following basic requisites are also given consideration in evolving a fundamental design pattern for a tug, whether it is to be used for ocean, harbor or inland tow purposes:

1. The main propulsion engine and auxiliary machinery should be capable of providing maximum power, when towing or pushing under full load or light load conditions.

2. The engine must be capable of being quickly maneuvered with a minimum of time expended while going from zero torque to full power.

3. The machinery must be completely reliable under all conditions of operation with a minimum of time lost (lay-up) due to breakdown. The main engine should be quickly and easily maneuverable using pilothouse control wherever possible or feasible.

4. The hull must be strongly-built and heavy enough to utilize the contained horsepower—a consideration of great importance in ocean tugs. The vessel must be rugged enough to withstand heavy usage with a minimum wear and tear to hull and appurtenances.

5. The vessel in toto must be readily maneuverable and capable of executing sharp turns within a minimum radius.

6. In conjunction with its maneuverability the tug should possess favorable stability characteristics under all conditions of loading and towing—fair weather or foul. Stability, it may be said, is perhaps the single most important sea-keeping characteristic a tug must possess, for there are critical times when the position of a tow can set up tripping moments which tend to capsize the tug. Hence, in addition to being able to ride easily in heavy seas, the tug must also resist any adverse stability conditions imposed upon it by a tow.

7. The tug must be economical to operate. Operating costs that must be kept at a minimum include fuel, crew wages, maintenance, fitting out and insurance.

In designing a tug the foregoing requisites in conjunction with other requirements dictated by the needs of the owner, type of trade, climatic and geographic location, combine with the laws of the country wherein the tug will operate to form a definite pattern from which the basic tug will evolve.

It may be seen how the foregoing factors plus local "know-how" have produced an infinite variety of tugs as diverse as the combinations of modifications on basic requisites.

Until fairly recent times there were few progressive improvements in the design of American tugs. The period of general stagnation and absence of imaginative innovations began around the turn of the century and lasted for a long period, basically because tug requirements had remained fairly constant.

The few design improvements made were generally limited to, and affected only, new machinery, horsepower output and navigational aids, but any improvements were usually housed in the same basic tug form. On river towboats, the stern-wheeler was in command until the advent of World War II. In harbors, the flush deck, long house tug held sway.

Coastal tugs were of similar construction to harbor tugs, but built to larger scale, and the same may be said of the scarce ocean, or deep-sea towing tug.

The cause of stagnation may be ascertained to some extent by observing that the tugboat designers' greatest problem through the years, as a result of owner needs, was and is to create a tug with maximum power at towing speeds and with maximum speed while running free. This generally applies to all tugs regardless of trade.

Fig. 17.   A clear unobstructed view aft is apparent at this outside steering and control station on an American harbor tug. Moran

The primary considerations of a tug company in America are those of speed and pounds-pull that a tug can exert on a tow hawser—speed because in the competitive U.S. economy, time is money and pounds-pull because it is taken as a measure of the tug to transport a payload.

American tugs have always been difficult to classify according to trade because of the general overlapping in the ability of tugs to perform jobs in more than one trade.

In general there is a unique need on all tugs and towboats for a clear open deck aft to provide adequate working space. The view from the pilothouse in a 360-degree circle should be unobstructed, as far as is practicable; in addition, the view from any outside maneuvering stations should be unobstructed whether they be located amidship, in the bridge wings, or aft as illustrated in Fig. 17.

HARBOR TUGS

Harbor tugs are designed to best meet the requirements for operating in each harbor. Few harbors are alike, consequently harbor tugs develop in a wide variety of design.

DOCKING TUGS

The docking tug is designed for operating alongside ships; "butting" in way of the flair of the bow and under the counter of the stern. Fitted with numerous wood, tire, or rubber side fenders and heavy bow and stern puddings of braided manila or preformed rubber, the tug is well protected from indents and excessive wear and tear resulting from continually operating close aboard large heavily constructed steel ships and barges. Figure 4 illustrates a typical docking tug showing these features.

Additionally, the following should be incorporated, to some extent, in the design of most harbor tugs in order to broaden their adaptability:

1. The superstructure set back from the sheer strake in a vertical line approximately 18″ for every 7 feet of height.

2. The forestay to be moveable or eliminated wherever possible.

3. Outside control (maneuvering) stations to improve "seeing" located on bridge wings and on a clear area of raised deck aft.

4. Hawse pipes set well back from the stem and recessed to seat flush-hulled a stockless anchor.

RIVER TOWBOATS

A river towboat design must take into consideration the following in order to meet the demands of river trade:

1. A pilothouse high enough to see above the tow which, in reality, is pushed in front.

2. Slanting pilothouse windows to reduce glare.

3. Searchlights; powerful and located to reduce glare, as well as to be readily operated from the pilot steering station.

4. Shallow draft; this requirement explains the broad beam of most river boats and, in turn, the broad beam explains the roomy appearance of the hotel-like superstructure.

5. Push-knees; well built into hull structurals with renewable rubber, wood or composition knee pads.

6. Horsepower and maneuverability.

Some stern-wheelers (tugs with paddle-wheel propulsion aft) still operate on the Ohio and Pacific Coast rivers; however, the latest designs of river tugs employ two, three or multiple propellers set in tunnels recessed into the hull bottoms to facilitate shallow water towing. These pusher-type tugs are known as towboats and they are secured to the rear of a long (some nearly ⅛ mile), tight, integrated tow. The towboat and all barges are secured as one unit with taut wires and chains so that the integrated tow is easily steered and maneuvered. The towboat is fitted with numerous steering and flanking (4–8) rudders so that judicious and skillful handling of a multiple screw and rudder towboat enables the operator to work the tow sideways on the river.

MANEUVERABILITY

The need to maneuver well is one of the most important considerations taken into account in tug design. The following design factors, singly and in combination, tend to improve or impede maneuverability; e.g., hull form, propulsive power, propellers, rudders. In addition, the location of tow engines, "H" bitts and tow hooks greatly affect maneuverability.

The ability to maneuver well is of prime importance for all tugs and towboats and especially for tugs required to accomplish ship docking work in confined areas. In addition, there are times when a towboat is required to turn a tow of greater length and displacement within a minimum radius. Long integrated river tows require towboats capable of a degree of steering and control not required in other tugs. On river towboats the use of multiple screws and rudders have proven more than satisfactory in improving maneuverability so that now a towboat can actually "walk" a tow sideways on a river. Earlier installations of temporary rudders placed at the head of a tow gave way to the more satisfactory results obtained by multiple and flanking rudders installed on the towboat itself.

Recessed hull tunnels for propellers and shafts, flat bottoms and special underwater body lines, as illustrated in Fig. 18, greatly improve the maneuvering performance of towboats by allowing a full free flow of water to propellers.

The ocean tug adapts well to twin-screw design and greater horsepower. Stability problems must always be given prime consideration when incorporating in an ocean tug any new underwater changes to improve maneuverability.

Tugs of normal body design including those operating in harbors, inland waters and canals have seen improvements in maneuverability by the adaption, singly and in combination, of new hull forms, hydroconic hull designs, Kort nozzles and controllable-pitch propellers.

Still, much remains to be done. The astern steering quality of most tugs is considered to be poor and in need of improvement, but the use of flanking rudders on tug bodies of normal design apparently is not the answer. New hull forms tending to shift the center of buoyancy forward or aft affect the performance of a tug and require in many cases a relocation of the tow connection point; i.e., tow engine, tow hook, tow "H" bitts, etc. In the selection of new hull forms, it should be kept in mind that a full body forward is necessary to keep a tug from driving under while running free at full speed. And, much can be done by a more widespread adaption of hydroconic hull designs, controllable-pitch propellers, Kort nozzles, and transverse maneuvering propellers.

Some design features that improve maneuverability of tugs operating in a particular service, in many cases, cannot be adapted to towboats in another service; e.g., ocean-going raised forecastle to harbor towing, or the push-knee and flat bottoms of river towboats to ocean or coastal towing.

To be effective most tugs should be capable of maneuvering quickly, and one authority indicates a satisfactory stopping time to be approximately 25 seconds from full speed to dead stop. (note 1)

The great control and maneuverability over a tow on our western rivers by the application of "push-towing" has attained such a degree of success that it has been adopted for integrated towing on the Niger and Benares rivers. (note 2) In time this effective method of "push-towing" will in all probability find wider areas for application.

NAVAL ARCHITECTURE

In this investigation, only those design features peculiar to tugs and towboats that affect operation and performance will be covered in a rather cursory manner, with the thought in mind to acquaint tugboatmen and rivermen with some aspects that are taken into consideration rather than to instruct and guide the naval architect in the solution of design problems. By acquiring a "nodding acquaintance" with these features, it is hoped that operating personnel may better understand the performance characteristics that affect maneuverability of their particular vessel.

Generally speaking, it is desirable to locate the center of buoyancy at approximately amidship or slightly aft thereof; a condition difficult to attain in design because of the unusually fine form of the afterbody—a form that is necessary to provide a full flow of water to the propeller. It is advantageous to make the towing connection at a point as near as possible to the center of buoyancy or slightly aft thereof in order to minimize the forces tending to adversely affect steering control. These forces work in a couple; the propeller force opposed to towline pull.

On American harbor tugs this couple could present a problem because the tow connection is farther aft than on British and European tugs; however, most of the time assistance is rendered with the American tug butting alongside so that the location of the tow connection does not become a problem until assistance is rendered at the end of a tow line.

On most European and British harbor tugs docking assistance is usually rendered at the end of a short tow line connected to a tow hook. The tow hook is located as near as possible to the center of buoyancy so that maneuverability of the tug will not be impeded. Although maneuverability of the tug is improved over the American counterpart, the chances of tripping or girding the tug are increased because of the elevation and forward position of the hook. Sudden adverse movements or maneuvers by either the tow or tug are dangerous and may spell disaster. The danger is minimal, however, when

Fig. 18. Most modern descendant of the original *Pioneer* is the 6,400-horsepower diesel towboat *Navigator*, built by Dravo for Union Barge Line Corp. Streamlined Kort nozzles are fitted into the stern; rudders, propellers and hull lines all are designed for maximum efficiency. Dravo

skilled pilots and tug captains are employed. And again, on an ocean tug the shifting of the tow hook even a slight amount forward to coincide with a shift in the center of buoyancy may seriously encroach upon space made available for living quarters, house and superstructure.

The long deckhouse, common to most early American harbor tugs and well illustrated in Fig. 3, has gradually given way to a shorter house. The long deckhouse once was required in order to house crew living spaces topside with adequate ventilation. Most American tugs expect to ply the coastal trade at one time or another and can, therefore, expect to operate in climates ranging from cold and temperate to hot and subtropical. Crew quarters below decks proved unbearable in hot weather. The quartering of crews above deck was considered a must and resulted in the rather long deckhouse.

On the other hand, it is mentioned in passing, the European tug never encountered this problem in its development because most European tugs are confined or they are limited to operating in the temperate zones of Europe and Great Britain; hence, the crews were always quartered below deck. As a result the deckhouse of the European tug is considerably shorter than that of the American tug.

It has been shown that the maneuverability of the tug is improved when the tow connection is made just aft of the center of buoyancy

Fig. 19. U.S.S. *Edenshaw*, YTB-752, starboard view. Official U.S. Navy photo

so that some considerable effort has been made in the design of American tugs to shorten the deckhouse. One example of this is illustrated in Fig. 19. Note how this deckhouse has been shortened considerably from the one installed on an earlier type shown in Fig. 20.

For all practical purposes, the problem of a deckhouse should be eliminated where the installation of air-conditioning equipment is feasible so that crews can be berthed below decks.

Freeboard. A rather basic measure of stability of a tug is its freeboard, or the distance from the water to main deck. The general rule of thumb followed to determine the required freeboard for different tugs is a minimum of approximately 10 per cent of the waterline beam; e.g., small harbor tug to about a 25 ft. beam–2 foot freeboard; large coastal and harbor tug to about 35 ft. beam–3 foot freeboard; ocean or salvage tug, depending upon beam—4 to 6 foot freeboard.

Stability. A range of stability from 60 to 70 degrees, necessary for tugs, is a condition that usually requires watertight doors on the midship house. The watertight doors are mounted above high coamings. Bulwarks approximately 36″ high, depending on requirements of regulatory agencies, with adequate freeing ports and scuppers, are installed on tugs to aid stability by restricting seawater flow to decks and by quickly freeing decks of any entrained water.

There should not be any nonwatertight doors or openings, and all watertight doors should open outward so that water pressure will tend to seat them more firmly—to prevent the pounding of green seas from forcing open or springing doors which may result in flooding and eventual sinking unless remedial measures are taken. All coffer-dam, fuel and water-tank vents must be extended high above the

Fig. 20.   U.S.S. *YTB-275*, port view. Official U.S. Navy photograph

main deck to insure freedom from flooding and contamination by salt water, and they must be fitted with ball checks.

A tug must possess good stability characteristics as defined by:

1. Curves of Statical Stability.
2. Dynamical Stability.
3. Metacentric Height, generally a minimum of 2 feet is required. GM, the distance from the center of gravity to the metacenter measured at small angles of heel, is the most commonly used measurement of a vessel's stability.

Several formulas have been developed to determine the GM of a tug and two examples follow:

$$GM = \frac{SHP \times h}{100 \ \Delta \ \dfrac{f}{B}} \qquad \text{(note 3)}$$

where

SHP = shaft horsepower
h = vertical distance from center of effort to the top of towing bitts
Δ = displacement in long tons (salt water)
B = extreme waterline beam in feet
f = minimum freeboard in feet

$$GM = \frac{BHP \times 15h}{\Delta \dfrac{f}{B}} \qquad \text{(note 4)}$$

where

Δ = displacement in pounds
BHP = brake horsepower
h = vertical distance from center of effort to the top of the towing bitts in feet
f = minimum freeboard in feet
B = waterline in feet

CONSTRUCTION

A tug or towboat hull and in particular the underwater body resistance in water, absorbs only a small per cent of the total power that the tug can produce. The major portion of power developed is applied to tow-line pull. This is true for all tugs and towboats except the river giants and largest coastal and ocean, seagoing salvage and rescue tugs, which might lead one to deduce that the hull form has only slight effect on towing speed. However, this is not completely true, for in addition to hull resistance, an equally important factor in towing and the forces involved and generated thereby, is performance of the propeller.

A full free flow of water to the propeller is essential and this can be brought about only by a thorough consideration and careful development of the underwater body. A full free flow of water to the propeller must be assured with a minimum of hull interference, whether the tug be towing at speed or applying a towing force while dead in the water.

A restricted or fouled water flow to the propeller produces a turbulence and agitation of the wake that decreases propeller effectiveness and results in loss of towing power. The power loss, it would appear, results from failure of the propeller to develop sufficient thrust by not operating in a full flow or fairly solid water mass.

A tug is generally heavily constructed with scantlings for plating and framing in excess of the requirements of classification societies. The reason for this becomes apparent when we consider the trade requirements in which a tug operates. Contact with other vessels and floating equipment and structures is a must. As a result there are numerous occasions for heavy wear and tear because some landings alongside other vessels, in reality, may be considered as strikings and the damage done can range from slight to excessive depending on the heaviness of construction of a particular tug.

Hydroconic Hull. A popular hull construction in Europe becoming more in demand in America for harbor work is the hydroconic hull. The hydroconic hull of patented design provides for a greater hydrodynamic propeller efficiency than a standard hull form. The body lines of a hydroconic hull are shaped so as to provide a straighter flow of water to the propeller, thereby increasing its overall efficiency through providing more uniform wake values and reduced turbulence permitting a reduction of propeller tip clearances. In turn a larger and more efficient propeller can be installed with a result that the static bollard pull increases approximately 30 per cent more than that for a tug of regular hull form. (note 5)

It would appear that the hydroconic hull form is at least a partial answer to the problem of underwater body shape that restricts the flow of water to a propeller.

The hull is easily, rapidly and cheaply constructed due to prefabrication methods employed. In addition sea-keeping qualities are at least equal to the standard hull form. (note 6)

Recently, the application of hydroconic hull form designs seems to have captured the imagination of most builders and operators.

Originally designed and built with an eye to economy, the double-chine construction of the hydroconic hull was found to provide better water flow patterns to the screw.

The absence of rounded bilges has eliminated the need for shaped plates and frames, furnaced plates and castings, all of which contribute to escalating the costs of vessel construction.

It is reported that the tug possesses an unusual ability to maintain speed under heavy weather conditions—a great advantage in tugs. The stability is reported to be good which would tend to indicate that the application of this hull design to tugboat construction is excellent. (note 7)

The guaranteed minimum bollard pull of 36#/shp for hydroconic hulls as compared to 28–30#/shp common to American tugs of similar size and horsepower enables less horsepower installations and a resulting savings in machinery costs. (note 8)

In summary, we have in hydroconic tugs a hull of double-chine construction capable of developing a static bollard pull of 36#/shp having good sea-keeping and stability characteristics and able to maintain speed in a rough sea. (note 9)

Superstructure. The construction of a superstructure will range from a very modest enclosure for the smallest tug to the sometimes elaborate hotel facilities of the giant river towboat.

The size and spaciousness of a tug, when not specified by the dictates of a classification society or government agency, will vary depending upon the trade in which a tug will be employed. A tug that ties up at night will have only the most meager accommodations for a day crew—barely more than to provide shelter during inclement weather.

If a crew is to live aboard, as in some deep-sea tugs, the accommodations become more elaborate; consequently, the superstructure begins to take on larger dimensions.

The largest ocean-going tugs, salvage vessels and river tugboats that accommodate year-around crews, require a housing containing all the conveniences of modern day living. Pilothouses must be built wherein the vessel is navigated. The view must be unobstructed, so the pilothouse usually tops the superstructure. Modern pilothouses contain all the latest in navigational aids, e.g., radar, auto-pilot, RDF, radio, Loran, Fathometer.

Engine control and vessel steering are under pilothouse control. In addition, one or more outside steering and control stations are installed to improve vision and command of any situation. A typical outside steering station is illustrated in Fig. 21. Some idea of the

Fig. 21. An outside steering and control station on a modern tug. The helm is on the left and engine control on the right. In between mounted at the railing are the whistle pull, emergency engine order bell signal, emergency engine stop and a speaking tube to engine room. Note also the convenient location of the floodlight and a spotlight for night operations.   Moran

evolution of the modern tug may be had from a comparison of Figs. 19 and 20. Note that in Fig. 19 the house has been shortened and shifted slightly forward so that it does not extend as far aft as the earlier model. These design innovations shifted the tow connection farther forward so that maneuverability is probably improved because the towing connection is now closer to the center of buoyancy and to the center of lateral resistance. Note also the self-closing freeing ports. Pilothouse vision has been greatly improved in the later model as can be seen by a comparison of the photographs.

Aluminum. The use of aluminum in the construction of tugs is finding ever wider application, principally because of low maintenance costs, lightness that reduces draft, and long life.

A light tug of corrosion resistant aluminum alloys built by Bryant Boats, Inc., was reported to have better maneuverability and developed more thrust than a steel tug of comparable power and dimensions, leading to the contention that a 58-ton aluminum tug is equal to an 83-ton steel tug. (note 10)

There can be little doubt that small tug construction with aluminum is cheaper overall than with steel. Light aluminum may be cut to size using portable power saws, which proves ideal for construction by small shipyards.

The elimination of expensive gases for cutting torches and faster welding in aluminum construction resulted in the expenditure of 30 per cent fewer man-hours than for a similar steel tug, although the materials cost approximately 5 per cent more than steel. (note 11)

Although the use of all-aluminum has been limited to small utility tugs, aluminum is finding ever wider areas for application in the superstructure of selected larger tugs and towboats.

Fenders and Guards. Fenders and guards are installed on a tug to protect the hull from damage that might result from contact with a tow, pier, or stationary structure. During an ocean tow a tug may be required to go alongside the tow several times during a voyage. First, while connecting (hooking up) to the tow, the tug will usually tie up alongside. During the approach to tie up, the tug may accidentally land heavily against the tow with enough force to cause hull damage. Later at sea, the tug may be required from time to time to lay alongside the tow to conduct inspections, take soundings, or pump bilges. And finally, while again coming alongside to disconnect after completion of a voyage, contact must be made.

A docking tug needs many side fenders and guards, as well as bow and stern fenders, to prevent damage to the hull while working alongside ships. Harbor tugs require hull protection of varying degrees of completeness depending on their type of service.

It can readily be seen that some form of protection must be provided to protect the hulls of all tugs from accidental damage that might occur on numerous occasions during the conduct of normal business.

Two means are employed to protect the hulls of tugs, viz., fenders and guards.

Fenders. The earliest fender system was one of wood logs hung vertically over the side when required and removed inboard while under way. Excellent for use on the olden low-powered wooden-hulled tugs, this log system did not hold up to the requirements of a later age. Greater horsepower, heavier tugs, and stricter owner requirements regarding hull damage spelled the end for the wood log fender. Figure 3, Chapter I, shows a steam tug fitted with log fenders.

Tires and hose sections have replaced the earlier log fenders to a great extent, primarily because of the abundance of old automobile tires which in modern times are easier to obtain than logs, and, secondly, because tires provide more complete protection.

Rope fenders. Figure 22 is noteworthy in that it shows two types of rope side fender. The all-rope fender on the tugboat in the photograph has largely been replaced by the combination rope and tire fender, several of which may be seen forward.

The *rope and tire fender* is simply a rope-filled tire with the center netted to secure the ropes that make up the fender. The whole is dressed off with standard rope whiskers.

The bow fender, perhaps the dressiest looking and one that smacks of the romance of tugboating, is all-rope, made from downgraded hawsers, lines, bits and small stuff, and it is dressed with rope whiskers. Indeed, in many tugs the vessel is not considered "shipshape" until the bow whiskers have been combed with a garden rake. Figure 23 shows the typical arrangements employed for securing

Fig. 22.   Side fenders, tug *Kings Point*. Curtis Bay Towing

the bow fender as well as the side fender. Note that the bow fender is hung with chain over the stem bitt and secured laterally by ropes tied to rings fitted in padeyes welded to the bulwark and sides.

Figure 24 illustrates a rope bow fender developed for push-towing on inland waterways. The fender is adapted to a tug of normal shaped bow, whereas the river towboat with push-knees on the bow presents a different problem.

Rubber bow fenders are becoming increasingly popular for tugboat use. Time will tell whether wear and adaptability of this type of fender will prove economical.

Figure 25 shows a comparison between a new type rubber bow fender and the older rope fender installed on two U. S. Navy YTB's.

Figure 26 illustrates another Navy *YTB* with an extruded rubber fender that is an all-rubber unit manufactured by Goodyear Tire and Rubber Company to U. S. Navy Bureau of Ships specifications.

A preformed type of rubber bow fender is illustrated in Fig. 27. On tug bow and stern installations preformed rubber fenders of this type can be properly curved before curing to take the shape of the ship being fitted.

Push-knee rubber fenders. Towboatmen report that it is easier to hold and maneuver tows against rubber knees than against the older type wood knees (which are fast becoming obsolete).

Fig. 23. Illustrating the methods used to secure the bow and side fenders of tug *Eugene F. Moran*. Moran

The *bumpers* are installed in strips (horizontally is preferred by most towboatmen) and bolted, to facilitate switching strips to areas of greater or lesser wear. The use of rubber stripping for push-knees helps to maintain machinery and main engine alignments by cushioning impacts during landings and while towing. Strip sections are made up in sizes of 10″ × 36″ × 2″ thick and 8.75″ × 36″ × 4.5″ thick, of high tensile strength rubber.

Although the initial cost is higher, it is reported that life expectancy is extended from two to six times the wood fenders.

Special fenders. One example of special fenders that are constantly being developed to fill particular needs is the white fender developed by Goodyear Tire and Rubber Company for tugs handling white-hulled cruise ships at the Panama Canal.

Fig. 24. This picture shows how the new type of fender, with "Turk's head" at the bottom, fits into the notch of a barge. Tug *Marie S. Moran* pushing Texaco's barge *396*. Moran

Guards. Split-pipe guards made of half-round pipe sections shaped to fit the curvature of a hull are installed in one or more strakes of plating either partially or completely around the hull. Periodically, repairs as found necessary are made by cropping out and partially renewing any damaged section. Damaged split-pipe guards are part of the wear and tear normally to be expected in towing operations.

Fig. 25. A picture is worth 1,000 words they say, and this photograph of two Navy tugs, berthed together, illustrates better than words the difference in fendering systems—rubber and fiber. Rectangular and cylindrical rubber fenders are used in combination on the *YBT 181*, at left, for all-around protection. Goodyear

Fig. 26. The Navy tug *Paducah* during trials by Southern Shipbuilding Co. This ship and three identical tugs are fendered with 12″ square bow fenders with a 5″ bore; 10″ by 12″ fender arranged on a 100-degree arc for stern protection, and 10″ cylindrical fenders mounted over stakes for lateral protection. The four ships are the most powerful the Navy has in use, developing a bollard pull of 35 pounds per brake horsepower. Goodyear

A split-pipe guard distributes any striking load over a greater area of hull plating, minimizing the effects of concentrated local strains, and results in damage to the guard rather than to hull plating.

At least one heavy guard of 4″ split-pipe should be installed completely around the periphery of a tug in way of the sheer with partial additional guards extending from forward to amidship or aft as required.

Another type of guard made of rubber is illustrated in Fig. 28. The rubber strake is continuous around the hull providing 360 degrees of protection.

Fig. 27. The 45-foot diesel tug *Torito* fitted with rubber bow fenders during construction by Equitable Equipment Co., Inc., at New Orleans. On tug bow and stern installations, rubber fenders can be properly curved before curing to take the shape of the ship being fitted. Goodyear

PROPULSION

Any discussion concerning tugboats must of necessity include the various methods employed for propulsion and their comparative merits and detractions. Probably the best approach will be to list the types and discuss them separately. The indulgence of the reader is requested in this investigation, since a final selection of the type of power will result from a consideration of the advantages and disadvantages weighed against the specific needs of the owner and capabilities of the builder.

The following is a partial list (though not in order of importance) of common types of propulsion installed in tugs:

Steam Reciprocating Engine. The reciprocating steam engine was for many years the mainstay of tug propulsion. Earlier slow-turning engines of heavy construction were directly connected through shafting to a large propeller. Later design improvements produced high-speed engines of light construction coupled to the shaft and propeller.

The selection of a slow-turning, direct-drive engine or a high-speed engine with reduction-gear drive was dictated strictly by requirements of the trade in which the tug was to be employed.

Fig. 28. The Brown and Root tug *Tiburon*, with a continuous rubber strake giving 360 degrees of protection. Fendering material is 8″ by 10″ rectangular extrusion with 3″ bore, rated at 21,000 ft/lbs of energy deflection per foot of length. Goodyear

In Great Britain the steam reciprocating engine was used as late as the 1930's to propel the side paddle-wheel tugs that were so popular for a great many years, not only because of their minimum draft for shallow water operation, but also because of their tremendous turning power, which is of prime importance for docking tugs.

Improvements in rudder, propeller and hull designs have caused the paddle-wheel tug to give way to the more efficient propeller-driven tug. (note 12)

The following is a partial list of the advantages and disadvantages of the steam reciprocating tug:

Advantages:
1. Slow turning engine.
2. Dependability.
3. Facility in making repairs.
4. A fouled propeller will not result in severe damage to shafting or engine bed, since engine will stop when boiler pressure equals the force applied to the shaft.

Disadvantages:
1. High initial cost.
2. Uneconomical. The boilers must be steamed continuously or if not they must be fired sufficiently in advance of getting under way to obtain a head of steam. Engines must be warmed up gradually, which requires a consumption of fuel oil that does no payload work.
3. Replacement parts are larger than diesel parts and are proportionately more expensive.
4. Additional personnel are required to fire the boilers.
5. More potential failures, due to crew negligence.
6. Increased maintenance and repair costs, due to the amount of auxiliary machinery.
7. Not readily available for operation at the proverbial "minute's notice" unless engines are kept continuously warmed-up.

In addition to the foregoing, the steam tug creates a fire hazard when handling tankers loaded with high-octane gas and fuels, necessitating the use of elaborate spark arresters at the stack. Smoke from a steam tug cannot be entirely eliminated and a clear stack is, for all practical purposes, impossible to attain especially while maneuvering. The smoke of a steam tug fouls paintwork and general cleanliness of vessels, which eliminates its use in handling passenger and cruise ships.

From a cursory perusal of the foregoing, it can readily be seen that the disadvantages seem, on the whole, to outweigh the advantages; however, this has not always been the case for as can be seen by the following example the prime importance of the advantages far outweighed the disadvantages in the particular trade cited:

A steam tug had proved for years to be of particular advantage for ocean and rescue towing. The dependability of a slow turning engine throwing a large wheel in a heavy boat was a combination that was for years unbeatable on long hazardous ocean tows where the loss of propulsive power could have easily spelled disaster during times of stress and inclement weather. This dependability of the steam engine has since been overcome by improvements in diesel engines.

Steam Turbine. The steam turbine was never given serious consideration as a means of tug propulsion due principally to the necessity of maintaining a high-turbine blade speed velocity to a low-propeller speed accomplished through the use of large reduction gears and the resultant increase in size of the plant.

Cross-compounding for efficiency further increases the size of a turbine plant so as to put it out of the picture completely as a means of propulsive power for all practical towing purposes.

Diesel Engine. In the diesel engine the industry has found the most practical means of propulsion adaptable to the towing trade. A quick glimpse at the following should show why:

Advantages:

1. Low initial cost.
2. Economical. Low fuel consumption to shp produced and cheap fuel.
3. Replacement parts are cheaper than steam reciprocating engine parts.
4. Fewer operating personnel required. Firemen eliminated.
5. Fewer auxiliaries result in less potential failures due to crew negligence.
6. Less maintenance costs although maintenance work on the main engine is increased.
7. Engines may be started immediately, and they are instantly available to apply any fuel consumption to payload work.
8. Readily adaptable to any remote control.
9. Minimum lay-up expense.
10. Cleaner tugs.

Disadvantages:

1. Repair work requires much dismantling of the engine and in many cases it is a time-consuming task.
2. Noise and vibration.

The adverse dependability factor in the diesel engine has been overcome down through the years to a great extent by constant improvements in design and performance so that today it is as reliable and in most cases more reliable than the older obsolete reciprocating engine. The foregoing is considered anathema by a hard core of steam engineers, but then, no argument would serve to convince them of the superiority of diesels in this field.

Figure 29 illustrates the clean and orderly appearance of a modern diesel tug engine room.

The engine must be securely mounted, particularly in a river towboat that operates continually in shallow waters and is subject to possible groundings.

The diesel engine should be fitted with manometers to measure turbo-inlet pressure, air manifold pressure, turbocharger suction and discharge pressures. Pyrometers are necessary to measure cylinder temperatures and turbocharger inlet temperature. A tachometer is desirable to measure turbocharger speeds. In order to determine engine performance, L. O. test instruments are needed to measure acidity, mulsification, fuel dilution, etc.

The noise and vibration produced by diesel engines are gradually being reduced as a result of continuous research and experiments conducted by engineering societies in America as well as in Britain and Europe. Although much has, been done in the past to reduce

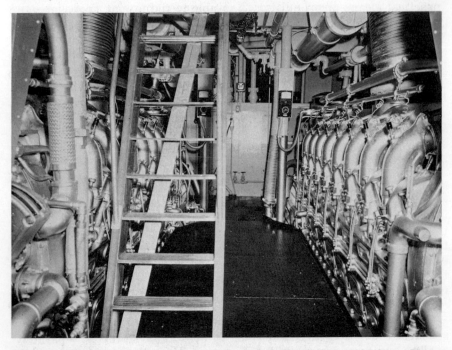

Fig. 29. The "shipshape" appearance of a modern diesel twin-engined tug. Moran

noise and vibration, there remains considerable room for improvement. These factors in the past were generally given secondary consideration in the selection of a diesel propulsive unit, if in fact they were considered at all. (note 13)

Passing on, we move quickly to a related subject and a close though rather more sophisticated cousin of diesel direct drive and reduction gear propulsion—the diesel-electric drive tug.

Diesel-Electric Drive. The diesel-electric drive tug, as its name implies, uses two drives in conjunction to produce the final propulsive power for the propeller.

The diesel drives a generator, of a size depending upon the choice of the owner and the requirements of the trade. The generator, in turn, produces electric current that is used to operate a main motor. The main motor is affixed to and drives the shaft that turns the propeller.

The extreme sensitivity of control over propeller speed required by harbor tugs can be provided by the expensive and inefficient diesel-electric drive.

The following should help to understand at a glance the factors involved in diesel-electric tugs. (note 14)

Advantages:

1. Provides a speed reduction between engine and propeller.
2. The propeller can be maneuvered—ahead, astern or stopped without stopping or reversing the engine.
3. Ability to maintain constant full power through all towing loads, resulting in greater bollard pull per bhp.
4. Electrical machinery can sustain large overloads at decreased propeller rpm without exceeding engine ratings.
5. Allows varied selection of propeller speed and engine speed, reducing high speed of engine to efficient slow propeller speeds.
6. The propeller speed affects only the motor size, weight and cost, whereas direct-drive diesel affects the weight of the entire plant.
7. Positive and accurate bridge control minimizes the chances of damage to hull and rope breakage while maneuvering. It is a time-saver and necessitates fewer engineers to operate.

The system allows the use of a relatively high-speed diesel engine that weighs less and requires less room than a low-speed engine of the same power, but this is offset by the added weight of electrical equipment. A propeller operates most efficiently at low speed so that the necessary speed reduction is accomplished by either a low-speed motor directly connected to the propeller shaft or a high-speed motor coupled to the propeller shaft through reduction gears.

High-speed engine and reduction gears weigh less than a low-speed engine. The direct-current, shunt-wound motor is separately excited and is reversed electrically, permitting the engine and gene-rator to run in the same direction at all times. This constant running of the engine requires no stops and reverses, and reduces maintenance costs considerably.

Disadvantages:

1. There are electric transmission losses, including electric engine-room auxiliaries, of 19 per cent. In other words, 19 per cent of the diesel engine ihp is *not* delivered to the propeller.
2. The first cost of machinery is greater than for other types of engines.
3. More machinery is installed than in a straight diesel tug, resulting in a heavier plant.
4. Electrical maintenance costs are increased.

The principal argument against diesel-electric, and it is an effective one, is its overall cost. Diesel-electric drive has the dubious distinction of having the highest initial cost as well as the greatest maintenance expense.

It would appear that many of the diesel-electric tug advantages can be matched favorably by a controllable-pitch propeller plant with some considerable savings in installation and maintenance costs.

PROPELLER

The selection of a propeller for a vessel must take into consideration the hull design of a tug. An efficiently designed propeller and a poorly designed hull will not combine to produce anything but an overall performance producing results somewhere between the designs of both.

The propeller must be built with sufficient strength to withstand minor damage that might be incurred while operating in harbors strewn with floating debris and by striking submerged objects on rivers or oceans.

Static bollard pull tests used as a criterion of hull and propeller design efficiency have emphasized the need for correlating hull, propeller and horsepower design characteristics to produce the most effective tug. (note 15)

Conventional Open Blade. A conventional propeller, or fixed propeller as it is also known, is "unable to absorb the correct power for more than one special condition" (note 16) of operation; i.e., free running or loaded—free running (speed) and loading (bollard pull).

Formerly propellers designed for towing speeds of 7 knots gave fairly good propeller efficiency at towing speeds and moderate free running speeds. However, this compromise did not provide maximum efficiency in either towing or free running conditions. As a result other forms and designs of propellers had to be investigated to produce a better and more efficient operation. A most effective result of these investigations was the design of the C-P or controllable-pitch propeller and its application to tugboats.

Controllable-pitch. The open, controllable-pitch propeller has an improved power-absorbing range under different loading conditions and it is well suited for tugs; however, the propeller is expensive, and it lacks sufficient thrust when operating astern. Continued design improvements should eventually increase astern thrust, particularly if the propeller is used in conjunction with other patented features, such as the Kort nozzle or hydroconic hull.

There are several patented controllable-pitch propellers, e.g., KAME-WA, Liaanen-Wegner and Baldwin-Lima-Hamilton, to name a few.

Some of the advantages of a C-P propeller are the following:

1. The engine need not be reversed, a practice which reduces engine maintenance costs, and eliminates the need for a clutch.

2. The propeller pitch is automatically controlled to settings coinciding with the engine's horsepower to maintain maximum performance under any condition of engine loading.

3. Tug maneuverability and adaptability are highly satisfactory which lends its use most suitably for docking tugs and to handling ships of any size in restricted waters.

On the Liaanen installation the propeller is of three-blade or other multi-blade stainless steel construction with automatic pitch compensation. Briefly, the pitch is controlled by a sliding rod fitted inside a hollow tailshaft. The rod is moved by a servo-motor piston which, in turn, is operated by varying oil pressure on either side of the piston through an adjustable valve gear, all enclosed in a casing.

Damages to a C-P propeller may cost more to repair than those on a conventional blade propeller which might tend to restrict its adaption for harbor tugs because of floating debris often found in harbors; however, it has been fitted on the British docking and harbor tug *Gower*, a prototype of tugs built by W. J. Yarwood & Sons, Ltd., for Alexandra Towing Co., Ltd., Liverpool (largest towing company in the United Kingdom).

The vessel is of raked keel design, flush deck sheered forward, elliptical stern and reinforced shaped stem for pushing. A set-back boat deck and raked bulwarks facilitate operating alongside ships under the flares of bows, shaped sterns, and while heeling alongside. This design avoids damage to superstructures by permitting a certain clearance while working in these overhand areas. Additional chafing gear is provided by installation of a solid rubber fender completely around the tug outboard of the stringer in way of the sheer and a double fender protecting the nosing piece in way of the stem. The whole fender system is of Firestone design. (note 17)

Twin-screw. The twin-screw tug for harbor use is not in favor with most owners because of the great danger of propeller damage while operating in harbors usually cluttered with debris and flotsam.

The twin-screw installation is better adapted to river, ocean and coastal towing needs. The failure of one engine does not mean the loss of control of a tow, an important consideration in offshore towing.

With the same power a twin-screw has greater maneuverability although developing less bollard pull because of smaller propellers. In order to turn a twin-screw tug quickly, it is sometimes necessary to stop one engine, and perhaps reverse it, which results in a loss of pull. On the other hand, a single-screw tug will turn fairly rapidly at most speeds and will not experience great difficulty in maintaining her head into the wind. The hydroconic hull is well adapted to twin-screw propulsion.

At least one authority believes that a future American tug may well be a twin-screw hydroconic hull of approximately 800 shp per screw with a two-speed reversible reduction gear. (note 18)

Perhaps the C-P propeller will play an increasingly important role in twin-screw tug design. Twin-screw propulsion has long been used on towboats in the western rivers trade.

Kort nozzles have been installed on many river towboats so that today it is rare to find a towboat hauled out that is not fitted with this effective propulsive aid. Figures 18 and 30 show two twin-screw installations of the Kort nozzle.

Fig. 30.   Kort nozzles of modern design installed on twin-screw tug fitted with multiple rudders, all in recessed shaft tunnels. Dravo

Voith-Schneider Cycloidal. The Voith-Schneider propeller is constructed of vertical blades rotating around the circumference of a circle. The blade angles are adjustable and varying the pitch angle enables the tug to turn around on its own axis and to stop within its own length from full speed.

The propulsion drive includes a reduction gear that permits the use of high-speed diesel engines. Because of the variable pitch angle of the propulsion blades, the thrust magnitude can be accurately regulated, as well as the direction of thrust.

Another feature of the Voith-Schneider is that no rudder is required because the thrust can be adjusted ahead, astern or sideways by varying the angle of the blades.

A flat-bottomed Voith-Schneider tug, called tractor, is usually twin-screw and applies the towing force aft of the propeller blades which tends to return the tug to its course.

The installation of the engine well forward would normally encroach upon crew living space; however, in Voith-Schneider installation the *tractors* are usually confined to operating on inland waters only, with crews that live ashore.

Tractors are smaller and lighter than conventional tugs, but the initial cost is high and maintenance costs are considered excessive. In addition to its complicated and expensive construction, the V-S propeller requires a flat-bottomed hull that in turn makes for poor sea-keeping characteristics.

Paddle Wheel. Although it has been many years beyond the recollection of most people since the side paddle-wheel tug was employed in America for towing, its use in Great Britain extends into our time. (note 12)

As recently as 1957, side paddle-wheel tugs were being built and delivered, with others on order, for the British Admiralty. The chief advantage of the side paddle-wheel tug is its great turning power, a definite and important advantage over a conventional tug when docking and maneuvering in small areas. Stern paddle-wheel towboats operated extensively on our western rivers system until recent times.

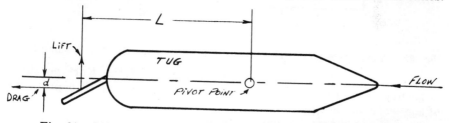

Fig. 31.   Lift, drag and pivot point of a tug maneuvering operation.

RUDDER

Conventional Blade Type. A rudder should produce a turning diameter of twice the vessel's length. The conventional blade or plate type rudder is the best design. The rudder area is approximately 5.5 per cent to 6.5 per cent of the immersed lateral plane.

The height to length ratio of a rudder is approximately 0.56. A rudder angle of 35 deg. is considered necessary for a tug, with a hard-over-port to hard-over-starboard speed of approximately 8 to 15 seconds. One authority recommends a rudder area to be from 6 to 6.5 per cent of the lateral plane. (note 19)

The conventional blade type rudder found on most tugs gives high lift going ahead, high drag, and it is excellent for maneuvering, although backing operation is unsatisfactory.

The terms lift, drag and pivot point are illustrated in Fig. 31.

Aerofoil. Aerofoil is the name given to a symmetrical aerodynamical rudder. The rudder provides a maximum lift to drag ratio but less lift than a blade type. The control obtained while backing is much better than for a blade type.

A typical aerofoil rudder is illustrated in Fig. 32.

Kort Nozzle. The Kort-nozzle rudder, a continuation of the design of the Kort nozzle, is a steel ring of fore and aft aerofoil section in which the propeller turns. The ring can be pivoted about a vertical rudder axis.

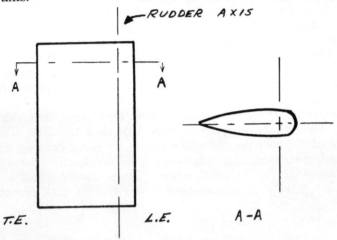

Fig. 32.   A typical aerofoil rudder. T. E. = Trailing Edge; L. E. = Leading Edge.

To better illustrate the operating principle of the Kort nozzle it is perhaps the best approach to describe the operation of a propeller of conventional design.

A propeller normally has to pump accelerated water through a propeller race section diameter smaller than the diameter of the propeller itself and at some distance aft of the propeller. The Kort-nozzle prevents this squeezing of the propeller race and the consequent slowdown of water, resulting in a greater volume of accelerated water mass producing a greater thrust.

See Fig. 30 for a Kort-nozzle installation on twin-screw vessel.

The effect of pumping water through the ring is to stabilize the flow during heavy weather, providing the propeller with improved thrust while pitching. Whereas an open-blade propeller will operate while pitching vertically up and down in a water mass of varying density and the resultant thrust is expended in diagonal or angular thrusts, the Kort-nozzle ring has a tendency to carry the entrained (confined) water mass and thus to effectively direct the thrust astern. Additionally, there is some considerable evidence to support the contention that the nozzle will improve towing efficiency of a tug and the maker claims a 50 per cent increase in static pull. One of the major advantages of the nozzle is its increasing efficiency with increasing slip—a condition most helpful to tugs; and the disadvantage is in the expensive heavier steering gear required. (note 20)

The Kort-nozzle rudder, a later development of the Kort nozzle, solved one of the objections to that nozzle by improving astern operation.

The Dravo Corporation installed the first Kort nozzle used in America on a river vessel, the 300-horsepower *Pioneer* in 1937, see

Fig. 33. The steel shroud around this towboat's propeller made marine history and helped the upsurge in inland river transportation. It was the first Kort nozzle ever used in this country. Installed on the 300-horsepower *Pioneer*, built by Dravo Corp., Pittsburgh, it had its trial run on May 13, 1937. The *Pioneer* is still in operation. Dravo

Fig. 33. The first tugs on the East Coast using fixed Kort nozzles and three rudder systems were also installed by the Dravo Corporation. The combination of three rudders and Kort nozzle provides a tug with greater maneuverability than a single rudder and open-blade propeller, especially while backing where a conventional tug exhibits loss of power and control. (note 21)

The installation of the 7-foot diameter propellers on the 1,230 hp *Superior* and the 1,000 hp *Colorado*, owned by Great Lakes Towing Co., of Cleveland, included the first American-built steering Kort nozzles to appear on the Great Lakes. The units weigh approximately 8,200 lbs. each. It is expected that the installation should give the vessels from 25 to 40 per cent more push or pull per engine horse-power.

Retractable Flanking.   Flanking rudders are installed on most western rivers towboats and to a lesser extent on other tugs. It is estimated that the rudders are in use only about 1 per cent of the total operating time; therefore, they are sometimes raised by hydraulic rams into recessed trunks to reduce the turbulence of water to propellers. To date no information is available regarding the effectiveness of this costly gear and whether or not the results obtained justify the expense.

Pleuger-active.   A Pleuger-active rudder consists of a motor from 50 to 800 hp, depending upon needs, driving a propeller in a centrally positioned streamlined nozzle. The direction of a tug's heading may be changed by varying the angle of the forced stream of water to either side by turning the rudders. During slow-speed maneuvering, the rudder can be moved up to 90 degrees port or starboard and affords a positive control over a vessel's heading.

TOW ENGINE

The term *tow engine* is used here to identify machinery that may be employed to handle towing hawsers of any type. The engine may be automatic, non-automatic, or a capstan.

Automatic. The automatic towing engine consists of one or more central reel drums for main tow hawsers and usually two gypsyheads, one located at either side, operated through a clutch arrangement.

The tow engine automatically maintains towline tension and towline length to predetermined settings. The engine prolongs the life of a hawser by paying out at times of excessive pull and by reeling in when the pull eases up. Movement of the tow hawser, at times almost continuous, reduces concentrated wear and tear of the tow hawser due to chafing at gunwale or over the towing bar, span or Dutch bar.

The main tow wire is wound on a central reel drum powered by an electric motor. When tug is running ahead of the tow the hawser is automatically veered on the winch in order to prevent sudden jerks on the line, jumping the line, and to prevent the tug from coming up short on a taut hawser.

The winch also provides greater control over docking vessels when used in docking operations.

For automatic operation the length of towline and tension are preset so that the hawser pays out upon exceeding the tension set and, upon tension being relieved, the winch reels in hawser to a pre-set distance. There is a general tendency for the winch to pay out excessively during heavy weather, or when a sea is running. As a result the main tow hawser is secured to the towing "H" bitts at these times.

Winch operations are thoroughly covered in the manufacturer's instruction books, and they should be read, studied and understood prior to operating the towing winch. In any event, do not use chafing gear on the hawser of an automatic towing engine, but do grease heavily the rail, gunwale, or Dutch towing bar (towing span).

Nonautomatic. A nonautomatic towing winch, as the name implies, pays out or shortens up in the tow hawser by manual control only. At other times towing is done from the towing "H" bitts.

Periodically inspect the foundations of all towing winches. Check particularly the bolts by rapping smartly with a test hammer to

Fig. 34. The Baker-Whiteley Towing Co.'s tug *Resolute* on starboard quarter of N.S. *Savannah* with tug *Britannia* assisting on port quarter, docking at Dundalk Marine Terminal, May 20, 1964.

check for loose or fractured bolts. Take up on the nuts of any loose hold-down bolts.

Capstan. On tugs not equipped with towing winches a capstan is usually installed as a means of handling the tow hawser. A capstan serves the same purpose as a nonautomatic tow winch except that the towing hawser is not wound around and stowed on a drum. A capstan is illustrated in Fig. 35. The capstan is used to heave in or pay out the tow hawser. Towing is done from towing "H" bitts and not from the capstan.

TOW "H" BITTS

Most long-distance towing is done with the main tow hawser secured to the towing "H" bitts, rather than on a nonautomatic towing engine or tow hook.

"H" bitts are best located as near as possible to the center of pivot of the tug, or slightly aft of the center of buoyancy.

An unstable couple is created with the "H" bitts forward and propeller aft that tends to set the tug off course. Conversely, placing the "H" bitts too far aft holds the tug to a steady course and impedes

Fig. 35. A capstan installed on a tug. The drive motor is usually mounted beneath the deck. The gear housing and hand brake are visible in this photograph.

maneuverability. On American tugs bitts are located slightly farther aft than on European and British tugs, primarily because the houses of American tugs extend farther aft. Generally, the engine room is covered with the extended house, whereas on European and British tugs, the engine-room skylight looks onto the after deck.

Tow "H" bitts may be seen in Figs. 12 and 28.

TOW HOOK

A tow hook is used as a simple means of connecting the towing hawser to a bitt or bollard on a tug.

Some European tugs and harbor towboats are fitted with non-automatic tow hooks with a tripping mechanism that may be operated from their bridges. In this way the release of a tow is directly under the control of the tug captain.

The towing hook may be tripped from the bridge by lanyard with towline in any position and under all loading (towline pull) conditions. Use of a tow hook requires that the after deck and fantail be clear of working personnel during maneuvering to prevent injuries when hook is tripped releasing the towline.

The tow hook usually is located just aft of amidship or as near the pivot point as possible so as not to impede maneuverability of the tug. Should the hook be placed too far aft, the tug cannot readily maneuver and steering is impeded so that when the steering wheel is put over to make a turn the tug tends to maintain its original course.

On a tug handling large ships in port docking operations, the hook is usually secured amidship above any obstructions in order to facilitate operating ahead or astern.

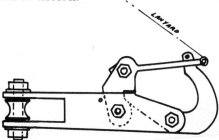

Fig. 36.   A standard tow hook.

Standard. The standard tow hook is illustrated in Fig. 36. The hook is secured to the tow bitts using a strop; in turn, the main tow hawser eye is connected to a short length of Manila that is inserted in the hook. Towing is then done on a hook that is capable of being released quickly causing an immediate disconnect between tug and tow, a condition that serves to resolve many different needs; e.g., to prevent tripping or girding of tug, to facilitate docking maneuvers, and to release a sinking tow—to name a few.

The towing hook must be rigidly secured and free to swing through a lateral arc of approximately 180 degrees. Foundation supports must be carried down into the hull structure.

Spring-loaded. Spring type tow hooks in the closed and tripped positions are illustrated in Figs. 37 and 38. Some hooks are designed to trip and release the tow when the pull or load exceeds a predetermined amount. The automatic disconnect feature of the spring-loaded

Fig. 37. Spring type tow hook in the closed position. Loveridge, Ltd.

Fig. 38. Patent slip type towing hook with short spring in the open, or released position. Loveridge, Ltd.

tow hook prevents tripping or girding of the tug by releasing the towline upon reaching a maximum strain. (note 22)

Two large hooks are illustrated in Figs. 39 and 40.

In any event, the position of the tow hook will to some extent be located just aft of the center of buoyancy, and should coincide with the center of lateral resistance—a sound position because the unstable couple (tending to set the tug off its course) created with the tow hook forward and propeller aft, increases as the tow hook is moved farther forward. Hooks placed at excessive heights tend to capsize or gird a tug, therefore, the height of a tow hook should be minimized to reduce stability problems.

So we find that the tow hook should be located as near the center of buoyancy as possible to improve maneuverability and as far aft

Fig. 39. Custom built tow hook made by Loveridge, Ltd., Cardiff, United Kingdom. Loveridge, Ltd.

Fig. 40. Patent slip type towing hook with long spring. An idea of its size can be gained by a comparison with the machinist. Loveridge, Ltd.

of the center of buoyancy as possible to improve transverse stability. Obviously a compromise is called for here.

In conclusion, the location of a towing hook is an important factor in tug design and it should theoretically coincide with the center of lateral resistance.

TOW SPAN

The tow span, sometimes termed *tow bar* or *Dutch tow bar*, is a steel shape curved to elliptical form that is fitted above the after deck between port and starboard gunwales. The shape spans the engine-room skylight. Its purpose is to prevent the tow hawser from snagging or becoming fouled on any deck construction.

The span directs the hawser up and clear of the deck as shown in Fig. 41, permitting tug personnel access to stern deck at all times.

Fig. 41.   Tow span or Dutch tow bar over the fantail of an ocean tug from gunwale to gunwale.

STATIC BOLLARD PULL

Static bollard pull is a measurement of the amount of force a tug is capable of applying to a tow under certain conditions.

Whereas in past years horsepower output of an engine has played the important role in tug requirements, the specification of static bollard pull lately has come into increasing prominence as a more logical measurement of a tug's power.

Static bollard pull being a result of the force of propeller jet area is a function of the propeller diameter, pitch, revolutions of shaft, and draft of tug, all in combination. It should be mentioned in passing that static bollard pull alone is not taken as the total criterion of a tug's ability to tow. Two other factors probably of equal weight in affecting that ability are displacement and maneuverability.

Aside from the United States Navy and a few American operators, Great Britain and Europe are the leading proponents for static bollard pull as an important measurement of a tug's force. It would appear that primary concern of the average American operator and underwriter with horsepower in tugs may have been a carry-over from the general American preoccupation with horsepower in other industries.

Test.   Generally, the static bollard test is conducted in waters exceeding one atmosphere in depth—the depth at which atmospheric pressure doubles, or approximately 33 feet.

A dynamometer, with a scale in excess of the maximum pull in tons expected, is made fast on dock and connected to an intermediate wire approximately 100–600 feet in length depending on space available and length of tug.

Considerable research has been done to determine the probable static bollard pulls of tugs from formulae resulting from the findings of tests.

To illustrate, the following are a few examples:

$$T = 1.3 \times \frac{BHP}{100}$$

where

T = static bollard pull   (note 23)

Hydroconic hulls: The observed bollard pull for this type of tug nearly equaled the open-water propeller thrust, and was recorded in excess of,

$$T = \frac{SHP}{61} \qquad \text{(note 24)}$$

Kort-nozzle tugs:

$$T = \frac{BHP}{57} \qquad \text{(note 25)}$$

Static bollard pull may also be estimated from the shaft horse-power. (note 26)

Standard hull: Approximately 4,400# plus 23.5# per bhp for open-blade propellers.

Hydroconic tugs of double chine construction: Approximately 36# per bhp.

Kort-nozzle tugs: Approximately 39# per bhp.

Voith-Schneider tugs: Approximately 25.5# per bhp, which is somewhat less than for conventional propellers.

In conclusion it may be said that static bollard pull should be given considerable thought in conjunction with displacement and maneuverability in ascertaining the suitability of a given tug to perform a particular job in the most efficient manner. And for immediate needs of an operator, the foregoing data should allow him to approximate the static bollard pull of a tug in the quickest possible time.

TUG HORSEPOWER

While horsepower is considered important when determining a tug's ability to do a job, it is by no means the only factor taken into account. Displacement and maneuverability are two additional factors that determine the tugability of a vessel.

European owners successfully operate tugs in Rotterdam, Antwerp, Hamburg, Bremen and most European ports with power between 450–750 bhp; a rather far cry from the engines of increased horsepower that have been installed recently in American tugs. Of course, in all fairness we must add that the newer American tugs are designed and built to handle much larger ships and heavier towing jobs with fewer tugs than in the past, hence the need for more power.

For general harbor towing and docking, 1,200 bhp or 1,560 ihp is considered more than adequate. (note 27)

Great Britain formerly saw tugs almost exclusively operating in the 350 to 750 bhp range; however, it would appear that the horsepower "bug" has caught up with our British friends also, as seen by the recent introduction in Britain of larger tugs ranging from 1,400 to 1,600-plus bhp.

Although from the foregoing this begins to take on the appearance of an antihorsepower campaign, it could be more truthfully characterized as a horsepower with "horse sense" admonition. Briefly stated, the case in point is, it is best not to consider powering or increasing the power of a tug without first taking under advisement the opinions of a qualified naval architect and marine engineer.

The following are a few of the horsepower indicators:

BHP = developed at the shaft
SHP = same as bhp
IHP = indicated at the engine cylinders (BHP × 1.3) (approximately)
DHP = delivered horsepower to the tow

Another term that has gained wide acceptance but explains little, is HP., apparently meaning *plain* horsepower but not stating whether delivered or produced. For our purposes, the expression HP will not be used since it explains nothing.

Simpson avers that when a towline pull and tow speed are known, the delivered horsepower can be approximated by his formula:

$$DHP = \frac{V \times P}{100}$$

where

V = speed in knots
P = towrope pull in pounds. (note 28)

To the value of DHP obtained in the foregoing formula, add the power required by the tug, to give a total power value. The BHP may then be estimated by:

BHP = k × (total power value from above)

where

k = 1.10 for direct-drive or geared diesel.
k = 1.25 for diesel-electric drive.

Bollard pull = 22.4 lbs. (0.01 tons) per SHP (any machinery). (note 29)

Torsionmeters are installed to indicate brake horsepower so that an operating engineer can know when his engine is running at the rated load.

BHP will again be taken into consideration in Chapter IV when we take up the problem of power, tow resistance, tonnage and hawser strength.

A capable captain is essential to the successful operation of a tug or towboat. He should be a man who knows local conditions, is aware of traffic patterns, and understands tides, currents, and channel conditions, in order to assure safe towing operations, render effective towing assistance, and provide efficient all-around tug service.

NOTES: CHAPTER II

1. P. Grieg, "Modern Harbour Tug Design," *Motor Ship*, v. 40, n. 475, February 1960, p. 436.

2. "Integrated Barge Train Runs Trials on Clyde," *Marine Engineer & Naval Architect*, v. 81, n. 984, August 1958, p. 298-300.

3. D. A. Argyriadis, "Modern Tug Design with Particular Emphasis on Propeller Design, Maneuverability and Endurance," *Society of Naval Architects and Marine Engineers*, Paper n. 7 for meeting Nov. 14–15, 1957, p. 371.

4. C. D. Roach, "Tugboat Design," Transactions, *Society of Naval Architects and Marine Engineers*, v. 62, 1954, pp. 593–626, 641–642, cited in Argyriadis, *loc. cit.*

5. "Demonstrates hydroconic hull tug," *Marine News*, Jan. 1961, p. 50.

6. R. Beattie, "Tug Design and Development," *Motor Ship*, v. 40, n. 475, February 1960, p. 448.

7. G. R. Knight, "Look at Hydroconic Design . . . Will This Development Improve Tugs?" *Marine Engineer/Log*, March 1958, v. 63, n. 3, p. 84–86.

8. J. J. McMullen, "Stagnation in Harbor Tug Design?" *Marine Engineer*, v. 63, n. 6, June 1958, p. 65.

9. Grieg, *op. cit., passim.*

10. "New Alabama Tug Is Almost All Aluminum," *Rivers and Harbors*, v. 43, n. 7, July 1958, pp. 26–28.

11. *Ibid., passim.*

12. For a fairly recent application of the paddle-wheel tug built for the British Admiralty see, "Diesel-Electric Paddle Tugs," *Marine Engineer and Naval Architect*, v. 80, n. 969, June 1957, pp. 214–216.

13. For one application of acoustical insulation to reduce noises in the engine room see, "1280 HP Tug 'Hustler 11'," D. P. Robinson, *Diesel Progress*, v. 24, n. 11, Nov. 1958, pp. 50–51.

14. Lester M. Goldsmith, "High Towing Efficiency of Diesel-Electric Tugs," *The Oil Forum*, v. 3, n. 4, April 1948, p. 40.

15. McMullen, *op. cit.*, pp. 64–65.

16. Grieg, *op. cit.*, p. 436.

17. "Liverpool Tug with Norwegian Controllable Pitch Propeller," *Motor Ship*, v. 42, n. 495, Oct. 1961, p. 303.

18. McMullen, *op. cit.*, p. 131.

19. Grieg, *op. cit.*, p. 436.

20. Grieg, *op. cit.*, p. 437. *See also* Beattie, *op. cit.*, p. 448.

21. "Two Lakes Tugs Get Steering Kort Nozzles," *Marine Engineering/Log*, August 1962.

22. R. Munro-Smith, *op. cit.*, p. 47, *cf. ibid.*, p. 51, a spring-loaded type hook of 30 tons test weighs 0.47 tons.

23. R. Munro-Smith, *op. cit.*, p. 50.

24. *Ibid.*, p. 52.

25. *Ibid.*, p. 53.

26. Grieg, *op. cit., passim.*

27. Beattie, *op. cit.*, p. 446.

28. D. S. Simpson, "Small Craft, Construction and Design," *Transactions-Society of Naval Architects and Marine Engineers*, v. 59, 1951, p. 578.

29. *Ibid.*, p. 579.

CHAPTER III

TOWING THEORY

Having covered a few of the basic factors to be considered in the design of tug and towboat, we may now pass on to a discussion of various equipment and the fitting out of vessels in the towing trade.

Lines, chain, splices, connections, line controls and mooring fittings will be covered first and then a general explanation of some practical seamanship exercises will follow.

Finally, we will investigate some methods of paying out and shortening up, as well as the forces exerted in, a tow hawser.

CLASSES OF TOWING EQUIPMENT

Towing equipment is usually classified in either one of two categories:

Protective. Hawser boards, chafing gear, seizing wire, rope yarn, marline, bolts, steel pins, canvas, wood.

Protective equipment, as the name implies, protects some additive equipment such as tow hawsers, bridles, pennants, turnbuckles, bolts, etc. Protective equipment prevents accidents resulting from breaks and failures due to chafing, rusting and inadvertent disconnecting.

Additive. Shackles, pennants, bridles, heavy lines and hawsers, thimbles, chain, swivels, tackle, etc.

Additive gear is used to connect a tug and tow, and to supplement the primary function of towing gear in facilitating and maintaining connections.

It may be said that protective equipment is basically *consumable* gear and that additive equipment is *expendable* gear.

An item of consumable gear is generally used only once before discarding, whereas a unit of expendable gear may be employed many successive times until eventually it is discarded after excessive wear and tear.

A running inventory of protective and additive gear will insure that an adequate stock is maintained and will prevent a "drought" or "overkill" in supplies kept on hand. In line with maintaining an adequate usable inventory, it is a good practice to remove from the vessel at the earliest opportunity all defective, damaged or badly worn expendables and discarded rope. Storing and saving of useless

61

or defective gear can only serve to occupy precious storage space that often could be put to better use. The operational effectiveness of a tug is usually considered to be in inverse proportion to the amount of useless gear aboard.

It is well to keep in mind the following when a decision is being made as to whether or not an item should be discarded:

1. Numerous man-hours are expended, not only by personnel in moving junk out of the way in order to get at useful gear, but also

Fig. 42. Stowage of ropes, anchors, hoses and spare parts in the hold of a modern salvage tug. Note anchors and hoses lashed with small stuff.

by new personnel in trying to acquaint themselves with the possible original uses of such junk.

2. A vessel, after a number of years in the collecting stage, begins to take on the appearance of a floating junk shop, while operationally it takes on the characteristics of one as time passes.

3. Excessive accumulations of useless gear add weight to a vessel and can limit its operational range. A coastal or ocean tug outfitting for distance towing may reach the deep load line before sufficient fuel, water and stores are aboard, often necessitating a stop at an intermediate port and the added expense that this involves. (note 1)

4. While junk is being collected, it in turn collects dirt and soon becomes a nesting place for rats, roaches and filth.

5. Finally, junk acts as a mental block to any seaman "worth his salt." It impedes his work and frustrates his efforts so that the sooner a vessel is cleaned and cleared of useless gear, the better will be its operational effectiveness as exemplified by performance, attitude and morale of the crew.

STOWAGE

Because of limited space aboard most tugs, the exercise of considerable ingenuity is often necessary so that storage spaces present neat appearances. Figures 42 and 43 show typical stowage patterns in a modern tug.

Wire reels are best stowed suspended off decks near overheads and supported on pipes passed through the center spool openings of reels.

Fig. 43.   A typical stowage pattern in a modern tug.

The wire is readily accessible and it is easily taken off the reel simply by unwinding the suspended reel.

Wire, cable and bridles that are used often are stowed on deck as shown in Fig. 44. Remember that few stowage patterns are alike and each reflects the experience and ingenuity of the individual tugboatman.

TOW HAWSERS

The main tow hawser is perhaps the most important item of gear employed in the towing trade and a successful towing operation depends to a great extent on its sound condition. The condition of the hawser, in turn, depends upon how it is handled, used and stowed, as well as its age.

The term *hawser*, formerly was defined as, ". . . a plain laid" rope of 4½″ circumference or larger, used for towing or mooring. Now,

Fig. 44.   Faking down a synthetic tow hawser showing how the lays of the rope are laid out to prevent snagging.   Moran

however, the term is applicable to wire, fiber and synthetic ropes used for the same purpose.

Tow hawsers that are *not* wound on drums of winches are to be flaked out on deck in a fore and aft direction with the bights of the lays laid abaft each other as shown in Fig. 44.

All bights of large hawsers are secured individually using stoppers of small stuff so that each bight will part (break) under a light strain, allowing the lays to pay out easily one at a time without fouling (snagging or knotting), when streaming a tow.

Wire. Wire hawsers, because of their great weight, are usually wound on the drums of, and used in conjunction with, a towing engine. Because they are not as elastic as fiber and synthetic hawsers, wire hawsers are often connected to *chain* bridles on the tow. Weight of a chain bridle in the make-up provides a spring effect that tends to cushion sudden shock-loading of the hawser; shock-loading that might result from heavy weather, high seas, strong winds and sharp turns. In addition, a shot of chain is sometimes shackled midlength in the hawser. This intermediate shot of chain will not suffer serious damage in the event that it drags bottom in shallow waters. And while a tow will ride and follow more easily and a fast tug can tow more quickly with this intermediate shot, the connecting and disconnecting operations are much more cumbersome and require the assistance of additional tugs when leaving and entering ports.

A few of the advantages of using wire rope over fiber rope as a tow hawser are:

1. Wire is easier to handle when coiled on the drum of a tow engine.
2. Less stowage space is required.
3. Less deterioration results when wire is properly dried and oiled.
4. Wire is more economical, due to its longer life when properly handled.
5. Greater strength.
6. The weight provides spring in the make-up.

A few of its disadvantages are noted for purposes of comparison:
1. Wire is more difficult to splice than most fibers and Manila.
2. Reels are heavier and consequently more difficult to handle.
3. Initially, wire is more costly.

Wire is employed for most ocean towing; however, in recent years synthetics have taken an increasingly greater percentage of the ocean tow load. The main tow wire on larger ocean-going tugs is usually in excess of 2″ in diameter and over 2,000 feet in length. The importance of sufficient length of a tow wire cannot be overstressed, especially for ocean towing and, to a lesser degree, for coastal towing. Splice in new wire when necessary to insure maintaining a hawser of adequate length.

A main tow wire requires proper attention and care if it is to provide long service with minimum wear. The wire must be thoroughly sluiced with oil and grease before and after each use. After some considerable service in salt water, the wire is hosed down with fresh water, then oiled and greased as usual. Inspect the tow wire when reeling in at the completion of each towing job. Note any damaged sections and make required repairs immediately, or as soon thereafter as possible. Necessary repairs are too often neglected and easily forgotten after wire is wound on a towing engine drum.

Inspect the heart of the wire by laying open a couple of strands using a marlinspike, thereby exposing the hemp core (heart). The core should appear moist and oily. A "dead" (dry and rotted) core will not provide necessary cushioning and lubrication of inner strands and will shorten the life of the wire by increasing wear and tear due to heat resulting from internal friction.

Periodically, but not exceeding a lapse of one year, *end-for-end* the main tow wire. End-for-end is a term that identifies the practice of removing wire completely from the drum of tow engine and placing the opposite end of the wire (towing end) on the drum and re-reeling so that the bitter end becomes the towing end.

Eventually, inspections of tow wires should result in *downgrading* of old tow wire for other purposes. Tow wire that appears to have "seen better days" need not be discarded completely, but should find its way into other uses on board the tug. Downgrading is an accepted economical practice. The establishment of adequate maintenance practices should result in extending the life of tow wire and a consequent savings in dollars.

A wire rope functions in a manner similar to a piece of machinery. There is movement between parts, causing friction. Strands rub, slide and squeeze onto each other as the rope is stressed, pulled, twisted or bent. This friction must be kept at a minimum because friction, as we know, produces heat and heat means expenditure of energy. Expended energy in this case results in wear and abrasion.

Friction between surfaces is minimized by lubrication as it is in any other machinery. Wire rope must be lubricated with oil or grease and, most important, the lubrication must penetrate to the vital core or heart where much of the energy of stress is absorbed. Failure to adequately lubricate internal parts as well as external surfaces will reduce the life of a wire rope and may eventually cause a failure. Sluice your wire rope often. Do not use crude oils and old crankcase oil. Consult your lube oil manufacturer's representative for the proper oil to apply.

Wire is used extensively in the towing trade for main tow hawsers, intermediate hawsers, back-up wires, large connections, etc. Wire rope is the most reliable of any rope used for a main tow hawser. Table I shows the strength and weight of various sizes of wire rope used in towing.

The steel used in wire rope is a composition resulting from a blending of different iron ores. Some steels used are iron, cast steel, extra strong cast steel, plow steel, improved plow steel and high-grade plow

Table I. Strength and Weight of Wire Rope Used for Towing.

Size (diam.)	6 × 12 (Mooring Lines) — Weight per ft in lbs	6 × 12 Galvanized — Improved Plow Steel	6 × 12 Galvanized — Plow Steel	6 × 24 (Towing Lines) — Weight per ft in lbs	6 × 24 Galvanized — Improved Plow Steel	6 × 24 Galvanized — Plow Steel	6 × 37 IMPROVED PLOW STEEL (Towing Lines) — Weight per ft in lbs IWRC[1]	6 × 37 — Weight per ft in lbs FC[2]	6 × 37 Bright — IWRC	6 × 37 Bright — FC	6 × 37 Galvanized — IWRC	6 × 37 Galvanized — FC
1/4	.10	4680	4080				.11	.10	5568	5180	5011	4662
5/16	.15	6720	5840				.18	.16	8664	8060	7798	7254
3/8	.20	9100	7900	.194	9540	8280	.24	.22	12400	11540	11160	10390
7/16	.26	11820	10280				.33	.30	16810	15640	15130	14080
1/2	.33	14900	12960	.35	16800	14600	.43	.39	21930	20400	19740	18360
9/16	.41	18320	15940				.54	.49	27730	25800	24960	23220
5/8	.59	26200	22800	.54	26000	22600	.67	.61	33970	31600	30570	28440
3/4	.69	30600	26600	.78	37200	32400	.96	.87	48590	45200	43730	40680
13/16	.80	35400	30800	.91	43600	38000						
7/8	1.05	46000	40000	1.06	50400	43800	1.31	1.19	65790	61200	59210	55080
1	1.19	51800	43000	1.38	65600	57000	1.70	1.55	85570	79600	77010	71640
1-1/16	1.33	58000	50400	1.56	73800	64200						
1-1/8	1.48	64400	56000	1.75	82400	71800	2.16	1.96	107700	100200	96940	90180
1-3/16	1.64	71200	61800	1.95	91800	79800						
1-1/4	1.99	85600	74400	2.16	101400	88200	2.66	2.42	132200	123000	119000	110700
1-3/8	2.17	93400	81200	2.61	122000	106200	3.22	2.93	159300	148200	143400	133400
1-7/16	2.36	101400	88200	2.85	133000	115800						
1-1/2	2.77	118400	102800	3.11	144600	125800	3.84	3.49	189000	175800	170000	158200
1-5/8	2.99	127200	110600	3.64	169000	146800	4.50	4.09	221400	206000	199300	185400
1-11/16	3.22	136600	118800	3.93	181800	158000						
1-3/4	3.45	146000	127000	4.23	195000	169600	5.23	4.75	255800	238000	230300	214200
1-13/16	3.94	166000	144400	4.53	208000	181600						
1-7/8	4.20	176400	153400	5.18	238000	206000	6.00	5.45	292400	272000	263200	244800
1-15/16	4.47	187200	162800	5.52	252000	220000						
2				5.87	268000	232000	6.82	6.20	331100	308000	298000	277200
2-1/16												
2-1/8							7.70	7.00	371900	346000	334700	311400
2-1/4							8.64	7.85	414900	386000	373400	347400
2-1/2							10.7	9.69	507400	472000	456700	424800
2-3/4							12.9	11.72	610600	568000	549500	511200
3							15.3	13.95	720200	670000	648200	603000

[1]IWRC = Independent Wire Rope Core; [2]FC = Fiber Core.

Courtesy: American Manufacturing Co., Inc.

steel. It is then processed through rolls into small rods of approximately ¼″ to ½″ in diameter. The rods are then drawn cold through dies to form wire of desired diameter. The cold drawn wire is annealed, lubricated, and quenched in order to offset the hardening effect of drawing which tends to make wire brittle.

Wire rope is approximately six times as strong as Manila rope. Table II shows by size comparative strengths of wire and Manila.

Table II. Comparative Strength of Wire and Manila Ropes.

Manila Rope		Spring Lay Wire Rope		6 × 12 Wire Rope Type "G"		6 × 24 Wire Rope Type "J"		6 × 37 Wire Rope Type "E"	
C Ins.	S Lbs.	D Ins.	S Lbs.	D Ins.	S Lbs.	D Ins.	S Lbs.	D Ins.	S Lbs.
4	15,000	3/4	17,500	5/8	17,700			1/2	18,600
5	22,500	1	29,300	3/4	25,400			9/16	23,200
6	31,000	1-1/8	37,100	7/8	34,500	3/4	36,900	3/4	40,000
7	41,000	1-3/8	54,600	1	44,800	7/8	49,300	7/8	53,400
8	52,000	1-1/2	70,200	1-1/8	56,700	1	64,000	1	69,400
9	64,000	1-5/8	81,900	1-1/4	69,400	1-1/16	72,200	1	
10	77,000	1-3/4	95,500	1-3/8	83,300	1-3/16	89,900	1-1/8	87,600
11	91,000	1-7/8	109,200	1-1/2	99,300	1-1/4	99,400	1/4	108,000
12	105,000	2	117,000	1-5/8	115,000	1-3/8	120,000	3/8	130,000

Note: C = Circumference; S = Strength; D = Diameter

A strand consists of six wires laid around a center wire and it is used for haulage rope. A strand wound with an additional layer of twelve wires forms a nineteen-strand wire rope used for hoisting. Strands are wound around a hemp or Manila core.

Wire rope is galvanized to provide temporary adequate protection from corrosion due to immersion in salt water. Once galvanizing has worn off, however, corrosive action on wire is greatly increased. A rule of thumb is to renew wire rope when the outer wires are worn down to half their original diameters.

Six-strand wire rope with seven (7) hemp cores is the most flexible and elastic wire rope made and therefore it is used for towing. The wire rope is made in 6 x 12, 6 x 24, 6 x 30, and 6 x 37. A main 6 x 37 tow wire is made of 37 wires in each of six (6) strands. There is no hemp in the strands but there is a hemp core. The 6 x 37 tow wire should not be galvanized.

A sharp nip may weaken a wire rope approximately 25 to 50%.

If a load is applied with a sudden jerk, the shock will have the effect of doubling the load and this must be calculated for, when determining the required rope size.

An estimation of the strength of wire rope can be made (if accurate information is not available) by applying the following formula:

$B = D^2 \times 25$ where

B = breaking stress in tons (2,240 pounds)

D = diameter of wire rope

Next observe the *condition* of wire rope and depending upon that analysis apply a *factor of safety* of from one-eighth to one-fourth of the breaking stress.

So much for breaking stress. For a *new* wire we determine the *safe working load* by the following formula:

$$P = \frac{D^2 \times 25}{6}$$

where P = safe working load D = diameter of wire rope

To the result of the formula add or subtract 30 per cent to the value of P, depending upon the service for which the wire is intended.

The approximate working load for wire rope is approximately equal to the breaking stress for the same size Manila rope.

Manila and Hemp. The sequence of listing the foregoing should not be construed to indicate the order of their importance, or acceptance, for each has a definite place in marine towing.

Uses. Generally speaking, Manila and hemp are not used extensively for heavy long-distance ocean towing. They have, however, maintained their place in inland, river and, to some extent, coastal towing.

The following types of fiber hawsers illustrated in Fig. 45 are in common usage:

Standard: a three-strand Manila towline

Sleevelay: manufactured by Plymouth Cordage Co., Plymouth, Mass., 5½″ to 12″ circumference

Four-strand   Cable-laid

**Standard manila   3 strand   4 strand
3 strand tow line   cable laid   manila rope**

Fig. 45. Some types of fiber hawsers.

1. ⠿⠿⠿⠿⠿⠿⠿⠿⠿⠿⠿⠿⠿⠿⠿ **SOFT**

2. ⠿⠿⠿⠿⠿⠿⠿⠿⠿⠿⠿⠿⠿⠿⠿ **STANDARD**

3. ⠿⠿⠿⠿⠿⠿⠿⠿⠿⠿⠿⠿⠿⠿⠿ **HARD**

Fig. 46. Typical fiber rope lays.

Note that in America wire size is measured in diameter and fiber is measured in circumference. Typical lays used in fiber rope are shown in Fig. 46. The angle of lay is greater in *hard lay* than in *standard lay* resulting in a hard, stiff rope that is compact and resistant to moisture absorption, but its breaking strain is reduced.

Some hemp and Manila tow hawsers on the smallest tugs are approximately 3″ to 4″ in circumference, whereas on coastal and ocean tugs the tow hawser may exceed 24″ in circumference.

Manila and hemp hawsers, when they fail, usually part at the eye. Investigations have revealed that the cause is principally dry rot at a point of failure between thimble and rope under parceling, where the rope seldom dries. After a long tow using Manila or hemp, it is

Fig. 47.   A correct method of uncoiling new rope as recommended by Wall Rope.

good practice to cut off the eyes and resplice new eyes to cancel out effects of rot, wear and tear.

Some early "Wallcore" hawsers made of three-strand Manila of 10″ to 15″ circumference up to approximately 265 fathoms (1,590 feet) proved of greatest value in deep-sea towing because they contained a special lubricant for the "give and take" needed in heavy tow loading. Today "Wallcore" hawsers are made up to 24″ circumference and larger for ocean towing. The increasing size of hawser used is one indicator of the greater size of the average ocean tow in tonnage pulled, as well as applied horsepower of tug.

Handling. Manila and hemp tow hawsers and intermediate hawsers must be properly handled and stowed to insure a long life:

1. Stow lines in wooden grated boxes that are raised above the deck a minimum of 6 inches. The space between box and deck will insure adequate air circulation necessary to prevent dry rot. (Dry rot results from factors that include dampness rather than dryness alone.)

2. Do not allow oils, greases, solvents, acids, etc., to come into contact with lines.

Fig. 48. Securing ropes and lines using small stuff. Note the wood grates installed to keep ropes off the deck and to allow for drainage and air circulation.
Moran

3. Periodically wash lines thoroughly using fresh water.

4. Do not stow lines in a damp or wet condition. Fake down and allow the lines to dry out first.

5. End-for-end lines at regular intervals to prevent excessive wear on either end.

Figure 47 illustrates a proper method of uncoiling rope.

Small stuff is a term generally used to identify rope yarn, bits of strand, pieces of hemp, etc., that serve innumerable purposes on any tug. To obtain rope yarn, unstrand a line for the yarn and cut it to size. Use rope yarn for lashing, securing chafing gear, seizings for fiber lines and for securing lights on inland tows. In fact, small stuff may be used for any one of countless minor lashing jobs. Figure 48 shows small stuff being used to secure ropes on deck. Note wood grating that keeps lines off deck.

Figure 49 illustrates the actual sizes of Manila rope in circumference and diameter. Some idea can be had of the actual size of a larger rope simply by projecting the sizes shown with caliper and rule.

Refer to Table III for the comparative strengths of fiber ropes.

Table III. Comparative Strength of Fiber Ropes.

Circum.	Diam.	Manila 100%	Composite 90%	Mixed Sisal 75%	Sisal Hemp 70%	Jute 60%
5/8	3/16	450		340	310	270
3/4	1/4	600		450	420	360
1	5/16	1,000		750	700	600
1-1/8	3/8	1,350		1,010	950	810
1-1/4	7/16	1,750		1,310	1,230	1,050
1-1/2	1/2	2,650		1,990	1,850	1,590
1-3/4	9/16	3,450		2,590	2,410	2,070
2	5/8	4,400		3,300	3,080	2,640
2-1/4	3/4	5,400		4,050	3,780	3,240
2-1/2	13/16	6,500		4,880	4,550	3,900
2-3/4	15/16	7,700		5,780	5,390	4,620
3	1	9,000		6,750	6,300	5,400
3-1/4	1-1/16	10,500		7,870	7,350	
3-1/2	1-1/8	12,000		9,000	8,400	
3-3/4	1-1/4	13,500		10,120	9,450	
4	1-5/16	15,000		11,250	10,500	
4-1/2	1-1/2	18,500	16,600	13,900	12,950	
5	1-5/8	22,500	20,300	16,900	15,800	
5-1/2	1-3/4	26,500	23,800	19,900	18,500	
6	2	31,000	27,900	23,200	21,700	
7	2-1/4	41,000	36,900	30,800	28,700	
8	2-5/8	52,000	46,800	39,000	36,400	
9	3	64,000	57,500	48,000	44,800	
10	3-1/4	77,000	69,300	57,800	53,900	
11	3-5/8	91,000	81,900	68,200	63,700	
12	4	105,000	94,500	78,800	73,500	

Occasionally it becomes necessary to renew rope. Old rope is discarded and new rope is acquired. The length, weight and strength of coils of various rope sizes should be known beforehand so that a correct purchase will be made. It is important to know the weight of a coil so that those accepting delivery will be better prepared to handle and stow the rope. This information is contained in Table IV.

Cautions. Exposing Manila rope to high temperature or stowing it wet will cause it to deteriorate rapidly; a well-made splice will weaken Manila approximately 5 to 10 per cent; a sharp nip may weaken Manila approximately 25 to 50 per cent.

The comparative strength of two similar ropes of different sizes is equal approximately to the squares of their circumferences, e.g., a three-inch rope is to a four-inch rope as 9 is to 16.

WALL MANILA ROPE
Actual Sizes

Circum- | Diam-
ference | eter

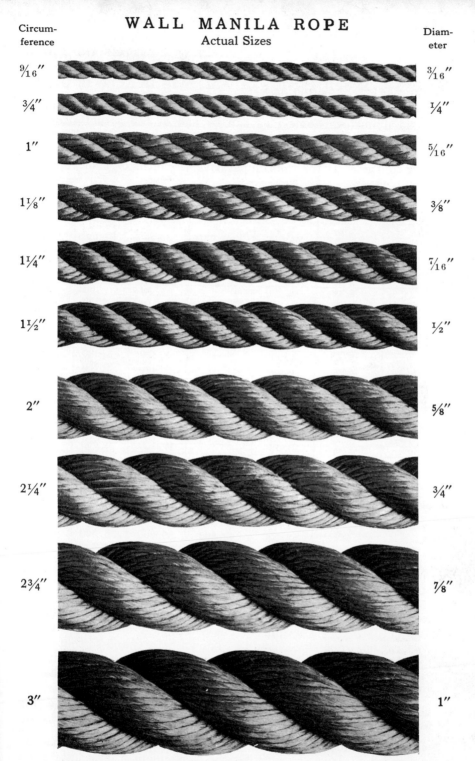

Circumference		Diameter
9/16″		3/16″
3/4″		1/4″
1″		5/16″
1 1/8″		3/8″
1 1/4″		7/16″
1 1/2″		1/2″
2″		5/8″
2 1/4″		3/4″
2 3/4″		7/8″
3″		1″

Fig. 49. A comparison of actual sizes of some rope. Wall Rope

Table IV. Specifications of Wall Manila Rope in U. S. and Metric Equivalents.

| Thread | SIZES In Inches and Millimeters | | | | GROSS WEIGHTS In Pounds and Kilograms | | | |
| | Diameter | | Circumference | | Full Coils | | Per Foot | |
	Inches	MM	Inches	MM	Pounds	Kilos	Pounds	Kilos
6-thd. fine	3/16	4.763	5/8	15.875	50	22.6796	.015	.0068
6-thd.	1/4	6.350	3/4	19.050	50	22.6796	.020	.0091
9-thd.	5/16	7.938	1	25.400	50	22.6796	.029	.0132
12-thd.	3/8	9.525	1 1/8	28.575	50	22.6796	.041	.0186
15-thd.	7/16	11.113	1 1/4	31.750	63	28.5763	.0525	.0238
18-thd.	15/32	11.906	1 3/8	34.925	75	34.0194	.0625	.0283
21-thd.	1/2	12.700	1 1/2	38.100	90	40.8233	.0750	.0340
	9/16	14.288	1 3/4	44.450	125	56.6990	.104	.0472
	5/8	15.875	2	50.800	160	72.5747	.133	.0603
	3/4	19.05	2 1/4	57.150	200	90.7184	.167	.0757
	13/16	20.638	2 1/2	63.500	234	106.1405	.195	.0885
	7/8	22.225	2 3/4	69.850	270	122.4698	.225	.10206
	1	25.400	3	76.200	324	146.9638	.270	.12247
	1 1/16	26.988	3 1/4	82.550	375	170.0970	.313	.14197
	1 1/8	28.575	3 1/2	88.900	432	195.9517	.360	.16329
	1 1/4	31.750	3 3/4	95.250	502	227.7032	.418	.18960
	1 5/16	33.338	4	101.600	576	261.2690	.480	.21772
	1 1/2	38.100	4 1/2	114.300	720	326.5862	.600	.27216
	1 5/8	41.275	5	127.000	893	405.0577	.744	.33747
	1 3/4	44.450	5 1/2	139.700	1,073	486.7042	.895	.40596
	2	50.800	6	152.400	1,290	585.1337	1.08	.48988
	2 1/8	53.975	6 1/2	165.100	1,503	681.7488	1.25	.56699
	2 1/4	57.150	7	177.800	1,752	794.6932	1.46	.66224
	2 1/2	63.500	7 1/2	190.500	2,004	908.9984	1.67	.75750
	2 5/8	66.675	8	203.200	2,290	1,038.7257	1.91	.86636
	2 7/8	73.025	8 1/2	215.900	2,580	1,170.2674	2.15	.97522
	3	76.200	9	228.600	2,900	1,315.4168	2.42	1.09769
	3 1/8	79.375	9 1/2	241.300	3,225	1,462.8342	2.69	1.22016
	3 1/4	82.550	10	254.000	3,590	1,628.3953	2.99	1.35624
	3 1/2	88.900	11	279.400	4,400	1,995.8048	3.67	1.66468
	3 3/4	95.250	12	304.800	5,225	2,370.0182	4.36	1.97766

4 Strand (Medium Lay) Averages Approximately 5% To 7% Heavier Than 3 Strand.

METRIC LENGTHS TABLE

1 millimeter (mm)	=	.03937 in.
10 millimeters = 1 centimeter (cm)	=	.3937 in.
10 centimeters = 1 decimeter	=	3.937 in.
10 decimeters = 1 meter (m)	=	1.093611 yd. = 3.2808 ft.
10 meters = 1 dekameter	=	10.93611 yd. = 32.808 ft.
100 meters = 1 hectometer	=	109.3611 yd.
1,000 meters = 1 kilometer	=	.62137 miles

1 inch	= 2.54 centimeters
1 foot	= .3048 meters
1 yard	= .914401 meters
1 fathom	= 1.8288 meters
1 mile	= 1.609347 kilometers

NOTE: To obtain the equivalent diameter or circumference of a rope in Centimeters, multiply the sizes given in inches by 2.54.

Courtesy: Wall Rope Co.

Synthetics. *Nylon*, a fairly recent newcomer in the field of marine towing, is for all practical purposes the "granddaddy" of a later crop of synthetic ropes that are daily giving birth to new applications.

Nylon costs more than Manila, lasts approximately five times longer, and requires the following special handling:

1. Keep clean and free of oil and grease by scrubbing with soap and water or by using light burning oils for cleaning.

2. If a line should freeze, thaw it out at moderate temperatures.

3. Whip strands with tape instead of seizing, and splice nylon the same as Manila except that one more tuck must be added. For heavy towing applications take an extra back tuck with each strand.

4. Although chafing and stretching may not alter the load-carrying ability of nylon, avoid chafing the line and take care to remove burrs from cleats, bitts, chocks, etc.

5. Coiling line in the same direction will unbalance the lay.

6. Stow away from sunlight, heat and chemicals.

Handling—Unreel nylon the same as wire rope. Nylon is stiff during first uses but this may be overcome by subjecting the rope to a stretch tension of approximately 30 per cent (for example, stretch a 100-foot length to approximately 130 feet) and holding for 20 minutes.

Stretch of nylon hawsers in service may be halved by doubling lines.

Dip the rope under the horn of bitts and cross the line upon itself to prevent elongation on the bitt while under strain. Take 2 or 3 round turns on a bitt before figure-eighting to gain control of the line. For heavy towing take six turns when on a capstan and two additional turns over the last four turns.

Nylon is not suitable for the following uses:

> Docking; too much stretch—polypropylene is better.
> Alongside towing; too elastic.

Nylon is suitable for end-to-end towing. It is also useful in place of Manila towing straps.

Cautions—The fusing of fibers due to heat of localized friction while rope is under heavy tension has a negligible effect on the rope's strength.

A normal safe working load will stretch nylon up to one-third its length.

All personnel should avoid the line of pull. Nylon rope parts at about 50 per cent stretch and the snap-back (back-lash) is excessive and dangerous.

Rope will usually part near the eye.

Cable-laid nylon hawsers will emit sharp cracking noises when under strain, and when wet under strain a steamlike vapor will issue forth; both are normal phenomena.

A 40 per cent stretching of nylon is considered to be the critical point.

Use only nylon stoppers on nylon hawsers.

Coil nylon line in a clockwise direction.

Table V. Strength Comparisons of Some Synthetic Ropes and Wire Rope.

SIZE		Fed. Spec. Minimum	WALL ROPE WORKS, INC. — AVERAGE TENSILE STRENGTH						PLYMOUTH CORDAGE CO. — APPROXIMATE TENSILE STRENGTH				
Diam.	Cir.	Manila	Nylon	Dacron	Poly E.	Polypropylene Monofil	Polypropylene Multifil	Poly-D.	Goldline & Nylon	Dacron	P/D	Poly-ethylene	Polypro-Monofil
3/16	9/16	450	960	720	700	800	870		1,100	1,300		700	800
1/4	3/4	600	1,500	1,150	1,200	1,300	1,200		1,950	2,150		1,200	1,350
5/16	1	1,000	2,400	1,750	1,750	1,900	2,050		2,960	3,300		1,750	1,960
3/8	1-1/8	1,350	3,400	2,450	2,500	2,750	2,700	3,600	4,200	4,500	3,050	2,500	2,650
7/16	1-1/4	1,750	4,800	3,400	3,400	3,500	3,280	4,500	5,550	6,000	3,800	3,400	3,350
15/32	1-3/8	2,250											
1/2	1-1/2	2,650	6,200	4,400	4,100	4,200	4,700	6,500	7,200	7,600	4,800	4,100	4,200
9/16	1-3/4	3,450	8,000	5,700	4,600	5,000	6,400	8,500	9,000	9,250	6,100	5,700	5,000
5/8	2	4,400	10,000	7,300	5,200	5,800	8,000	12,000	11,000	11,250	6,700	7,800	5,700
3/4	2-1/4	5,400	14,000	10,000	7,400	8,200	10,200	15,000	15,300	15,600	8,900	11,000	8,200
13/16	2-1/2	6,500	19,000	13,600	10,400	11,500	15,000		21,000	20,000	11,500	13,300	11,200
7/8	2-3/4	7,000	24,000	16,500	12,600	14,000	16,500		26,500	25,000	14,000	16,500	14,000
1	3	9,000	31,500	21,600	16,500	18,300	22,000	19,300	36,000	26,900	21,000	18,600	18,300
1-1/16	3-1/4	10,500											
1-1/8	3-1/2	12,000	36,000	24,400	18,600	20,700	24,500	22,000	41,500	30,600	24,000	21,200	20,700
1-1/4	3-3/4	13,000	42,000	28,000	21,200	23,500	27,300	25,000	47,500	35,000	27,000	26,700	23,500
1-5/16	4	15,000											
1-1/2	4-1/2	18,500	51,000	34,500	26,700	29,700	35,500	31,300	60,000	45,000	34,000	32,700	29,700
1-5/8	5	22,500	62,000	41,500	32,700	36,300	42,300	38,300	74,000	56,300	42,000	39,500	36,300
1-3/4	5-1/2	26,500	75,000	51,000	39,500	43,900	51,000	46,500	90,000	66,300	50,000	47,700	43,900
2	6	31,000	89,500	61,000	47,700	53,000	61,000	56,500	107,000	77,000	60,000	55,800	53,000
2-1/8	6-1/2	36,000											
2-1/4	7	41,000	104,000	70,200	55,800	62,000	72,000	65,500	125,000	91,000	70,000	63,000	62,000
2-1/2	7-1/2	46,500	120,000	81,000	63,000	70,000	85,000	74,000	145,000	106,900	80,000	72,500	70,000
2-5/8	8	52,000	138,000	92,500	72,500	80,500	95,000	86,000	166,000	120,000	92,000	81,000	80,500
2-7/8	8-1/2	58,000	154,000	103,000	81,000	90,000	108,000	96,000	190,000	137,500	105,000	91,800	90,000
3	9	64,000	195,000	130,000	103,000	114,000	134,000	120,000	240,000	180,000	130,000	103,000	102,000
3-1/8	9-1/2	71,000											114,000
3-1/4	10	77,000	238,000	160,000	123,000	137,000	165,000	144,000	300,000	221,000	163,000	123,000	137,000
3-1/2	11	91,000	288,000	195,000	146,000	162,000	200,000	170,000	360,000	270,000		146,000	162,000
4	12	105,000	342,000	230,000	171,000	190,000	231,000	200,000	430,000	324,000		171,000	190,000

Table V. (Continued)

| | | Fed. Spec. Minimum | AMERICAN MANUFACTURING CO., INC. MINIMUM BREAKING STRENGTH | | | | | | WIRE ROPE APPROXIMATE TENSILE STRENGTH | | | |
| SIZE | | | Nylon | | Dacron | | Floterope | | | | | |
Diam.	Cir.	Manila	Reg. Const.	Pyc. Ampycor	Reg. Const.	Pyc. Ampycor	Poly-ethylene	Polypropylene	Spring Lay	6 × 12	6 × 24	6 × 37
3/16	9/16	450	960		700		700					
1/4	3/4	600	1,500		1,200		1,200					
5/16	1	1,000	2,400		1,850		1,750					
3/8	1-1/8	1,350	3,400		2,600		2,500					
7/16	1-1/4	1,750	4,800		3,500		3,400					
15/32	1-3/8	2,250										
1/2	1-1/2	2,650	5,500	6,200	4,400		4,100	5,000		17,700		18,600
9/16	1-3/4	3,450	7,200	8,000	5,700		4,600	5,800		25,400		23,200
5/8	2	4,400	9,000	10,000	7,200		5,200					
3/4	2-1/4	5,400	12,500	14,000	10,000		7,400	8,200	17,500	34,500	36,900	40,000
13/16	2-1/2	6,500	14,500	16,000	11,500		8,900	9,900			49,300	
7/8	2-3/4	7,700	17,000	19,000	13,500		10,400	11,500	29,300	44,800	64,000	53,400
1	3	9,000	21,500	24,000		18,000	12,600	14,000		56,700	72,200	69,400
1-1/16	3-1/4	10,500										
1-1/8	3-1/2	12,000	29,000	32,000		21,200	16,500	18,300	37,100	69,400	99,400	87,600
1-1/4	3-3/4	13,500	32,500	36,000		24,400	18,600	20,700		83,200	118,000	108,000
1-5/16	4	15,000		42,000		27,000	21,200	23,500	54,000	99,300		
1-1/2	4-1/2	18,500		51,000		34,200	26,700	29,700	70,200	115,000		132,000
1-5/8	5	22,500		62,000		41,500	32,700	36,300	81,900			
1-3/4	5-1/2	26,500		75,000		50,500	39,500	43,900	95,500			
2	6	31,000		89,500		60,300	47,800	53,000	117,000			
2-1/8	6-1/2	36,000		104,000		70,200	55,800	62,000				
2-1/4	7	41,000		120,000		81,000	63,000	70,000				
2-1/2	7-1/2	46,500		137,000		92,500	72,500	80,500				
2-5/8	8	52,000		154,000		103,000	81,000	90,000				
2-7/8	8-1/2	58,000					91,800	102,000				
3	9	64,000		195,000		130,000	103,000	114,000				
3-1/8	9-1/2	71,000										
3-1/4	10	77,000		238,000		160,000	123,000	137,000				
3-1/2	11	91,000					146,000	162,000				
4	12	105,000		342,000		228,000	171,000	190,000				

Polypropylene rope labeled "PNX" was developed by American Manufacturing Co., Inc., and designed especially for tugboat use without the excessive stretching found in nylon. Stretch is comparable to that of Manila or Dacron.

The rope is treated during manufacture with an agent known as Resistex, making the rope highly resistant to heat, water and abrasion. "PNX," a highly refined rope owing its virtues to its polypropylene antecedents, is lightweight, is not water-absorbent, floats, is twice as strong as Manila, will not rot or mildew, resists chemical attack and is inert to most acids, alkalies, organic solvents and petroleum products at normal service temperatures.

"PNX" is readily adaptable to alongside towing, docking and push-towing although nylon is better for end-to-end towing. Because it resists electric conduction (low di-electric loss), it may be used on tankers.

Although the strands are easy to splice and to lay open for inspection, a heavy surface and internal friction causes heat and often melting at the bitts—not a desirable reaction.

In conclusion, it may be said that this rope shows good qualities for use as an all-around rope not requiring elasticity.

Docrylene rope, manufactured by Cating Rope Works, Inc., of Maspeth, N.Y., is made of individual jackets of Dacron over polypropylene cores to combine the stretch and flotation qualities of polypropylene with the appearance and handling characteristics of Dacron.

Since docrylene appeared on the market in the spring of 1960, many towing firms have expressed satisfaction with its use. The rope will not stretch and, therefore, it is suitable for alongside towing and docking service.

Dacron jackets around polypropylene fibers act as heat insulators to prevent melting at the bitts (a fault of straight polypropylene rope). In addition, the rope provides greater resistance to abrasion and rubbing wear. It has the look and feel of Dacron although it will float, and it is lighter and less expensive.

Docrylene rope will not rot, shrink, mildew, freeze or foul propellers (it floats).

Goldine, a synthetic rope developed for use as a main tow hawser by Plymouth Cordage Co., averages 20 per cent stronger than nylon. The fibers are produced from Caprolan, a nylon type fiber manufactured from corncobs.

Table V shows strength comparisons of some synthetic ropes and wire rope.

It is sometimes advantageous for a tug crew to know beforehand the approximate size mooring lines they are likely to be handling during a docking operation. Table VI shows recommended sizes of mooring lines for ships of different tonnages. While there is no guarantee that a particular vessel will employ the exact size line, still some idea of the size that they are likely to use may be had from this.

Table VI. Mooring Line Sizes for Ships of Various Tonnages.

Gross Tons of Ship	Manila	Nylon	Dacron	Poly-ethylene	Poly-propylene
1,000 - 2,500	6	4	4-1/2	5-1/2	5-1/2
2,600 - 5,000	6-1/2	4-1/2	5	6	6
5,100 - 8,900	7	5	5-1/2	6-1/2	6-1/2
9,000 - 12,900	8	5-1/2	6	7	7
13,000 - 17,900	9	6	6-1/2	7-1/2	7-1/2
18,000 - 22,900	9-1/2	7	7-1/2	8	8
23,000 - 28,900	10	8	8-1/2	9	9
29,000 - 35,000	11	9	9-1/2	10	10
36,000 - 45,000	12	10	10	11	11

(Wall Rope Co.)

A list follows showing types of lines that may be used for different purposes in the towing trade:

Mooring lines—Manila, nylon, Dacron, polypropylene
Heaving lines—hemp, polyethylene, polypropylene
Towline—Manila, nylon, polypropylene
Head line—Manila, Dacron
Stern line—Manila, Dacron
Gate lines—Manila, nylon, Dacron, polypropylene
Deck lines—Manila, polypropylene
Side straps—Manila, Dacron

The foregoing can change rapidly as new products are marketed; so that it is best to consult with your local rope representatives for information regarding your specific needs.

Table VII. Property Comparisons of Different Ropes.

	Manila	Nylon	Dacron	Poly-"E"	Poly-Pro
Relative Strength	1	5	4	2	3
Relative Weights	4	3	5	2	1
% Elongation Dry	9.0	24.5	12.5	15.5	15.0
@ 20% Load Wet	21.5	29.0	13.0	20.5	18.0
Relative Resistance to Impact Loading	1	5	2	3	4
Mildew Resistance	Poor	Excel.	Excel.	Excel.	Excel.
Acid Resistance	Poor	Fair	Fair	Excel.	Excel.
Alkali Resistance	Poor	Excel.	Excel.	Excel.	Excel.
Sunlight Resistance	Fair	Fair	Good	Fair	Fair
Organic Solvent Resistance	Good	Good	Good	Fair	Fair
Critical Temp.	380°F	410°F	410°F	265°F	300°F
Floating Time	82 hrs	1 min	2 mins	Indef.	Indef.
Abrasion Resistance	1	5	3	2	4

Numbered Ratings: 1 - Lowest to 5 - Highest   (Wall Rope Co.)

An interesting chart developed by Wall Rope Co., showing property comparisons of different ropes, is shown in Table VII. There is hardly a tug afloat that has not seen the need, from time to time, for splicing ropes. New sections are spliced into tow hawsers to replace worn or damaged sections. Straps often need renewing and they are made aboard to the desired length for particular needs. In short, the splicing of lines, ropes and hawsers is a vital function of a deck crew on any tug or towboat. Consequently, some fundamental information concerning the joining of ropes is included here to refresh the memory of the reader and to remind him of some problems involved. The reader may refer to any one of numerous and more concise books on seamanship wherein this and other pertinent information is presented in much greater detail.

The following shows the percentage of total rope strength that can be had by various methods of fastening ropes:

METHOD OF ROPE FASTENING	PERCENTAGE OF TOTAL ROPE STRENGTH
Wire rope socket (attached with zinc)	100
Thimble or eye splice in rope with four or five tucks	90
Thimble placed in the end of rope and fastened with wire rope clips	85
Three wire rope clamps	75

WIRE STRAPS

A wire strap is a short piece of wire cut to required length with eyes spliced in both ends. Eyes may or may not be fitted with thimbles depending on the purpose of the strap.

Where the largest shackle available will not pass through a thimble in the eye of a tow hawser, a strap is sometimes substituted for the

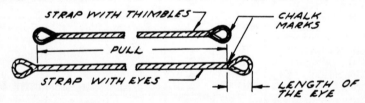

Fig. 50.   Measurement of wire strap.

shackle. In a connection of this type, the strap should equal or exceed the strength of the tow hawser to which it is connected and it may be doubled if necessary. A wire strap in place of a shackle on the main tow hawser must be restricted in use to emergency situations only.

Wire straps are put to numerous other uses on a tug and we will record here some useful information regarding their fabrication. The eyes of wire straps may be spliced plain or they may be fitted with thimbles. Wire straps are always measured from pull to pull in a straight line, as shown in Fig. 50.

Splices. Observe the following to make a strap that is to be fitted with thimbles:

1. Lay off on wire rope the length needed for tucking plus one-half the distance around the thimble. Chalk this point.

2. From the chalk mark lay off the length required for the strap plus three times the diameter of the wire for each thimble. Chalk this point.

3. From this last chalk mark measure off the distance around the thimble plus the length needed for tucking. Indicate this point using a clove hitch where the cut will be made.

4. Insure that the bitter end is prepared for cutting and splicing. See Fig. 51.

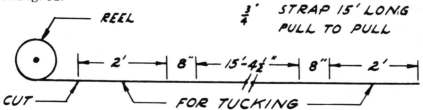

Fig. 51.   Method of making a strap to be fitted with thimbles.

In order to determine the length of rope to allow for tucking when making an *eye splice* consult the following table:

EYE SPLICE IN WIRE ROPE

Diameter of Rope, in Inches	Length to Allow for Tucking, in Feet
¼" to ⅜"	1'
½"	1½'
⅝" to ¾"	2'
⅞" to 1"	2½'
1⅛"	3'
1¼"	3½'
1½"	4'

After an eye splice is made it should be wormed, parceled and served as illustrated in Fig. 52.

The recommended *servings* for different size ropes is shown below:

SERVINGS

Size of Wire Rope	Serve With
⅜"	marline
½"	marline
⅝"	marline
¾"	houseline
*1"	thread seizing stuff

* One-inch wires and larger should be wormed before parceling and serving.

Seizing, as the name implies, is a method of binding the ends of a wire to prevent unraveling when the wire is cut. Seizings are applied before the cut is made, as shown in Fig. 53.

The following is a formula for the *Liverpool eye splice* shown in Fig. 54. Measure 2 to 4 feet from the end of a rope; seize the wire at this point to prevent unraveling while splice is being made. Unlay strands back to the seizing. Cut out the heart (core) at a point close to the seized end and then whip the ends of each of the six strands.

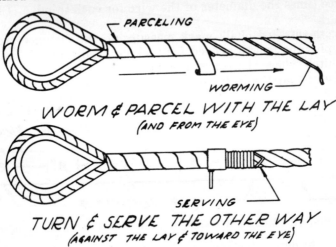

Fig. 52. Worming, parceling and serving of an eye splice.

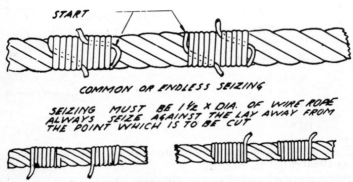

Fig. 53. Seizing a wire rope.

The recommended specifications for seizings are shown below:

SEIZINGS RECOMMENDED

Rope Diameter in Inches	Number of Seizings	Length of Seizings in Inches	Distance Between Seizings in Inches	Approximate Size of Seizing Wire in Inches
½ and smaller	2	½	1	.020-.030
9/16 to ⅞	3	1	2	.040-.060
1 to 1¼	3	1½	2	.060-.090
1⅜ to 1⅝	4	2	2	.080-.125
1¾ to 2	4	3	2	.105-.125
2½ and larger	4	4	3	.105-.125

Referring to Fig. 54, proceed as follows:

6	under	DE	With butt of spike (the rest go in with the point).
5	"	D	
1	"	ABC	
2	"	BC	
3	"	C	
Heart	"	ABC	
4	around	D	This is first tuck.
5	"	E	
6	"	F	
5	"	E	
4	"	D	Run up four and five tucks.
Heart inside splice			Even-numbered strands get five tucks.
3	"	C	Odd-numbered strands get four tucks.
2	"	B	
1	"	A	

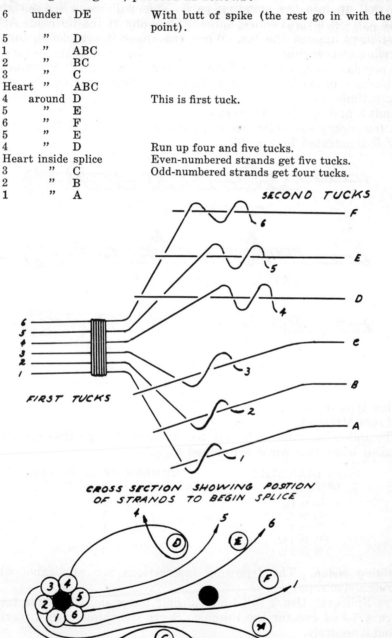

Fig. 54. Liverpool eye splice.

Using a nonferrous mallet, pound the splice away from the thimble and well up into the standing part. This will make for a tighter splice. To get a tight splice, spread the points of the thimble. Apply all seizings against the lay. When the splice is completed, tar the parceling and serving.

A popular variation of the Liverpool eye splice is made by reversing the position of strands 3 and 4. In the merchant marine, this splice is sometimes referred to as a "lock splice" because, by reversing strands 3 and 4, a lock is formed.

A *temporary eye splice* with thimble and secured with wire rope clips is illustrated in Fig. 55.

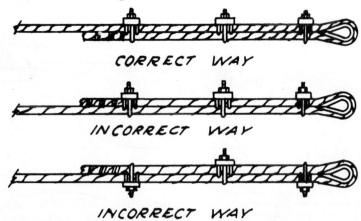

Fig. 55.   Correct and incorrect way of eye splicing a wire rope.

This type of fastening will hold to approximately 85 per cent of total rope strength.

The following table indicates the number of clips that should be installed when two wires are joined together:

ROPE DIAMETER IN INCHES	NUMBER OF CLIPS FOR EACH END OF ROPE
³⁄₁₆ to ⁷⁄₁₆	2
½ to ¾	3
⅞ to 1	4
1⅛ to 1¼	5
1⅜ to 2½	6

Splicing Nylon. The following instructions are applicable when splicing nylon rope.

Eye Splices: Use 3 full tucks, 2 half tucks and 2 quarter tucks. Splice a 3-foot eye for the thimble. Serve the thimble with marline to hold it securely.

Short Splices: Use a tapered splice. Make 3 full tucks, and then taper each side with 2 half tucks and 2 quarter tucks.

Preparatory to splicing and before cutting, a strand should be taped using friction or adhesive tape. A clean cut is made and yarn ends are then fused by applying a flame, blowtorch, or hot iron. This melting and fusing of the yarn ends prevents fraying while rope is in service.

TOWING GEAR

Chain. Types of chain are named from a description of their construction, e.g., open link, stud link, Di-Lok, etc.

Di-Lok chain is a patented chain originally manufactured to Navy specifications. It is now widely used in the commercial towing trade.

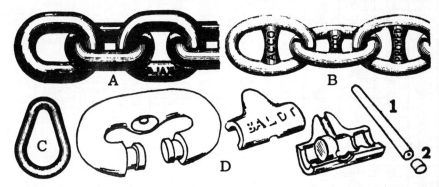

Fig. 56. Some types of chain. A: Ajax dredge chain; B: Stud link chain; C: Sling links, for thimble or chain; D: Detachable link. The tapered locking pin (1) is held in place by a lead plug (2).

Chain is an essential part of the make-up of any offshore tow, but it is seldom if ever used on inland and harbor tows.

A very important asset in a tow make-up for offshore towing is weight. The weight of a length of chain added in a towline provides a flexibility and cushioning that is not inherent in straight wire rope towing, except to a minor degree. A weighty chain, whether used for long bridles or as an intermediate length in the towline, provides a resistance to sudden surges and shock loading on the tow wire resulting from action of: running in a seaway, heavy weather, waves, sudden changes of speed, sharp turns, etc. Sharp turns are included because an added strain is placed on the towline while a tug and tow are turning.

Chain is extremely rugged, long wearing and dependable; on the other hand, it is hard to handle, difficult to stow and expensive to replace.

Figure 56 illustrates some chain types.

Table VIII is most valuable in that it not only lists the proof and break tests in pounds but it also provides information regarding weight, length and link dimensions for most stud link chain sizes.

Table VIII. Stud Link Chain Dimensions and Test Requirements.

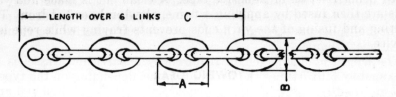

CHAIN SIZE	LINK LENGTH A	LINK WIDTH B	LENGTH OVER SIX LINKS C	LINKS PER 15 FATHOM SHOT	WEIGHT PER 15 FATHOM SHOT APPROX.	WROUGHT IRON		HIGH STRENGTH STEEL		DI-LOK	
						PROOF TEST POUNDS	BREAK TEST POUNDS	PROOF TEST POUNDS	BREAK TEST POUNDS	PROOF TEST POUNDS	BREAK TEST POUNDS
½	3	1 15/16	13	535	340	10,300	15,400	15,900	22,300	22,100	34,000
9/16	3 3/8	2	14 5/8	475	358	13,000	19,450	19,950	27,900	27,900	42,400
5/8	3 3/4	2 3/16	16 1/4	427	385	15,680	23,560	24,560	34,380	32,300	52,200
11/16	4 1/8	2 3/16	17 5/8	389	425	19,040	28,560	29,400	41,160	41,300	61,800
3/4	4 1/2	2 5/8	19 1/2	357	505	22,680	33,880	34,680	48,550	48,000	75,000
13/16	4 7/8	2 7/8	21 1/8	329	600	26,600	39,872	40,430	56,600	56,000	86,500
7/8	5 1/4	3 1/8	22 3/4	305	700	30,800	46,200	46,630	65,280	64,000	98,000
15/16	5 5/8	3 5/16	24 3/8	285	795	35,392	53,088	53,280	74,590	74,000	113,500
1	6	3 5/16	26	267	900	40,320	60,480	60,360	84,500	84,000	129,000
1 1/16	6 3/8	3 3/4	27 5/8	251	1,020	45,472	68,096	67,850	94,990	95,000	145,000
1 1/8	6 3/4	4	29 1/4	237	1,140	50,960	76,440	75,770	106,080	106,000	161,000
1 3/16	7 1/8	4 1/4	30 7/8	225	1,275	56,840	85,120	84,120	117,770	118,000	179,500
1 1/4	7 1/2	4 1/2	32 1/2	213	1,415	63,000	94,360	92,910	130,070	130,000	198,000
1 5/16	7 7/8	4 3/4	34 1/8	203	1,560	69,440	104,160	102,090	142,930	143,500	216,500
1 3/8	8 1/4	4 15/16	35 3/4	195	1,705	76,120	114,240	111,660	156,330	157,000	235,000
1 7/16	8 5/8	5 3/16	37 3/8	187	1,865	83,160	124,600	121,720	170,430	171,000	257,500
1 1/2	9	5 3/8	39	179	2,035	90,720	131,488	132,190	185,060	185,000	280,000
1 9/16	9 3/8	5 5/8	40 5/8	171	2,195	98,336	137,536	143,050	200,270	200,500	302,500
1 5/8	9 3/4	5 7/8	42 1/8	165	2,345	106,400	148,960	154,310	216,030	216,000	325,000
1 11/16	10 1/8	6 1/8	43 7/8	159	2,530	114,800	160,720	165,960	232,360	232,500	352,500
1 3/4	10 1/2	6 5/16	45 1/2	153	2,720	123,480	172,760	178,000	249,210	249,000	380,000
1 13/16	10 7/8	6 1/2	47 1/8	147	2,925	132,440	185,360	190,430	266,620	267,000	406,000
1 7/8	11 1/4	6 3/4	48 3/4	143	3,125	141,680	198,240	203,250	284,540	285,000	432,000
1 15/16	11 5/8	7	50 3/8	139	3,335	151,200	211,680	216,430	303,000	303,500	460,000
2	12	7 3/16	52	133	3,525	161,280	225,792	230,000	322,000	322,000	488,000
2 1/16	12 3/8	7 7/16	53 5/8	129	3,750	171,360	239,904	243,930	341,510	342,000	518,000
2 1/8	12 3/4	7 5/8	55 1/4	125	3,975	182,000	254,800	258,240	361,530	362,000	548,000
2 3/16	13 1/8	7 7/8	56 7/8	123	4,215	192,920	269,920	272,910	382,060	382,500	579,100
2 1/4	13 1/2	8 1/8	58 1/2	119	4,460	204,120	285,600	287,930	403,100	403,000	610,000
2 5/16	13 7/8	8 5/16	60 1/8	117	4,710	215,600	301,840	303,320	424,630	425,000	642,500
2 3/8	14 1/4	8 1/2	61 3/4	113	4,960	227,360	318,304	319,050	446,660	447,000	675,000
2 7/16	14 5/8	8 3/4	63 3/8	111	5,210	239,456	335,160	335,130	469,180	469,500	709,500
2 1/2	15	9	65	107	5,528	252,000	352,800	351,560	492,190	492,000	744,000
2 9/16	15 3/8	9 1/4	66 5/8	105	5,810	261,408	365,960	368,340	515,670	516,000	778,500
2 5/8	15 3/4	9 1/4	68 1/4	103	6,105	270,816	379,120	385,440	539,620	540,000	813,000
2 11/16	16 1/8	9 11/16	69 7/8	99	6,410	280,224	392,280	402,890	564,040	565,000	849,000
2 3/4	16 1/2	9 7/8	71 1/2	97	6,725	289,632	405,440	420,660	588,930	590,000	885,000
2 13/16	16 7/8	10 1/8	73 1/8	95	7,040	298,816	418,320	438,760	614,260	615,000	925,000
2 7/8	17 1/4	10 3/8	74 3/8	93	7,365	308,224	431,480	457,190	640,070	640,000	965,000
2 15/16	17 5/8	10 5/16	76 5/8	91	7,696	317,408	444,360	475,940	666,310	666,500	1,005,000
3	18	10 9/16	78	89	8,035	326,592	457,184	495,000	693,000	693,000	1,045,000
3 1/16	18 3/8	11	79 5/8	87	8,379	335,552	469,728	514,380	720,130	720,500	1,086,000
3 1/8	18 3/4	11 1/4	81 1/4	85	8,736	344,400	482,160	534,060	747,680	748,000	1,128,000
3 3/16	19 1/8	11 1/2	82 7/8	85	9,093	353,248	494,480	554,050	775,670	776,050	1,169,000
3 1/4	19 1/2	11 11/16	84 1/2	83	9,460	361,984	506,688	574,340	804,070	804,100	1,210,000
3 5/16	19 7/8	11 15/16	86 1/8	81	9,828	370,496	518,560	594,920	832,890	833,150	1,253,000
3 3/8	20 1/4	12 1/8	87 3/4	79	10,210	378,840	530,320	615,800	862,130	862,200	1,296,000
3 7/16	20 5/8	12 3/8	89 3/8	77	10,599	386,960	541,632	636,970	891,770	892,100	1,339,550
3 1/2	21	12 5/8	91	77	10,998	395,136	553,056	658,440	921,810	922,000	1,383,100
3 5/8	21 3/4	12 15/16	94 1/4	73	11,607	410,253	570,688	702,755	983,850	1,021,000	1,566,000
3 3/4	22 1/2	13 3/8	97 1/2	71	12,626	425,370	588,320	747,070	1,045,900	1,120,000	1,750,000

Courtesy: Baldt Anchor and Chain Co.

All dimensions in inches. To convert to millimeters, multiply inches by 25.4.

The length of a standard "shot" of chain is 15 fathoms (90 feet or 1,080 inches). The safe working load for chain is theoretically as-proximately 5 to 7 times the depth of water, depending on the type of chain multiplies its strength by 4; however, in practice the result is slightly less than 4.

The length of anchor chain required by a particular vessel is ap-proximately 5 to 7 times the depth of water, depending on the type of bottom, weather, sea conditions, displacement of vessel, hull sail area, and other conditions that can affect the holding power of chain.

Table IX. Sizes of Di-Lok Chain and Stud Link Chain.

All Dimensions in Inches

Ordinary Iron or Steel Chain	Baldt Di-Lok Chain	Ordinary Iron or Steel Chain	Baldt Di-Lok Chain	Ordinary Iron or Steel Chain	Baldt Di-Lok Chain
3/4	11/16	1-11/16	1-7/16	2-5/8	2-1/4
13/16	3/4	1-3/4	1-1/2	2-11/16	2-5/16
7/8	13/16	1-13/16	1-9/16	2-3/4	2-3/8
15/16	7/8	1-7/8	1-5/8	2-13/16	2-7/8
1	7/8	1-15/16	1-11/16	2-7/8	2-1/2
1-1/16	15/16	2	1-3/4	2-5/16	2-9/16
1-1/8	1	2-1/16	1-13/16	3	2-5/8
1-3/16	1-1/16	2-1/8	1-13/16	3-1/16	2-11/16
1-1/4	1-1/8	2-3/16	1-7/8	3-1/16	2-3/4
1-5/16	1-3/16	2-1/4	1-15/16	3-3/16	2-3/4
1-3/8	1-3/16	2-5/16	2	3-1/4	2-13/16
1-7/16	1-1/4	2-3/8	2-1/16	3-5/16	2-7/8
1-1/2	1-5/16	2-7/16	2-1/8	3-3/8	2-15/16
1-9/16	1-3/8	2-1/2	2-3/16	3-7/16	3
1-5/8	1-7/16	2-9/16	2-1/4	3-1/2	3-1/16

At regular intervals (the usual practice is not to exceed 18 months or each dry-dock period), anchor chain should be ranged, examined for damage and excessive wear and tear; links should be sounded with a test hammer. Occasionally, shots are shifted from sections of greater wear to sections of lesser wear. Connecting links should be disassembled and recoated inside with a mixture of white lead and tallow.

Because Di-Lok chain is stronger than ordinary iron or steel stud link chain, all testing societies permit the use of smaller diameter Di-Lok.

Table IX shows dimensions of ordinary iron or steel stud link chain and the reduced size of Baldt Di-Lok chain that may be used as a substitute.

Chain should be inspected carefully before it is connected to a tow. Any damage or excessive wear and tear noted should be given par-ticular attention. If there is any doubt, dimensions should be taken and the chain renewed when worn to the mean diameter listed in

Table X. These dimensions are in accordance with *American Bureau of Shipping Rules for Building and Classing Steel Vessels* and *Lloyd's Register of Shipping Rules and Regulations.*

Table X. Minimum Dimensions for Chain Renewal.

Original Diam. of Cable Inches	Mean Diam. Needs Renewal Inches	Original Diam. of Cable Inches	Mean Diam. Needs Renewal Inches
11/16	5/8	2-1/8	1-29/32
3/4	21/32	2-3/16	1-31/32
13/16	23/32	2-1/4	2
7/8	25/32	2-5/16	2-1/16
15/16	27/32	2-3/8	2-1/8
1	29/32	2-7/16	2-3/16
1-1/16	15/16	2-1/2	2-1/4
1-1/8	1	2-9/16	2-9/32
1-3/16	1-1/16	2-5/8	2-11/32
1-1/4	1-1/8	2-11/16	2-13/32
1-5/16	1-3/16	2-3/4	2-15/32
1-3/8	1-7/32	2-13/16	2-17/32
1-7/16	1-9/32	2-7/8	2-9/16
1-1/2	1-11/32	2-15/16	2-5/8
1-9/16	1-13/32	3	2-11/16
1-5/8	1-15/32	3-1/16	2-3/4
1-11/16	1-1/2	3-1/8	2-13/16
1-3/4	1-9/16	3-3/16	2-7/8
1-13/16	1-5/8	3-1/4	2-15/16
1-7/8	1-11/16	3-5/16	2-31/32
1-15/16	1-23/32	3-3/8	3-1/32
2	1-25/32	3-7/16	3-1/16
2-1/16	1-27/32	3-1/2	3-1/8

Shackles. As might be expected there is considerable controversy and a diversity of opinion concerning the advantages and disadvantages of different types and designs of shackles for use in the tow hook-up.

We will briefly look into some of the requirements of towing connections and, from a further study of the types of shackles available, we may then reach some sort of conclusion as to which are most suitable for particular needs.

Towing connections require that the shackle possess the following attributes: Strength, ease in connecting and disconnecting, remain connected, resist distortion, ruggedness, and long-exposed use with a minimum of maintenance.

Shackles connect the tow make-up at towing padeyes, intermediate hawsers, and fishplates. Occasionally on a light tow a heart-shaped shackle, as shown in **D** of Fig. 57, is used instead of a fishplate, connecting the main tow hawser and bridle legs. The width of the opening in a heart-shaped shackle receives easily the thimbles of a main tow hawser and two bridle legs.

Keep in mind the following when selecting a shackle for a particular use:

1. A safety shackle is fitted with a threaded bolt drilled through the end of the bolt to receive a pin and cotter key, as illustrated in **G** of Fig. 57. The bolt is inserted in the shackle and a nut is screwed

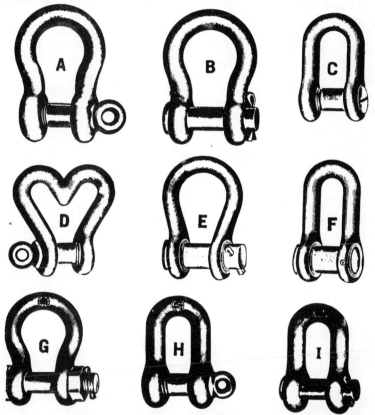

Fig. 57. Types of shackles. A: Screw anchor shackle, weldless drop forged steel or drop forged bronze; B: Round pin anchor shackle, weldless drop forged steel; C: Carver, drop forged steel; D: Heart, drop forged steel; E: Anchor type, drop forged steel; F: Chain type, drop forged steel; G: Safety shackle, weldless drop forged steel; H: Screw pin chain shackle, weldless drop forged steel; I: Round pin chain shackle, weldless drop forged steel.

on the threaded end. In addition, nut and bolt are often drilled through to receive a small pin. The pin keeps the nut from turning and backing off to the cotter key.

2. An oval pin shackle, as illustrated in **E**, is readily adaptable to a 2-inch main towing hawser, but the oval pin cannot fit through the round holes of a fishplate. A wedged forelock key driven into the

slot snubs the pin head tight against the body of the shackle. The key is then bolted and held by split-tailing.

3. When used for towing, a drop-forged screw pin anchor shackle is made of nickel steel.

4. For light towing a nonferrous nut on a screw pin shackle may be used to facilitate removal of the nut.

5. Should it ever become necessary to use a screw pin shackle, weld the pin to the body and, as an added precaution, wire the pin securely to prevent turning.

6. The round pins of shackles illustrated in **B** and **I** are free to turn and wear the pin and key while towing; consequently, they should not be connected outboard of tow hook-up where they cannot be inspected.

The strength of a shackle may be estimated, when exact information is not available, by use of the following formula:

$$P = 3D^2 \text{ tons}$$

where

$$P = \text{ strength of shackle}$$
$$D = \text{ diameter at sides}$$

Fishplates. A fishplate is a triangular shaped heavy steel plate with three holes, one at each corner. Figure 58 illustrates a typical fabricated fishplate. The hole at **A** in the drawing is of sufficient size to receive the shackle of a main tow hawser or intermediate spring.

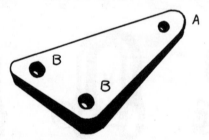

Fig. 58. Fishplate.

Each leg of the towing bridle extending from a barge or tow is shackled into the remaining two holes at **B–B**.

The height of the triangular fishplate measured from the base **B–B** to the apex **A** is greater than the width of the base.

The three-fold purpose of the fishplate is to add strength at the connections, add weight to the make-up and maintain a horizontal position under water while towing, thereby preventing twisting of the hawser and bridles.

Rings. A ring, as the name implies, is a circular piece of steel of small or large cross section shaped to form a ring. A ring serves numerous useful purposes, but it should not be used in the ocean towing hook-up. There seems to be a tendency in certain locales to use a ring in place of a fishplate—a practice that is not condoned.

Pelican Hooks. A pelican hook, as illustrated in Fig. 59, is sometimes employed as a quick-release hook. The hook is connected to a

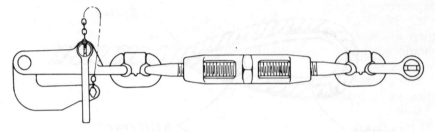

Fig. 59.   Pelican hook type chain stopper.

heavy solid turnbuckle and several links of anchor chain and secured to towing "H" bitts. The eye of a thimble on a tow hawser is inserted in the hook.

Thimbles. A thimble is a steel or galvanized iron, grooved, heart-shaped insert that is fitted into eye splices to provide strength and

Fig. 60.   Thimbles. A: Wire rope; B: Solid; C: Heavy wire rope.

to minimize wear and tear due to chafing action. Some thimbles are illustrated in Fig. 60.

Thimbled splices permit joining two lines with shackles.

The thimble with stiffener, shown in Fig. 61, prevents chafing of the eye, supports the thimble and prevents crimping of the eye.

For towing, use heavy duty thimbles. The solid or filled center thimble is excellent for use at the outer end of a tow hawser. The ideal thimble for use in towing is one with a thick base at the split groove and square-ended to prevent points from interfering with the first tuck of splice.

Swivels. Swivels are sometimes connected in the make-up of light towing jobs. A typical connection is shown in Fig. 62.

Stoppers. Stopper is a term used to define any one of a number of various items of equipment used to secure a rope or chain. These items include the carpenter stopper, chain stopper, gob rope and lizard stopper, to name a few.

One type of carpenter stopper is illustrated in Fig. 63. The grooved wedge secures the stopper to wire rope so that line pull tends to fasten the stopper more securely.

Chain stoppers are suitable for all-purpose work.

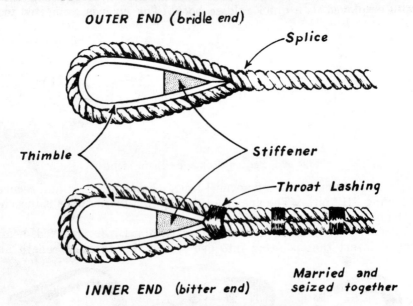

Fig. 61.   Thimbles with stiffeners.

Fig. 62.   Swivel connecting hawsers.

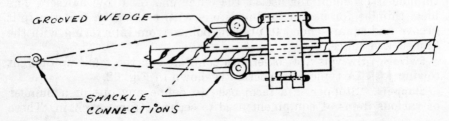

Fig. 63.   Hawser stopper.

A Manila or hemp gob rope of from 2-inch to 4-inch circumference is a short piece of line used as a stopper to hold the tow hawser amidship during times of rough weather.

A lizard stopper of wire fitted with a shackle or clamp for the tow hawser serves the same purpose as a gob rope.

The gob rope and lizard stopper may be substituted for a maneuvering bridle or Liverpool bridle in light towing work. A gob rope is shown in Fig. 131, a stopper in Fig. 130, a chain stopper in Fig. 59.

Blocks and Tackles. Blocks and tackles are mechanical devices used to gain advantage and multiply purchase power.

The parts of a block, as well as several types of blocks, are shown in Fig. 64.

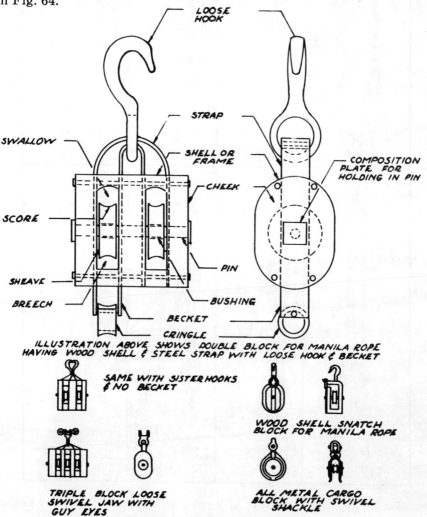

Fig. 64. Parts of a block.

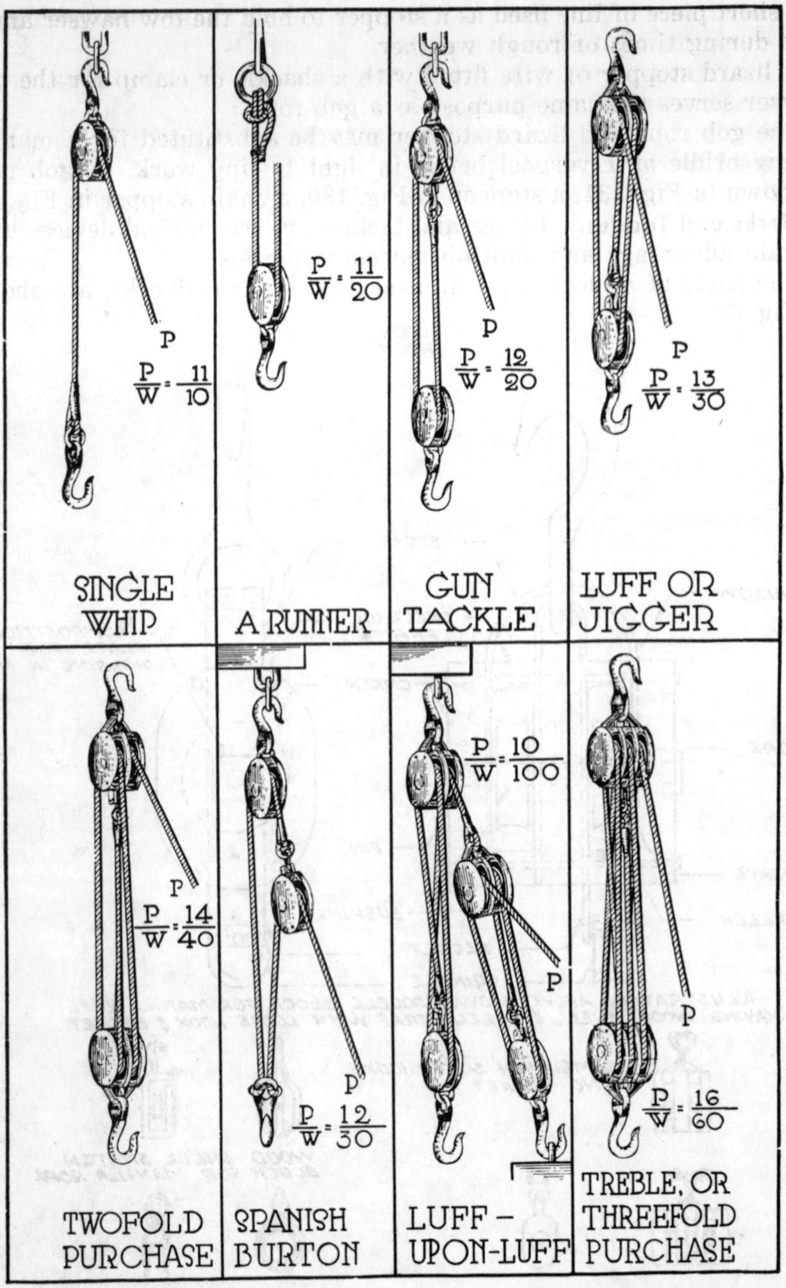

Fig. 65. Tackle. Ratios of Power to Weight, $\frac{P}{W}$, show the efficiency of tackles including allowance for friction losses. Wall Rope

To determine the power developed by blocks, count the number of lines leading to and from the movable block and multiply by the power applied to the hauling part.

The following nomenclature is used to describe tackles:

Falls. The rope of a tackle.

Handy-billy. A small light tackle with blocks of steel or wood that is used for miscellaneous small jobs.

Hauling part. The part of falls to which power is applied.

Overhaul. To separate and lay off blocks in preparation for hauling.

Reeve. To rig a purchase by reeving falls through swallows and over the sheaves of blocks.

Standing part. The bitter end of falls that is made fast to one of the blocks.

Two-blocked. When the two blocks are close together after hauling; sometimes called "chock-a-block."

Typical tackles are illustrated in Fig. 65.

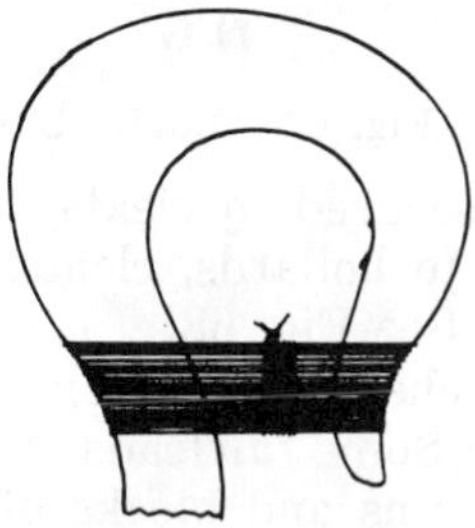

Fig. 66. Hook of a tackle "moused" with wire.

Care should be exercised to insure that rope is sheaved correctly. The sheave width should be at least 25 per cent greater than diameter of the rope. The correct rope diameter to block size is shown in the following table:

Size of Blocks Designated by Length of Shell In Inches	Size of Rope Diameter	Size of Blocks Designated by Length of Shell in Inches	Size of Rope Diameter
3″	⅜″	14″	1⅜″
4″	½″	15″	1½″
5″	9⁄16″-⅝″	16″	1⅝″
6″	¾″	Wood Snatch Blocks	
7″	13⁄16″-⅞″		
8″	⅞″-1″	6″	¾″-⅞″
9″	1″	8″	1″-1⅛″
10″	1⅛″	10″	1¼″
12″	1¼″	12″	1½″

(Courtesy of Wall Rope Works, 48 South Street, N.Y.C. 5)

Good seamanship practice dictates that the hook of a tackle be "moused" with wire as shown in Fig. 66. A better arrangement would be to replace the hook with a shackle for greater strength. A shackle is approximately five times as strong as a hook.

Bitts. Now we will consider the means whereby lines and hawsers are secured aboard tugs and tows. A bitt is usually made of two capped extra heavy pipes of large diameter mounted on built-up foundations and doubler plates.

Figure 67 illustrates three typical double bitts. **A** is the bitt found aboard most vessels. **B** is designed to prevent a line from jumping off the bitts, but its shape often results in jamming the rope. **C** serves the same purpose as **A**, allowing the line to be veered without jamming, and it also prevents the line from jumping off the bitts.

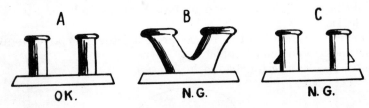

Fig. 67. Double bitts.

In addition, lines are secured to cleats, cavels and Samson posts. Ashore they are secured to bollards, cleats, Samson posts, piles and dolphins, to name a few. See Fig. 68.

Fairleads are used to change direction of pull on a line without undue chafing or friction. Some fairleads are shown in Fig. 68. These are chocks, but Norman pins and blocks of many types often serve the same purpose.

Padeyes. A padeye is a half circle of steel rod the ends of which are welded to a pad or doubler plate. The doubler in turn is welded at a convenient location so that the padeye may then be used as a means of securing blocks, shackles, lines, fairleads, etc. A padeye is as strong as the material in its component parts and the quality of workmanship of the weld attachment. See Fig. 121 for a typical towing padeye.

Doublers. A doubler is a piece of steel, usually rectangular in shape, used as a base, pad, or foundation for padeyes, cleats, bitts, etc. A doubler is also used to patch small wasted areas of structure to provide strength and stiffening.

The doubler derives its name from the fact that it doubles the number of foundation plates, but it does not necessarily double the thickness.

Doublers should be continuously welded and, when fitted with pad-eyes, cleats, etc., they should be mounted in way of structural stiffeners, brackets, frames or beams.

LINE HANDLING

All too often one of the most important functions on any tug, regardless of its trade, turns out to be one of the most hazardous.

Line handling, by its very nature, is dangerous and it is necessary to maintain constant vigilance in order to avoid stepping into a maiming predicament. Even under the best of circumstances when using the most modern equipment, forming of coils and loops of line

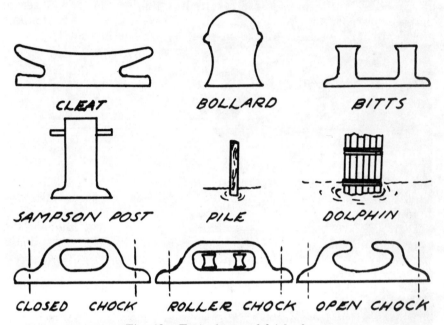

Fig. 68.   Fastenings and fairleads.

on deck is unavoidable when lines are being run out to hook-up or disconnect a tow, as illustrated in Fig. 69. Line handling requires skill, agility and practice on the part of the line handler to be mastered safely.

When handling heaving lines in port there is a need for speed and proficiency in order to tie up (dock) a vessel quickly. The forces of tide, winds, weight and horsepower are very often in constant interaction and they may at any time cause adverse movement of vessel or tug.

Heaving lines should be in good condition and not rotted. Tarred hemp, 15 to 20 fathoms in length, is best suited for the task. Signal halyard, lead line, Manila, or log line are not suitable, although in practice their use is sometimes condoned.

Fig. 69.   Line handling aboard a modern seagoing tug. Moran

Monkey's fists and sandbags secured to the throwing end of heaving lines are dangerous. The next time one is observed being thrown, notice how the receiver tends to "dodge" the weight to avoid getting hit. This reaction is the cause for as many "misses" as is the inaccuracy of the thrower.

To throw a heaving line:

1. Wet the line.
2. Loop the amount required in small coils in one hand.

3. Take less than half of the looped coils in the hand of pitching arm and heave out on a full swing. Allow the coils in the balance arm to pay out freely, but hold on to the bitter end. Bend the heaving line onto a hawser using a long bowline. This permits the men on the tow to get a better grip as the hawser passes over the fairlead at gunwale—where it is heaviest.

A proper method of paying out a line to a vessel is shown in Fig. 70. One man tends the line as another backs him up by taking up slack or paying out the line.

Fig. 70.   Line handling between tug and tow.   Moran

Figure 71 illustrates the correct and incorrect ways of securing bridle legs to a heaving line. Note that in the correct method both feet of the seaman are kept on deck for balance. In the incorrect method the seaman's foot is braced against the bitt for increased leverage. If his foot should slip off the curved surface of the bitt, he may lose his balance and fall. As a result he may injure himself or lose the lines.

One correct method of securing a towline to the "H" bitts is illustrated in Fig. 72. Note that the line is first dipped under the horn before a round turn is taken. The horn prevents the towline from "jumping the bitt."

Before the start of a tow it is well to take a few precautions as far as the "H" bitts are concerned. Prior to putting a bitt to use:

1. Check the foundation for signs of deterioration, structural weakness and strain.

2. Inspect holding down bolts for tightness.

3. Inspect deck doublers, underdeck stiffeners in way of framing and deck beams for wastage and cracks.

4. If in doubt concerning the strength of any doubler or stiffener, crop out any wastage using a torch and partially renew the suspect section by welding. Carry back the new piece to the nearest sound structural member.

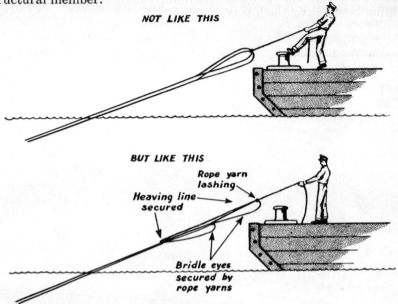

Fig. 71. Securing heaving line to legs of a bridle.

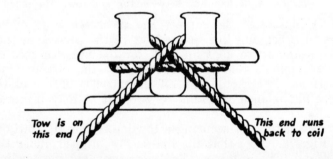

Fig. 72. A correct method of securing a towline on the "H" bitts.

5. Always take the strain of towing on bitts and not on winches or capstans, with the exception of automatic towing engines designed to control the amount of strain and length of hawser. And, too, this does not apply to towing hooks.

6. When a wire is to be secured on a bitt, first take a round turn nearest the pull in order to avoid a "parbuckle" on the bitts, then figure-eight the wire. Stress of a "parbuckle" may cause a strain and result in a fracture. Figure 73 shows a correct method of securing a line to a bitt.

7. When a nylon towline is secured to "H" bitts it will tend to elongate on the bitts when under tension; therefore, dip the hawser under a horn of the bitt, take a full turn and cross the line back onto itself. Then take two or three additional round turns before "figure-eighting" the line on the bitts.

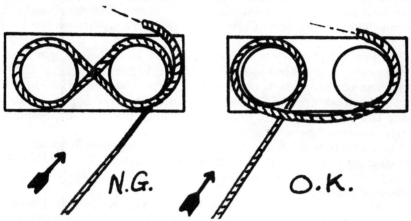

Fig. 73. A correct method of securing a line to a bitt.

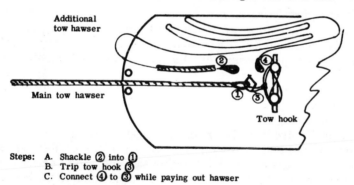

Steps: A. Shackle ② into ①
        B. Trip tow hook ③
        C. Connect ④ to ③ while paying out hawser

Fig. 74. Adding a length of hawser to a towline.

British and European Practice.

Adding a length of hawser to a towline. The tow bridle is connected directly to the tow hook or tow strap until tug and tow reach open water. The thimble of a hawser that is to be added is shackled into the plate shackle, fishplate or heart-shaped anchor shackle connected to the bridle legs. The tow hook is then tripped, allowing the additional length of hawser to pay out. Meanwhile the bitter end of this added length of hawser is connected to the tow hook. Additional lengths of hawser are connected as needed in the same manner, viz., shackle hawsers thimble to thimble, trip tow hook, connect bitter end to tow hook, pay out the added hawser. See Fig. 74.

When a tow is streamed to the required distance for towing, the last length of tow hawser is figure-eighted on the tow "H" bitts. Towing is *not* done from a standard tow hook.

Shortening a hawser using a capstan. Assume a tug is equipped with a capstan but not with a tow winch. The tow is at the end of a long towline made up of several lengths of tow hawser shackled end to end. The inboard end of tow hawser is figure-eighted on the towing "H" bitts.

The general practice is to have a coil of 3- to 4-inch coir rope on a reel near the tow hook and "H" bitts ready for recovery of the towline. The coir rope is bent onto tow hawser at the bulwark, a few turns are taken around the capstan and the hawser is heaved aboard using the power capstan. Recovery is completed after numerous successive shortening operations.

Upon shortening up the tow hawser, tow is eased in close aboard the stern of the tug until the bridle comes aboard. The bridle is then secured to the hook, the hawser disconnected and stowed away.

General practice.

Shortening a hawser using a winch. The hawser is heaved in slowly on the winch while tug proceeds ahead slowly. After shortening up, the hawser is resecured to the "H" bitts.

Handling nylon hawser on a capstan. When temporarily securing a nylon tow hawser on a capstan while heaving in or paying out, take at least six turns on the drum with the last two turns overlaying four turns, so that surging of the hawser on the capstan will be reduced.

Of Hawsers, Horsepower and Tonnage. Any discussion of towing hawser size must also take into consideration horsepower and displacement of a tug, as well as size and tonnage of the tow. All four factors basically are interdependent because the resistance and weight of the tow on one end of towline is opposed to the pulling power and weight of tug on the other end, thereby stressing the hawser connecting the two opposite forces. Therefore the hawser must be of sufficient strength to withstand the stress. In addition, these forces are affected to a great extent by towing speed, sea and weather conditions.

Lacking proof to the contrary it may be estimated that a tug of standard hull form without Kort-nozzle can pull approximately one (1) ton for every 100 bhp of the main engine. Each ton expressed in pounds should indicate the breaking strength of the towline to be used. But, according to this reasoning, a 100 bhp tug should be able to tow on a 1⅜" circumference Manila line (18-thread) that has a breaking strength of 2,250 lbs; however, any seaman will tell you that it cannot be done. He is correct—the line may hold while applying a static pull in quiet waters tied to a dock, but the slightest passing ripple or wave will cause the tug to surge on the line. Surging, however slight, will bring to bear an additional strain (weight of tug) that undoubtedly will result in a parted line.

Because of the foregoing, the usual marine practice is to add a factor of safety to the calculations by multiplying the result by 5.

Example:

$$\frac{bhp}{100} = \text{Tons}$$

Breaking Strength
of Hawser   = Tons × 2,000 × 5 (safety factor)

For our 100 bhp tug mentioned above, we then would have,

$$\frac{100 \ bhp}{100} = 1 \ \text{ton}$$

Breaking Strength
of Hawser   = 1 × 2,000 × 5
               = 10,000 pounds
               = 3¼-inch circumference, 3-strand Manila
                 rope (10,500 pounds breaking strength)

The static bollard pull for most tugs of conventional design is greater than 50 per cent of the towline pull exerted at maximum towing horsepower. Excluding external forces, the towline pull is at a maximum when starting from a dead stop. Pull reduces as speed increases to the maximum attainable at delivered horsepower.

For tugs other than those fitted with Kort-nozzles or those of hydroconic hull body lines, the maximum towing horsepower is available at approximately 60–65% of the free-running speed and approximately 40–45% of the brake horsepower. Under these towing conditions rpm of the engine is approximately 90–95% of free-running speed rpm.

It is the usual practice to multiply static bollard pull in pounds by a safety factor of 5, as stated above, to determine the breaking strength of the tow hawser. For a tug of normal body lines the size of tow hawser required may be estimated simply by adding two (2) zeros to the maximum brake horsepower of the main engine(s) in order to arrive at the breaking strength of the tow hawser. However, this method cannot be used for vessels fitted with Kort-nozzles, or vessels of hydroconic hull design.

Vessels of a given brake horsepower fitted with Kort-nozzles or designed with hydroconic hull lines will produce a greater pull than tugs of the same brake horsepower of conventional design; therefore, if the static bollard pull is not known for a tug of other than conventional design, a static bollard pull test should be conducted.

Knowing static bollard pull, the breaking strength of the required hawser may then be found by multiplying the bollard pull in pounds by the safety factor of 5.

It has been determined that a vessel of approximately 29,000 tons being towed at a speed of approximately 6 knots developed a hawser strain of approximately 11 tons. (note 2) Now say, for instance, that the towing tug can develop a dead-weight pull of 50 tons. From Table I, we see that a 1½-inch diameter wire hawser we have aboard has a breaking strain of approximately 70 tons. It can readily be seen that the tug cannot break the 1½-inch wire on a static bollard pull (barring, of course, the condition known as "jumping the line"), because there is a 20-ton additional loading margin that may be applied before the hawser will break. Connected to the foregoing tow of 29,000 tons, the total strain developed equals 61 tons at 6 knots. Because the breaking strain of the wire is 70 tons and the total strain on the tow hawser is 61 tons, we therefore have a 9-ton factor of safety.

Now to the foregoing strain on the tow hawser must be added the additional strain imposed by variables, such as: weather, sea conditions, sudden loading shocks, surging on the line (commonly called "jumping on the line"), and yaw. The estimates of these variables may range from 10–100%, depending upon prevailing conditions along the proposed route and the experience of the tugboatman.

Ocean Towing.

Vessels of from 30,000 tons to 45,000 tons. For the foregoing tow, use three (3) tugs of 2,000 ihp each, approximately; two tugs to tow in tandem on one hawser and one tug to tow independently on an additional hawser.

Vessels over 45,000 tons. For the foregoing tow use four (4) tugs of 2,000 ihp each. The tow would be made up of the four tugs towing in double tandem.

All these arrangements are based on 2,000 ihp tugs; however, where tugs of greater power are employed, the number of tugs may be reduced proportionately to the total ihp developed.

Coastal Towing. A 600 ihp tug may safely tow two (2) stone-loaded barges using a 10-inch Manila main tow hawser and an 8-inch intermediate hawser between barges.

Inland Towing. The same 600 ihp tug may safely tow from 10 to 25 stone-loaded barges on rivers and in harbors using two (2) long (over 600 feet) 6-inch Manila hawsers.

A quick glimpse at the foregoing examples will illustrate the considerable margin for safety between the two types of tows. It can readily be seen that factors adversely affecting an outside tow such as sea conditions, weather, currents, etc., greatly reduce the effective payload that may be towed with safety.

Tow Hawser Loading. Much has been said concerning the tow hawser—its size, strength, composition, and characteristics. There remains to be told some information about how the hawser behaves during different evolutions of tug and tow.

During the course of a normal tow, a tow hawser leads aft to the tow, not in a straight line but, rather, with a dip in the line, termed *catenary*. The catenary of a tow hawser, as illustrated in Fig. 75, serves several important functions.

The dip in the line acts as a reserve length of line that comes into play during periods of surging of tug and tow and prevents the hawser from coming up short and taut. Upon surging, the amount of catenary simply decreases and after the surge subsides, the catenary again seeks its towing depth.

Because of the additional weight of line that makes up the catenary, a hawser possesses a certain amount of spring that tends to absorb some of the energy of surging on the line.

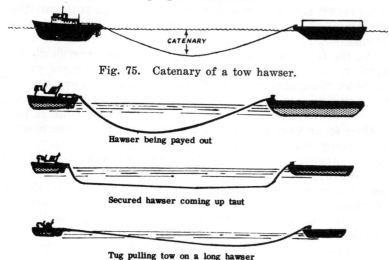

Fig. 75.   Catenary of a tow hawser.

Hawser being payed out

Secured hawser coming up taut

Tug pulling tow on a long hawser

Fig. 76.   Catenary of a tow hawser during different conditions of loading and scope.

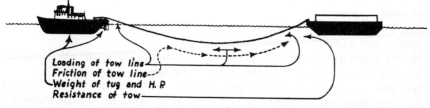

Loading of tow line
Friction of tow line
Weight of tug and H. P.
Resistance of tow

Fig. 77.   Forces exerted in hawser towing.

The distance between the tug and tow can be measured by using a stadimeter. This distance, in turn, is compared with the length of towline streamed to approximate the amount of catenary. Knowing the amount of catenary at any given time should enable tug personnel to estimate roughly the amount of strain on the hawser.

It is important to know the amount of catenary of tow hawser at all times and this is particularly true when tug and tow are entering or leaving port and when operating in shallow water. Excessive catenary may cause a hawser to drag along the bottom and chafe badly. There is also the possibility that the hawser may snag and become fouled on a sunken or submerged object.

During static periods of loading, catenary increases with an increase in the length of a towline; the reverse is also true. Now it appears obvious that in order to reduce the amount of catenary we can do one of two things, or both; i.e., shorten the hawser, or increase the load on towline by speeding up the tug.

Again, in connection with the hawser dragging along the bottom, there is a distinct possibility that a tug may find herself "in irons" and unable to proceed ahead if the amount of hawser on bottom produces a ground reaction sufficient to overcome the power of the tug. Usually this will occur only when a tug simultaneously slows down and commences reeling in *slowly*. In view of the foregoing it is perhaps a better policy to maintain the speed of tug while shortening up the hawser. In any case, a tug should always slow down gradually.

Figure 76 illustrates some behavior patterns of catenary.

The several factors that come into play and exert force on the main tow hawser are illustrated in Fig. 77. Some of these forces produce little effect in an easy tow and, therefore, the total force exerted on a towline is generally considered to be one ton pull for every 100 bhp of the tug applied to towing under favorable conditions. At other times, however, the effects of some of these forces are greatly increased, particularly during periods of heavy weather, while towing in a running sea or when tug and tow are not in synchronous towing; i.e., crest of wave to crest of wave and trough to trough. At such times these increased forces often work against each other so that the total force exerted on towline can exceed the breaking strength of the tow hawser.

Obviously then, some course of action must be taken to reduce the strain on a hawser during these adverse times. Several things can be done:

1. The tug can slow down or reduce the brake horsepower applied to towline.

2. The towline can be lengthened to provide more spring, thereby reducing the chances of "jumping on the line."

3. The tug may alter course so that by steering on a different heading the effects of running in an adverse seaway may be reduced.

While under way a tug develops a trimming moment by the stern produced by a couple resulting from tow resistance and propeller thrust on one end as opposed to resistance of the tug on the other end. Weight of a tow wire also produces a slight trim by the stern.

NOTES: CHAPTER III

1. Depending upon the type of tow, fuel and stores can sometimes be loaded aboard the tow for later transfer to the tug at sea. Adequate storage space and transfer equipment (pumps, etc.) aboard the tow are required. Prevailing weather conditions along the proposed route must also be studied to determine whether or not a transfer can actually be made.

2. W. Prince, *Seamanship As Applied To Towing*, J. D. Potter, London, 1934, p. 62.

CHAPTER IV

INLAND TOWING

BREASTED TOWING

This study encompasses some methods of breasted towing as practiced in harbors, on canals, rivers, bays and lakes; in fact, on most navigable inland waters.

Before demonstrating the practical side of breasted towing, we will describe and study some forces that come into play during a tow of this type.

In order to move a body, it is necessary to apply a sufficient force in the direction of and parallel to the required movement. Therefore, to move a tow forward, the tug is best positioned either directly ahead and towing, or directly behind and pushing.

The general practice is to position a tug ahead and towing on broad rivers, harbors, lakes and offshore; it is positioned astern and pushing, on canals, Western rivers, and intracoastal waterways. At other times, when these towing methods cannot be applied because of operating restrictions due to space limitations, the tug is often tied up alongside the tow, usually with the tug's stern extending aft of the tow in order to obtain better steering control.

We will digress briefly to review some fundamental principles before we go on to explain the forces and interactions involved in a tow of this type.

When a tug is tied up alongside and towing a parallelogram of forces, problem is brought into play. First, we know that a line to which a pull is applied will exert a force along its length.

Second, we know that in order for a tow to move ahead, we must apply a force parallel to and along the length of its keel in the direction of required movement.

Figure 78 illustrates this graphically. As long as the positions of both keel and line remain at right angles to each other, there will not, theoretically, be any forward movement. However, as the tug moves ahead, the line tends aft and assumes a more acute angle than 90 degrees. As a result, some of the force in the line will be exerted in a direction slightly forward of right angle, causing some forward movement. See Fig. 79. Simply stated, we may say that the nearer

107

a force is applied in a fore and aft direction, the more efficient will
be the tow.

Now, in the tow illustrated in Fig. 80, a longer towline is secured
farther aft thereby reducing the angle of line pull to keel, resulting

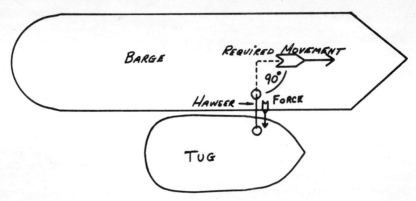

Fig. 78.   Tug and tow, no movement.

in a straighter pull and consequently more forward movement imparted to tow and less likelihood that the line might part. An additional diagonal line is secured from aft to forward in order to reduce
surging.

Continuing on, if two lines are added aft, as shown in Fig. 81, we
can improve steering by obtaining better control and prevent surging.

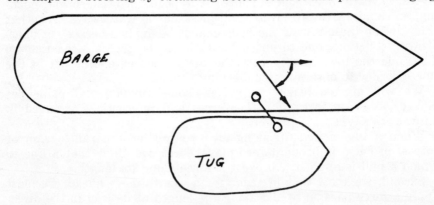

Figure 79.

Finally, the tow pattern shown in Fig. 82 is evolved. Rather than
position the tug forward, it is shifted to the stern of the tow and
secured as illustrated for better maneuvering control. Propeller and
rudder of the tug are now aft of the tow resulting in an ideal breasted

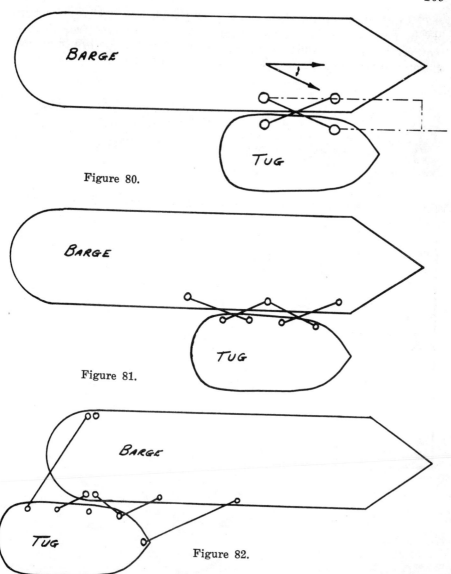

Figure 80.

Figure 81.

Figure 82.

hook-up. Of course, in many cases the hook-up will not duplicate exactly the one illustrated. Variations will depend upon the size of a tug and tow, location of bitts, cleats and fairleads, etc. But, regardless of the combinations of bow, spring and surge lines, the elementary principles must be adhered to; i.e., resolving parallel forces and control aft.

The tow hook-up illustrated in Fig. 83 is used extensively for towing in harbors and on broad rivers. An uncongested free area is required to permit sufficient maneuvering space for the breasted tow, thereby proscribing its use on narrow rivers and canals.

Fig. 83. Tug *Blanche T. Rogers* breast-towing acid barge *Rockland II.* Harbor Towing

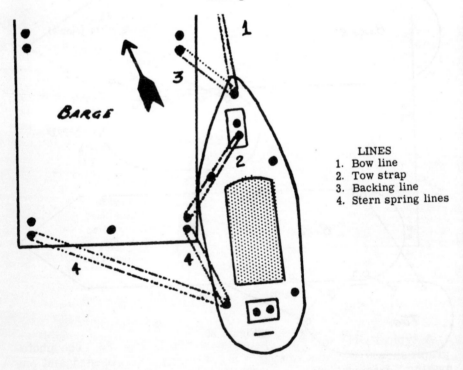

LINES
1. Bow line
2. Tow strap
3. Backing line
4. Stern spring lines

Fig. 84. Lines for towing heavy barges and lighters.

Figure 84 shows the nomenclature of the lines of a tow similar to the one in Fig. 83.

Number 1, bow line, and No. 4, stern line, are the side spring lines. Number 2 is a tow strap on which the towing pull is applied. Number 3 is a backing line on which the towing pull is applied during astern movement.

The barge is snubbed in to reduce the amount of water flowing between tug and tow.

Figure 85 shows a simplified method of hook-up for towing light barges and dump scows. The oblique angle of tug to tow causes the tow to run off the port bow, lessening side pull.

It is advisable not to use nylon for alongside towing because of its great elasticity. Sleevelay is better. When securing lines, make fast the forward and backing lines as near to each other as possible, as shown in Figs. 84 and 85, so that when one line is under tension, the slack may handily be taken out of the other line. Slowing down a tug that is secured with synthetic lines to its breasted tow may cause the tow to snap forward; so be prepared to reverse the tug's engine if necessary, in order to control a surging tow.

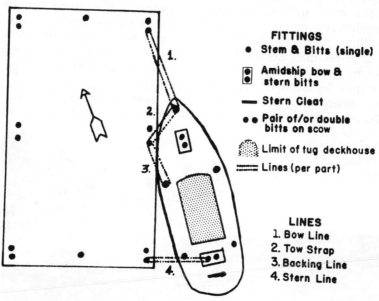

FITTINGS

● Stem & Bitts (single)

◙ Amidship bow & stern bitts

— Stern Cleat

●● Pair of/or double bitts on scow

Limit of tug deckhouse

Lines (per part)

LINES

1. Bow Line
2. Tow Strap
3. Backing Line
4. Stern Line

Fig. 85. Lines for towing light barges and dump scows.

PULL-TOWING

A typical river and harbor tow is shown in Fig. 86. The photograph shows two tugs towing a heavy barge, one breasted and one pulling. A typical pull-tow would exclude the breasted tug. The tow hawser is connected to a fiber or wire bridle on the barge. Towing is done on a short hawser with minimal distance between tug and tow.

Figure 87 illustrates the amount of catenary of a towline when towing at full speed or slow speed. Bear in mind that when a tug slows down, the increased catenary that results may cause the hawser to drag along the bottom which can put the tug "in irons" and anchor it effectively. Because of catenary, towing should be done on a short hawser in shallow waters. Again, slowing down and shortening up nonfloatable hawsers should be considered synonymous.

A light tow is shown in Fig. 88. Notice that towing is done on two short hawsers. The two lines are connected separately to capstan or winch drums to permit veering either line as necessary to offset any tendency of the tow to "yaw."

A 600 ihp tug can tow a number of sand, stone or brick-loaded scows (10 to 30) using two (2) long 6" circumference stern lines in protected waters. However, the same tug must use a minimum of 10" circumference hawser and 8" circumference intermediate hawsers between scows when proceeding offshore to a dumping ground.

For further information regarding towing on two (2) parallel towlines, see **Yaw**, Chapter VI.

Manila rope and, more recently, synthetic fiber rope bridles are used exclusively on small tugs for harbor and canal work. The bridles are seldom over 60 feet in length when used with tugs of 80 to 300 ihp.

When it becomes necessary to change from pull-towing to breasted towing in order to gain greater control over tow, the following procedure may be followed (refer to Fig. 89):

Slow down gradually while slowly heaving in on tow hawser.
(1) Be careful *not* to allow tow to override the tug, or to get "in

Fig. 86.   River and harbor pull tow. Moran

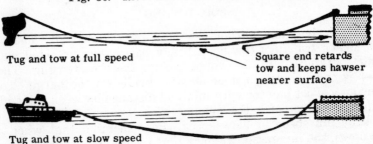

Tug and tow at full speed

Square end retards
tow and keeps hawser
nearer surface

Tug and tow at slow speed

Fig. 87.   Catenary of towline.

Fig. 88.   Barge *Texaco 397* towing light behind tug *Marie S. Moran* on the
Hudson River. F. C. Shipley

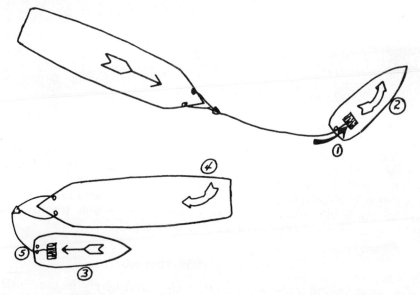

Fig. 89.   Maneuvering from pull-towing to breasted towing.

irons." When the hawser is shortened to within 50 feet or less, put the helm over, (2) stop the engines and allow tug and tow to stop and lie dead in the water at the angle indicated in the illustration.

Reverse the engines slowly and upon backing down (3) tow should lie easily alongside tug as shown (4). The main towline should be directed over the stern of tug by fairleading through stern rollers (5). Lacking stern rollers, the hawser should be led through Norman

Fig. 90.   Integrated shaped bow tow locking through the Erie Canal. Moran

pins, or held in a median position by the use of a gob rope or lizard stopper. This procedure should prevent the hawser from leading off to the side of tug, an event that would foul the maneuver.

An equally effective method is to shorten up, stop dead in the water, cast off the bridle and then maneuver the tug alongside the tow and make up a proper breasted towing connection.

SHAPED BOW PUSH-TOWING

On many inland waterways and canals, particularly in the Northeast, shaped bow tugs are adapted to push barges that have specially

shaped stern recesses to receive the bow of a tug. The tug applies a
motive force by butting its bow against the barge and pushing. A
tow of this nature may be made up of one barge or of a single file of
several barges.

Figure 90 shows a single barge tow of this type locking through a
canal in our inland waterways system.

A diagrammatic arrangement of the connections is illustrated in
Fig. 91. The main connection is made up from the after side bitts of
tug to the outboard stern bitts or cavels of barge, on both port and

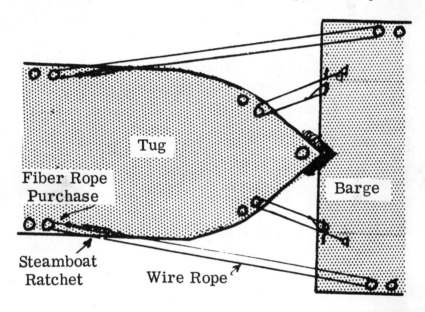

Fig. 91.   Connections of a shaped bow pusher tow.

starboard sides, as shown clearly in the photograph of Fig. 92. A
wire pendant is secured to the fiber hawser or strap using an intermediate connection consisting of a steamboat ratchet or other type
of screw ratchet. When connections are made up the fiber rope is led
to a capstan or drum of a winch and hauled in until all slack is taken
out of the line. The fiber rope hawser or strap is then stopped off and
secured to towing bitts at the sides of the tug. After both sides are
thus made up, the steamboat ratchets are tightened up to take any
remaining slack out of hawsers and bridles. This procedure then
locks in the tug against the barge. The barge has, for all practical
purposes, now acquired an integrated propulsion plant, propeller and
rudder.

It can readily be seen from the foregoing that any play in the joint
of the make-up (between tug and tow) will reduce the effective
maneuverability of the unit as a whole.

When more than one barge is to be locked through and towed on a canal the barges are tied together securely with short, heavy, *lug ropes*.

PUSH-KNEE TOWING

The push-knee towboat in canal and river service is a tug of normal shaped bow fitted with push-knees, that bear against the square stern of a barge. The connection is similar to the method described in the foregoing for shaped bow tugs.

Figure 93 illustrates the connections of a typical push-knee tow. Note that steamboat ratchets are located on the deck of the barge

Fig. 92.   Tug *William J. Moran* secured to a tow. A steamboat ratchet is clearly visible on the main starboard side towline. Note also the low silhouette of the tug necessary to permit access under low bridges. Moran

while in a shaped bow tow the ratchets are located on the tug. The methods of connection are interchangeable.

The tug butts its push-knees against a tow and secures two pendants from its stern quarters to the after corners of tow. Ratchets take up all slack and the tug becomes an integral part of the tow.

WESTERN RIVERS TOWBOATS

Towboating on the Western Rivers Systems is done by the push-knee method, which, in turn is a development of the early days of stern paddle-wheel river boats. In those beginning days, the stern paddle wheel did not permit a proper connection for the hawser needed for pull-towing. The paddle wheel extended completely across the

stern and its height often exceeded that of the upper deck. As a
result, the towboat was brought to the rear of the tow, fitted with
push-knees, and push-boating was on its way.

Because most rivers are shallow in many places and accessible
tributaries that extend operations over vast areas are of minimal
depths, the river towboat is a shallow-draft vessel. Winding rivers
of constantly varying depth require a degree of maneuverability not
needed in other types of towing.

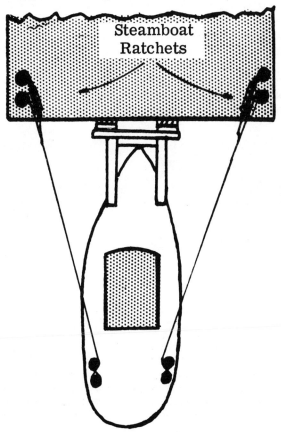

Fig. 93.   Main connections of a push-knee tug.

Operating continuously against river currents requires power
whose efficiency can spell the difference between profit and loss. The
diesel engine has served to provide the efficient power required in this
trade.

A tow, because of limited navigable width of some rivers, is comprised of up to 30 or more barges either in single file or in multiple
rows. Push-towing permits maximum sized tows using a minimum
of power. On large rivers the tow may be up to six units wide.

A multiple tow permits the tug to bank a damaged or sinking unit and continue a voyage without undue delay. The abandoned barge is later seen to by the returning tug, or more likely by another tug. After repairs the unit may be integrated in another tow. The foregoing procedure allows for a completely flexible operation that can adapt to most emergency situations. The banking, mooring and leaving of a damaged barge is called "hanging a barge off" and the principle is similar to the railroad practice of leaving a damaged freight car on a siding while a train continues its trip. When "hanging a barge off" care must be taken to insure that it is safely moored. Do *not* tie up to trees, boulders, logs, or utility poles. Instead, pour a concrete "dead man" ashore to which the barge can be moored using a minimum of 1" improved plow steel wire rope.

Figure 94 shows two typical river integrated tows.

The connection between towboat and integrated barge train is similar to that of push-knee canal tows.

Fig. 94. Two of the most powerful towboats in the world passing each other at Mile 596, or 66 miles above Greenville, Miss., on Dec. 14, 1960. M/V *United States*, northbound on the right, had a tow of 21 loads and 3 empties for a total tonnage of 21,651 tons. These cargoes from New Orleans, Mobile, Texas and foreign ports were destined for Chicago, St. Louis, Cincinnati, Pittsburgh, Evansville and Gary, Indiana.

M/V *America*, southbound on the left, had a tow of 24 loads for a total tonnage of 26,170 tons. The southbound tow originated in the Great Lakes area, and was destined for New Orleans, Mobile, Texas ports, and for transfer to steamships at New Orleans for delivery to many foreign ports. Federal Barge Lines

The river integrated tow requires regular inspections of all tow connections during a trip. This in itself is no small task when we stop to consider that an inspection around a large tow may require a walk of nearly a mile.

Hook-up. The hook-up of a river tow requires considerable planning and preparation. Barges are made up temporarily with fiber line to conform to the general shape that the final tow will take. Some facts taken into consideration and the ultimate results required are probably best presented in the colloquial language of a riverman: "First thing to make up a tow, the mate and the master get together.

They come to a full understandin' just where they're gonna pick up each barge and where each barge is gonna be placed in the tow. You try to put your heavy barges in the center and back next to the boat. Your light stuff, you put that on the edge. You gotta figure out what you're gonna let off, and at the same time you gotta make a tow that balances. And in the Ohio River we gotta figure on lockin'." (note 1) Get the picture?

There is a general trend toward coordinated towing wherein barges of the same destination are made up in the same tow.

Each unit of a tow is secured by wire rope pennants and turnbuckles tightened to make up a rigid integrated tow. A tight tow is necessary to facilitate maneuverability. The multiple propellers and rudders of the push towboat provide a greater degree of control than can be had in the end-for-end tow.

The total resistance of an integrated tow is everchanging and resistance shifts quickly between barges and towboat hull as towing conditions change. It has been found that spoon-shaped bow barges offer the least resistance and are the most practical for river tows. In recent times the spoon bow has been exaggerated to combine with ends of extraordinary rake.

As the size of a barge fleet affects the push required at a given speed, so also does the towboat hull design play an important part in the push required to move the tow at that particular speed. Therefore, it is impractical to apply horsepower, resistance and speed to represent a curve or set of values that will be true for all tows. Varying factors that result in changes affecting total resistance of tow and towboat performance include draft of towboat, mixed draft of towed units, and displacement and location of barges in the tow.

As a result of the constant shifting of tow resistance, the connections securing barges and towboat must have adequate strength to prevent parting—a strength difficult to calculate. In river towing practice there are no hard and fast rules regarding the make-up connections for an integrated tow. In the words of a riverman, "There's no two mates work alike. I seen some mates use a lot of iron. And others don't. Put enough out there, enough wires and riggin' so's we won't be bustin' the tow all the time, that's what I say." (note 2) A good idea in practice, but to estimate the sizes of rope necessary, calculate for the maximum strain you are liable to encounter in towing (exclusive of forces produced by collision). Apply the results to the tables of rope strengths found in Chapter III and employ the type and size rope or chain indicated. Barge connections are now made in three standard lengths of chain and ratchets.

An odd thing about the language of the riverman is his peculiar adaption of landsman's terms to marine practice. For instance, a few worth noting are: the use of "upstairs" and "downstairs"; identifying a propeller as a *wheel* and lately as a *screw*; all rope is called *line*; and steel cables are called *wire*, regardless of size.

Barge rigging, wire ropes, shackles, ratchets and hardware used in making up a tow are known as the river "jewelry."

The bow of a river towboat is called the "head."

Barge Rigging. Barge-connecting wires are usually made up in varying lengths, but commonly are found in three standard lengths, approximately 11 feet, 25 feet and 65 feet. Other barge rigging includes wire straps, shackles, lengths of chain, ratchets, "toothpicks," cheater bars and Manila and fiber line.

Barge wires are connected and slack taken out by using ratchets with "toothpicks." When taking up on a ratchet, face outboard and pull inboard on the "toothpick." In this way if you or the ratchet slip, you will not fall overboard or, worse yet, fall between barges. Slipping and falling are perhaps the worst accidents that can befall a deck hand. Another accident quite as bad is the hazard of a parted connecting wire. The snapback (backlash) is swift and lethal. A tight integrated tow on taut connecting wires will prevent, to a great extent, the surging that leads to breaking wires. If you hear a strained wire emitting popping noises, watch out! On the other hand, it is often said (not with verification) that a man seldom hears the line part that kills him. Amen.

Barge "jewelry" is usually stowed on the towboat foredeck. Wires are matched according to length. They are coiled and secured using small stuff and laid in neat piles toward the after end of the foredeck, out of the way. Ratchets are stowed farthest forward in square crisscross piles. Manila and fiber ropes are coiled or faked down on deck. All other "jewelry" is stowed in a forward locker, or under the tow knee ladders. All this gear stowed well forward on the towboat makes it readily available for immediate transfer to barges with a minimum of lost motion. Portable ladders are used to climb from one barge to another of different height.

Handling of ropes and rigging is facilitated by the use of a capstan, one or more of which are installed on the forward deck of a towboat.

The stubby posts on decks of barges used to secure and connect a tow are called *timberheads*. In marine parlance these fittings are known as bitts. Originally made of wood, the timberhead has been replaced by steel bitts on steel barges. Most rivermen persist in calling the bitt a timberhead.

Stern Lines. Stern lines are the heavy lines leading from the quarters of the after outboard barges to the head (bow) of a towboat. Stern lines prevent the tow from spreading out when backing down.

As previously mentioned, damaged or sinking barges are disconnected and left tied along the bank for later repair. Rivermen are required to climb onto banks of rivers in order to secure and moor any barge that is to be left behind. At such times they are likely to encounter snakes, mud, rain, snow or what-have-you—normal hazards to be expected when "hanging a barge off."

DOCKING TUGS

To grasp an idea of the fundamental maneuvers necessary to render assistance to a docking vessel it is perhaps the best approach to first demonstrate the effects that line handling, momentum, propeller thrust, and rudder have on a vessel.

Figure 95 illustrates two effects of line handling.

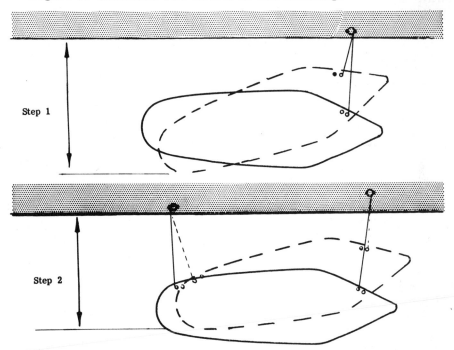

Fig. 95.   Effects of line handling.

Step 1. A bow line is hauled in while the vessel lies dead in the water causing vessel's bow to close with the dock, but meanwhile the distance between stern and dock increases because the vessel pivots about, or near, the center of gravity.

Step 2. A line is secured to the stern as well as the bow. The vessel now pivots from the stern when bow line is hauled in, causing the ship to close diagonally with the dock along its entire length. Heaving in on both lines simultaneously requires a greater force and the vessel is hauled toward the dock sideways and parallel on breasted lines.

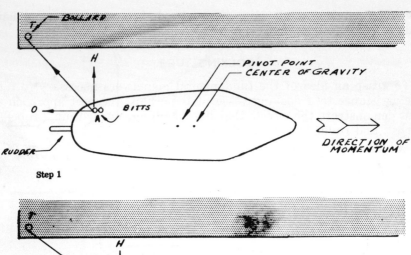

Step 1

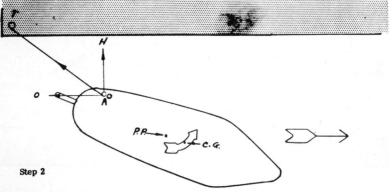

Step 2

Fig. 96.   Effect of momentum and a stern spring line on movement.

Figure 96 illustrates the effects of momentum.

Step 1. A vessel enters a slip. Assume that the rudder is amidship,
propeller is stopped and the vessel is making headway only through
momentum. A stern spring line is secured ashore. Now the spring
line, unlike the breast line, brings into play additional forces on
the vessel other than the single tension along the direction of the
line. The spring line force exerted along the line **AT** is resolved
into two components, **AO** and **AH**.

AO opposes momentum and retards progress of the vessel along
the direction of momentum. **AH**, on the other hand, hauls the stern
of vessel in toward the dock, while the bow is thrown out as a result
of the vessel swinging around its pivot point. However, the momentum which is concentrated in the center of gravity located slightly
forward of the pivot point tends to carry the vessel forward producing a small couple that acts around the pivot point and sets bow
toward the dock. As a result, the vessel should close with the dock
at an angle similar to that illustrated in Step 2.

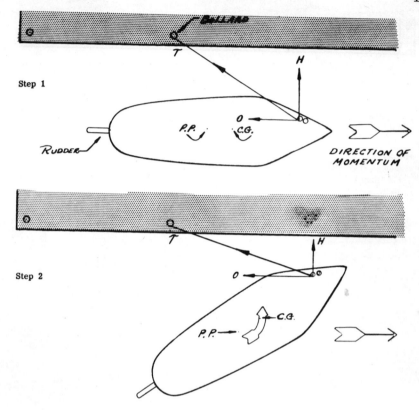

Fig. 97. Effect of momentum and a bow spring line on movement.

A tug secured under the starboard bow and butting would aid in laying the vessel easily alongside and prevent a heavy landing against dock by the use of backing power.

Figure 97 illustrates the effects of momentum and a bow spring line.

Step 1. A vessel enters a slip with rudder amidship, propeller stopped, and vessel making headway only through momentum. A bow spring line is secured ashore.

Step 2. The momentum increases the turning effect of the line causing bow to head sharply in toward dock while the vessel's swinging around the pivot point throws stern off the dock.

Port (left) rudder will increase turning effect and starboard (right) rudder will oppose but not overcome turning effect.

A tug placed aft and pushing on the starboard quarter would aid in laying the vessel easily alongside.

Location of a Stern Line. A stern line secured close to the rudder on the quarter, as illustrated in Fig. 98, will do little to improve

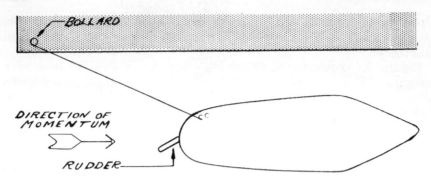

Fig. 98.   Location of stern line.

Fig. 99.   Tug *Kings Point* assisting ship *Finnboston* at bow. Note short wire
pendant shackled to bow line (backing line) of tug. Curtis Bay Towing

maneuverability. When the rudder is put hard over, there is little
steering effect; however, if the same line is secured at any point
along the middle one-third of vessel's length, the turning effect of
the rudder is greatly improved thereby gaining greater control over
vessel.

Docking Practice.   The usual practice in New York harbor for tugs
rendering docking assistance is for one tug to secure to the offshore
side of the bow of a docking vessel that is proceeding upstream.

Upon coming abreast of the pier or berth, a tug pushes against bow at right angle to the upstream movement, forcing the bow to turn into the slip.

Figure 99 shows the position of a tug secured to the bow of a freighter. The position of a bow tug alongside a liner is about the same.

A tug is often secured to vessel with an 8″ Manila line (size depending on tug horsepower and vessel displacement). The line is tied to the after end of forward main bitts of tug, as shown in Fig. 100.

Fig. 100. A method of securing a butting tug for pushing-backing operation.

Synthetic lines are often substituted as previously described in Chapter III. This line is frequently connected to a short wire pendant that is passed to the vessel and secured on board. The wire passes over gunwale, deck edges or other chafing areas on the vessel and better withstands this wear and tear than does Manila or fiber. Whereas wire is better suited to use aboard the vessel, it is easier to handle and make fast Manila or fiber lines to bitts on the tug; therefore, both are combined for use on a docking tug. Any other tugs deployed alongside a vessel and used for butting and backing are similarly tied up. The number of tugs employed in and required for a particular docking job depends upon the size of the vessel to be berthed.

Figure 101 shows a large passenger liner berthing using two tugs on the bow and two tugs controlling the stern. The tug pushing at the stern is secured in a butting position as described in the foregoing and the towing tug is secured on a short hawser stern-to-stern for pulling. The lateral position of ship is controlled by tugs, rudder and mooring lines while fore and aft movement is mainly controlled by the ship's propellers and tugs.

Another undocking operation is shown in Fig. 102. Note the varied disposition of all tugs.

In general, it is more desirable to use many tugs of lesser horsepower than fewer tugs of greater horsepower. For example, in the event that the service of one tug is eliminated because of an accident, the loss will have a greater or lesser effect on the operation depending upon how many tugs are employed.

West Coast docking practices parallel to some extent those of the East Coast. The West Coast tug is generally referred to as a towboat. There is one practice that is an outstanding exception to ordinary docking maneuvers that had its beginnings principally on the West Coast. That practice is known as a "west coast tugboat," a slang term used to identify the dropping and paying out of the outshore anchor when a vessel enters a slip preparatory to docking.

A vessel entering a slip bow-first drops its outshore anchor at a location near the head of the pier. By judiciously paying out and taking a strain on this anchor cable, the bow of the vessel may be kept under some degree of control and held off the dock against adverse currents, prevailing winds and tides to prevent a heavy landing. Conversely, upon undocking, hauling in on the anchor cable will pull the vessel's bow off the dock.

GREAT LAKES TUGS

Great Lakes tugs handle ships in a manner similar to the British and European practice.

The bitter end of a pendant is shackled to a padeye near the deep load line in the stem of a vessel to be towed. The thimble end of pendant is married to a heaving line received from tug and pendant is then paid out. When the pendant is aboard the tug, the bight of a tug's line is passed through the thimble and led to a winch or capstan. The tug adjusts length of the line by working the winch or capstan.

The pendant is retrieved by the vessel using a messenger (retrieving line) that is attached at all times to the thimble end of the pendant. Figure 103 shows this type of connection. Note pendant near

Fig. 101. Aerial view of the liner *Flandre* docking with the assistance of four (4) Moran tugs. Moran

Fig. 102. Tugs *Lambert Point* and *Tern* assisting U.S. Navy tugs to undock U.S.S. *America*. Curtis Bay Towing

Fig. 103. The Great Lakes 678-foot steamer *Wilfred Sykes*, owned by Inland Steel Corp., being escorted out of Black River to Lake Erie, Lorain, Ohio on her maiden voyage, April 19, 1950. Floyd Lynch

the deep load line and retrieving line extending higher up. The steam tugs in the picture were built with low pilothouses to enable passage under low fixed bridges.

BRITISH AND EUROPEAN TUGS

Given a particular set of circumstances, such as distance and material development differences, it is not surprising that the towing techniques of Britain and Europe have not paralleled our own. Although the results desired on both sides of the Atlantic are similar, the means to the ends have developed along divergent paths.

While the methods developed on both sides serve well their particular trade, it is believed that each side may profit from a knowledge of the other's basic techniques. With these thoughts in mind, we will look into the matter of British and European towing more to learn something from their methods rather than to presume to teach them anything about those methods.

Docking operations in Britain and Europe are hampered to some extent by the lack of really adequate room for maneuvering. Many ports do not have natural harbors in the strictest sense and they are man-made. Through Britain and much of Northern Europe there are high tides. The change from high to low tide can drain most of the water from harbors. To overcome this tidal phenomenon many ports are fitted with locks and dams to confine flood waters within dredged harbors so that any vessels within will remain afloat during an ebb tide. As a result of these limited harbors, every foot (or meter) of available harbor space must be used to the best advantage; consequently, docks are closely spaced, they are often not uniformly spaced or parallel (they conform to existing shore lines) and, as a result, access channels are narrow.

It is not uncommon for a turning basin to be an integral part of harbor design. A vessel is towed to an enlarged basin, turned by tugs and its direction reversed.

An excellent example of a turning basin in America may be seen in Houston, Texas. The Houston Ship Channel was carved out of a stream giving birth to the flourishing Port of Houston. Because it is man-made, the port, like many in Britain and Europe, has a limited maneuvering space. A turning basin of sufficient diameter to handle the largest vessels was dredged upstream. Here ships are taken and turned rapidly with the assistance of tugs.

Harbor Tugs. The harbor tug assists in docking and undocking vessels. Upon completion of an undocking operation it is the usual practice for two tugs to escort and assist a vessel down rivers and estuaries to the open sea.

Harbor tugs are usually fitted with a tow hook. A short, Manila 13″ to 19″ cable-laid hawser (nylon of equivalent strength may be substituted) is connected to the hook and extends to approximately six feet beyond the stern rail. The thimble at the outboard end of the hawser is fitted with a ring to which is shackled a length of tow wire that is passed to a ship. Any strain is absorbed by the stretch of the short cable-laid Manila hawser and the spring of the hook. The purpose of the length of tow wire is the same for American practice, i.e., to extend the life of the make-up in heavy chafing areas.

One tug is connected to the bow of vessel with a short towline connected to the tow hook. The acute upward angle of towline to the high bow of a vessel requires a free upward movement of tow hook and a clear open visibility aft on the tug.

Another tug is located aft with a tow rope secured between the Samson post, or tow bitt, just aft of the tug's stem and the stern of

Fig. 104.   Coming alongside the Tilbury Ocean stage. Port of London Authority

the ship. The Samson post is high enough to clear bulwarks by about two feet.

Figure 104 shows a bow tug towing. Note the acute angle of tow rope and hook. A towed vessel should never overtake a bow tug. In the event of any overriding situation, the bow tug must slip its tow hawser immediately by releasing the tow hook. A towed passenger liner can be seen on a short taut towline of tug in the background of the photograph.

The first sign of an overtaking condition is slackening of the hawser and it should warn those on the tug of imminent danger. The towline must be tripped. Herein lies one important advantage of the tow hook's functional design that enables it to be released and disconnected from the hawser at a remote vantage point on the bridge of the tug and under the direct control of the tug captain.

Another potentially hazardous operation is the turning of a towed vessel. Turn increments should be small and the towed vessel must slacken speed and reduce forward motion to a minimum. If necessary, the ship should ring an astern bell so as to brake forward momentum and slow down sufficiently before reaching the turning point—all of this to prevent *girding (tripping)* of the tug doing the towing. Should a tug find itself in a *girding* predicament, the tug captain must immediately release the tow hook.

A ship arriving at a port proceeds up the estuary while the tug(s) that is to assist at docking makes its approach. The approach is made at a large angle, as shown in Step 1 of Fig. 105, in order to allow sufficient time to hook-up while the vessel proceeds ahead.

Step 2 shows the sequence of events employed in securing the tug. Although the tug engine is turning ahead slowly, there is not enough power applied to its propeller to cause any movement or turning force to the vessel.

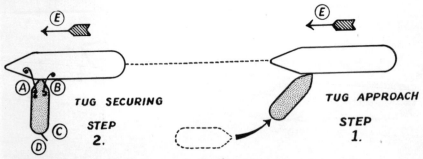

TUG SECURING   TUG APPROACH

STEP   STEP
2.   1.

Ⓐ   Line secured *taut* on bollards
Ⓑ   Line secured to gypsyhead of winch or capstan
Ⓒ   Rudder hard to starboard
Ⓓ   Tug engine slow ahead
Ⓔ   Ship moving slowly ahead

Fig. 105. Docking tug tying up to assist a vessel in berthing.

DOCKING PRACTICE

Docking to Windward—One Tug. In rendering assistance to a berthing vessel (refer to Fig. 106) against an adverse wind, the procedure is as follows:

1. The tug tows ahead on a short hawser connected between tug's tow hook and vessel's bow.

2. The ship (assuming a right-handed propeller) operates its main engine slowly astern as required. A vessel will normally back into the wind on an astern bell. Briefly, the procedure is that tug holds the bow to windward while at the same time astern bells on the ship

cut the stern to port. The result is that the ship is held "in irons" and kept up to windward while berthing. Stern movement of the ship inshore is checked by "kicking" ahead the ship's engine. The ship's stern can be moved outshore by ahead movement of the ship with helm to port (left rudder).

Docking to Windward, Stern-First—One Tug.   To berth a vessel stern-first with the assistance of one tug against an adverse wind, refer to Fig. 107 and proceed as follows:

1.   The tug secured at the bow operates its engine full ahead and pushes against the bow of the vessel.

2.   The ship operates its main engine dead slow ahead. The combination of forces thus created causes vessel to move straight back.

3.   The ship's rudder is used to steer the stern and guide the vessel alongside. A vessel can be berthed in this manner even against an adverse wind.

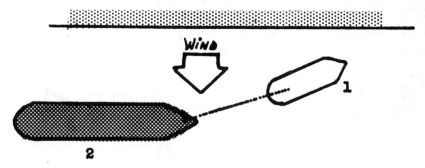

Fig. 106.   Docking to windward, bow first, assisted by one tug.

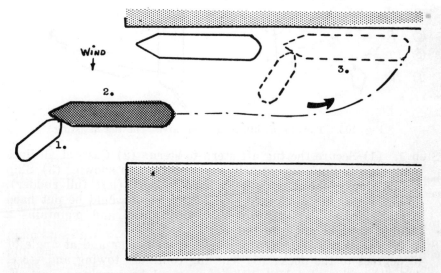

Fig. 107.   Docking to windward, stern first, assisted by one tug.

Turning in a small area. To turn a vessel completely in a small area, refer to Fig. 108 and proceed as follows:

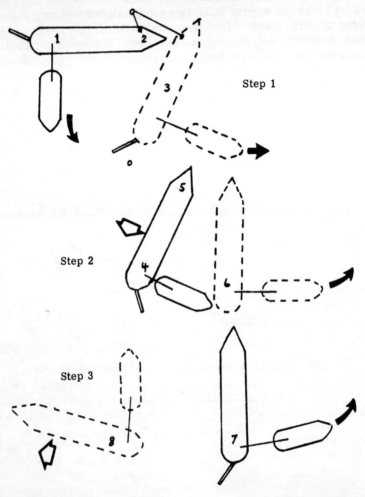

Fig. 108.   Turning a ship in a small area—one tug assisting.

Step 1. (1) Secure the tug aft stern to stern. (2) Cast off all lines tying ship to dock except a bow spring line, as shown. (3) Ship steams slowly ahead with helm hard to port (left full rudder). (When vessel lies starboard side to, the helm would be put hard to starboard.) Tug commences towing ahead and maintains a heading at right angle to the ship.

Step 2. (4) When the stern of vessel is well clear and at angle of 45 degrees to the dock: (5) The tug continues towing and vessel stops its engine, the ship's helm is reversed, bow spring is cast off, then a slow astern bell is rung. (6) When vessel is at right angle to dock (90 deg.) the ship's engine is stopped and helm is reversed again (port helm—left full rudder).

Step 3.   (7) Ship's engine is rung up half ahead and tug commences towing at full speed. The ship will now turn rapidly. (8) The vessel should be prepared to steady up on the desired heading and to cast off tug. Take care not to overturn.

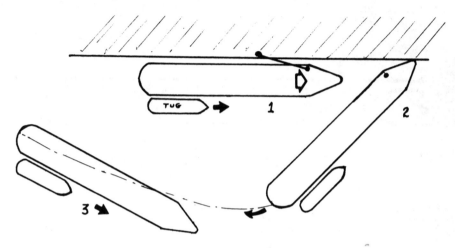

Fig. 109.   Undocking a vessel with extended propellers.

Undocking vessels with extended propellers.   Refer to Fig. 109 and proceed as follows:

1.   It is impractical to back spring because of extended propellers that can strike the dock; therefore, the vessel proceeds dead slow ahead on a bow spring only. A fender is placed between dock and stem.

2.   Vessel pivots on the dock to an angle of approximately 45 degrees, then tug backs down (half, or full speed astern) after letting go the bow spring.

3.   The tow should describe a semicircular turn as indicated, whereupon it is ready to proceed ahead when clear of dock and other vessels.

Undocking a Vessel in a Slip—One Tug.   Refer to Fig. 110. Secure the stern tow hawser of tug just forward of the bridge of vessel to be undocked. The hawser is on a tow hook. The tug pulls gently and the vessel will commence to ease off the pier.

In order to keep the stern of the vessel from rubbing on the pier apron as it pivots, put the ship's helm over hard right (right full rudder) and "kick" the engine ahead lively. The combination of tug pull and engine maneuver should lay the ship off the pier smartly.

A "kick" on an engine is just enough power to start the vessel moving. Depending on the particular characteristics, such as horse-power, rpm, and propeller size, the amount of "kick" will vary with different vessels. Usually a full ahead or half ahead bell is sufficient for a period of time lasting long enough to get the shaft up to speed . . . say, approximately 15 seconds but not exceeding one minute.

If there is any doubt about the amount of "kick" to give a vessel, remember that several "kicks" of short duration are better than one prolonged "kick."

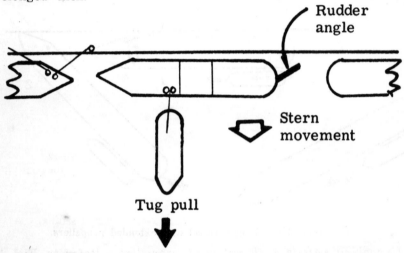

Fig. 110.   Undocking a vessel in a slip—one tug assisting.

Undocking a Vessel in a Slip—Two Tugs. See Fig. 111. Connect both tugs to bow an stern of vessel. Hawsers are on tow hooks.

Step 1. Both tugs commence towing vessel off the dock.
Step 2. When vessel is clear, lead tug tows in the direction of re-quired movement and second tug becomes the "towed" unit. The second tug secures its tow hawser aft of the tow hook using a gob rope or lizard stopper to prevent girding and it is pulled into line behind the tow. In this position the second tug can apply steering control. When the stern of a tow requires pulling to port the sec-ond tug is ordered to steer to starboard. If the tow's way is to be checked, stopped or pulled astern the second tug is signalled three short blasts of the whistle.

Note that a distinction is made between the "stern of a *tow*" and the "stern of a *vessel*." In the illustration in Fig. 111 the stern of the tow is the bow of the vessel while in Fig. 112 the stern of the tow is also the stern of the vessel.

Docking Large Vessels. To assist in docking large vessels to approximately 45,000 tons it is usual to employ a total of five (5) tugs. Two (2) ahead (one on each side of the bow); two (2) astern (one on each quarter); and one (1) tug pivoting at about amidship.

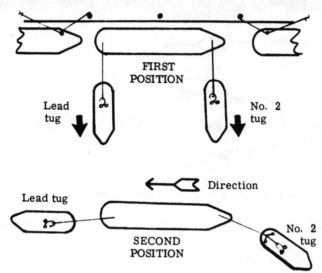

Fig. 111. Undocking a vessel in a slip—two tugs assisting.

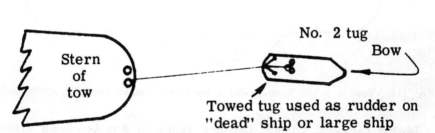

Fig. 112. Towed tug used for steering control.

Large vessels are escorted to clear waters as shown in Fig. 113. A pilot on the ship indicates the direction of turn to the lead tug only. The lead tug in turn then signals the maneuvering orders to side tugs:

Port tug:	Two (2) short blasts
Stbd tug:	One (1) short blast
Orders:	One (1) short blast—"Stop"
	Two (2) short blasts—"Go ahead"
	Three (3) short blasts—"Go astern"

The tug receiving orders acknowledges by repeating the "Order"
signal only.

Example: Order: "Port tug go astern"
       Signal: Two (2) short blasts, pause—then three (3)
            short blasts.

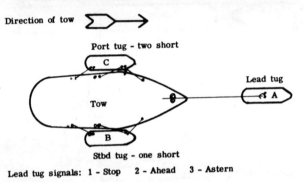

Fig. 113. Signals for tugs assisting large vessels to the open sea.

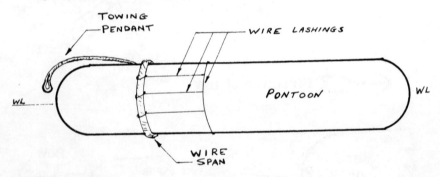

Fig. 114. Towing bridle hook-up for a pontoon or other low-lying cylindrical
object.

**Towing Pontoons, Camels, Caissons, Tanks, or Any Low-lying Cylin-
drical Body.** In harbor work the towing of camels is a common occurrence. Camels are used to fender off ships and liners from docks and
piers. Caissons are towed in the vicinity of construction sites of
bridges, tunnels, and at dredging sites, etc. Pontoons supporting
pipe lines and those used for ship salvage are also towed to and from
work areas.

To prepare for towing any low-lying cylindrical body, sling the
body with a length of wire span and secure it with wire lashings,
shackles or clamps. The wire span is then, for all practical purposes,
a bridle to which the tow hawser is attached. Figure 114 illustrates
a typical towing connection for these low-lying cumbersome tows.

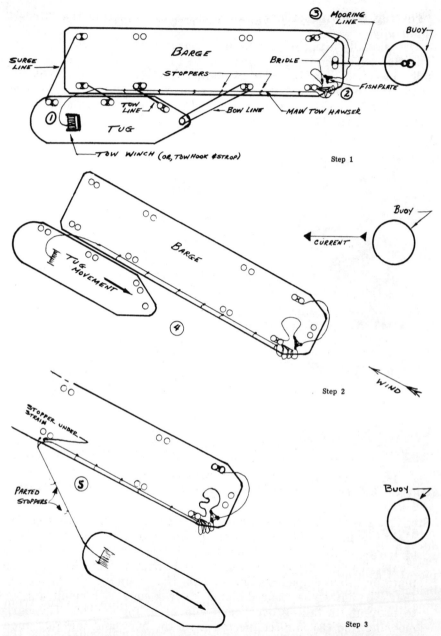

Fig. 115.   (Top, Step 1): Tug taking under tow a barge moored to buoy. (Center, Step 2): Mooring lines cast off. Tug has moved barge into wind, cast off all tow-lines and proceeds slowly ahead. (Bottom, Step 3): Proceeding ahead, tug parts stoppers holding main tow hawser on deck. Main towline falls overboard and streams aft of tug.

TOWING BARGE MOORED TO BUOY

Occasionally a tug must pick up a barge that is moored to a buoy. The plan is for the tug to commence the tow with barge tied up alongside (breasted tow) in order to maintain effective control while maneuvering in close quarters, but later on, when the tow reaches clear water, the barge is to be streamed and towed astern on the main tow hawser. Figure 115 is an illustration of this type of operation with the barge moored to a buoy.

Fig. 115A. Tug *Progress* of the The Baker-Whiteley Towing Co., Baltimore, sailing S.S. *Export Bay* from Dundalk Marine Terminal, Baltimore, February 3, 1966.

Step 1. The tug is secured alongside aft as in a normal breasted tow. Main tow hawser (1) is led forward and laid along the outside edge of barge, outboard and clear of all obstructions such as bitts and cleats. Towing end of the main tow hawser is shackled to a fishplate or heart-shaped anchor shackle that connects the bridle legs (2). The hawser is secured along the deck edge with hemp stoppers to prevent its falling overboard and becoming fouled. The barge mooring line (3) is disconnected from the buoy and tug gets under way with the barge as a breasted tow.

Step 2. Tug then maneuvers tow into the wind upon reaching clear water and, while lying stopped in that heading, casts off all breasted towlines (4) including bow and surge lines.

Step 3. Proceeding slowly ahead, the movement of the tug will cause
the hemp stoppers to part (break) one at a time from stern to bow
(5) allowing the main tow hawser to fall overboard and the barge
to stream astern of the forward moving tug. The bridle stoppers
part last, allowing the bridle legs and fishplate to drop overboard.
Tug may then veer the main tow hawser to the desired scope for
towing the barge astern.

LUMBER TUGS

The lumber tug is usually a small utility tug of shallow draft that
is used to tow rafts of lumber downriver to a sawmill site. A shallow

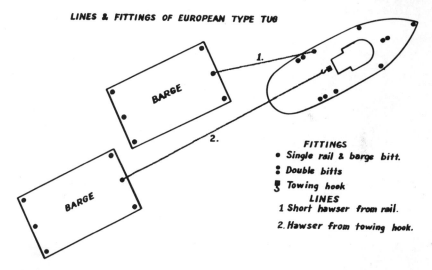

Fig. 116.   Lines and fittings of some British and European type tugs.

draft is necessary because of shallow waters in which the tug is required to operate. The closer a tug approaches headwaters of a river,
the shallower is the water. Therefore, a minimum draft will extend
the range of a lumber tug and bring it closer to the lumber source.
An important factor in the amount of draft of a tug is its displacement. The displacement in turn is determined by the weight of the
tug. A weight reduction reduces displacement and draft. Because of
this factor, lumber tugs have lent themselves well to aluminum construction with its light weight.

Log rafts are made up by securing logs together with three-strand
raft ropes. The floating log rafts are towed on the river to a sawmill. This procedure eliminates to a certain extent the building of
expensive access roads.

RIVER AND CANAL—BRITISH AND EUROPEAN METHOD

The usual practice of British and European towing on rivers and canals is illustrated in Fig. 116.

Single towing is done from a tow hook. Tandem towing is done from two separate lines, one hawser on the tow hook and the other on a short hawser tied to a single *rail and barge bitt*.

NOTES: CHAPTER IV

1. Edwin and Louise Rosskam, *Towboat River*, N. Y., Duel, Sloan and Pierce, 1948, p. 164.
2. *Ibid.*, p. 184.

CHAPTER V

OFFSHORE TOWING

TOWING PREPARATIONS

Towing preparations required for an offshore tow include securing and inspecting the tow, ballasting, connecting bridles and tow hawser, applying chafing gear, rigging maneuvering bridles and tow running lights, tests of equipment, towing engine and navigational aids, and providing quarters and subsistence for a riding crew.

Towing preparations vary widely for coastal and ocean tows. Because there are no two tows exactly alike, an attempt has not been made to describe all possible towing situations that may be encountered which will vary the preparations for tow. Any or all of these preparations may be necessary depending upon the requirements of a particular tow.

The fact that all tows are somewhat different requires the services of a third impartial party (first the owner, second the tug company), who has no interest in the venture. A surveyor should inspect the tow to see that all necessary preparations have been carried out. He must also make recommendations concerning any preparations needed for a safe and successful venture. The surveyor often bases his opinions and recommendations on past experience and therefore his services should be sought.

Securing and Inspecting the Tow. In preparing a tow for sea it must first be secured in all respects. Securing means lashing down any movable objects as well as obtaining a watertight hull. The adequacy of preparations is determined by the inspection survey of a marine surveyor.

1. *Hull.* The hull must be watertight or made so. This sounds rather like a simple statement to make, but there have been a number of tows that have departed leaking and in a slow sinking condition. Leaking slowly—yes, but sinking nevertheless!

Wasted and deteriorated plates should be cropped out and renewed. Cracks must be veed out, stopped and welded. Severely set-up sections of the bottom and heavily indented side shell plating should be faired to original shape, where practicable, by releasing internals, heating the plate and bumping to shape using heavy mauls or drawing to shape using strong-backs. In minor instances of damage, a hole is

141

blown in the center of an indent using a torch; the area is heated and faired by bumping and working the peened metal toward the center-hole. The practice insures a permanent final set and reduces stresses in the metal.

It should be remembered that on barges, indents and set-up bottom plating are considered, in most cases, to be a part of the normal wear and tear to which a barge is subjected during her routine labors and unless there is evidence of serious structural faults, fractures or failures, remedial action is usually not deemed necessary.

On large vessels in class and registered with classification societies, the allowable indents and disposition thereof are subject to the approval of a Classification Society Surveyor.

2. *Machinery and valves.* Sea valves must be closed. Double sea valves, where installed, are to be wired shut. A good safe practice for securing single skin valves is to close the valve, wire it shut and insert a blank flange in the joint on the shell side of the valve.

Overboard valves above the water line should either be blanked off or stoppered by driving wooden plugs from outside into the hull connection. Any portion of the plug extending beyond the shell plating must then be cut and trimmed flush with the hull.

Chain locker hawse pipes should be cemented to insure a watertight closure.

Main shafting must be secured to prevent turning by the propeller while under tow. Perhaps the simplest method is to unbolt and remove the upper half of a line shaft bearing cap near the stern tube. Insert burlap, canvas, or cloth over the journal and reinstall the upper bearing cap. Tightening down on the bolts connecting upper and lower halves will squeeze the material between journal and bearing causing a tight fit that prevents turning of the shaft. The last line shaft bearing is thus clamped to minimize the length of shafting that will be subjected to torque. It is necessary to keep the shaft from turning in order to prevent wiping of any bearings.

3. *Superstructure.* Any topside superstructure (structure built above a main or weather deck) must be protected against possible damage from heavy weather, or from the results of excessive towing speed.

Windows, where installed, must be boarded. Port light covers should be closed and dogged tight. Ventilators are often removed and deck openings boarded up. Doors and access openings are closed, dogged and secured watertight. Hatches are closed, secured and shored where necessary. All internal furnishings and fittings should be secured to prevent movement.

A canvas metal or wood cover is fitted over the stack and adequately lashed. Any structure of flimsy construction should be boarded up and shored as found necessary.

4. *Breakwaters* are constructed of wood bolted to metal framing and mounted on the forward deck of a barge or vessel to protect any

machinery, structure or cargo aboard from damage due to the pounding of heavy seas breaking over the bow or rake end.

A breakwater is usually vee-shaped with the apex of the vee forward towards the bow on centerline of a vessel. The sides of the breakwater are extended diagonally aft and outward to the stringer plate or sheer strake. The walls of a breakwater are not vertically straight up and down, but are sloped slightly inboard. Figure 117 illustrates a typical breakwater installed on a barge to protect deck cargo.

A breakwater in effect breaks up any sea passing over the bow onto the deck and prevents the full force of the sea from pounding deck machinery, cargo and superstructure.

Fig. 117. Breakwater installed on bow of a barge built by Equitable Equipment Co., Inc., Shipbuilding Division, New Orleans, La., for Compania De Acero Del Pacifico, S.A., Chile.

A satisfactory breakwater is made of horizontal transverse 4″ × 12″ timbers secured to vertical steel framing consisting of angle, channel, or other suitable shape, spaced on four foot centers. The height of a breakwater varies from, say, approximately 3′ 6″ to over 8′ 0″, depending upon the amount of protection needed.

5. *Rake packing* is installed to strengthen rake compartments of barges and to stiffen the blunt bows of shaped vessels in order that they may better resist damage that often results from sea pressure differentials due to pitching and pounding while under tow.

An inland barge is generally rectangular in shape and constructed lightly for operation in protected waters. The bow end is raked from deck line downward and aft presenting a form that makes an easy entrance to the water during forward progress. The broad rake ends thus formed are susceptible to damage while under sea tow because of the following:

a. The light construction normal to an inland barge.

b. The broad surface of rake exposed to the force of pounding seas while under tow in a running sea.

In addition to packing the rakes in order to prevent damage, two other methods are sometimes employed to achieve the same results. Scantlings are "beefed-up" (structurals, stiffeners, brackets, clips and plating are added), and the ends are ballasted.

The first alternative is not usually feasible because building up scantlings would in effect require much rebuilding and construction work. If, for instance, the rake ends were sufficiently strengthened to withstand the adverse effects of being towed in heavy seas, then it is likely that the remainder of the barge would be structurally inadequate to tie into the "beefed-up" rake ends.

A barge is ballasted at times for short light towing, but the practice should not be condoned for general towing because the weight of the entrained water can place an excessive stress on the rake ends that may result in structural failures or hull fractures. In addition, ballasting eliminates a certain amount of reserve buoyancy that is considered to be essential in any offshore towing operation. There is also the possibility that any free surface effect of the entrained water resulting from nonwatertight centerline longitudinal bulkheads in the rake ends may set up adverse torsional stresses at the barge ends that tend to twist, distort and fracture.

Having cancelled out both alternatives, for all practical purposes, by applying a minimal reasoning dissent, we may again take into detailed consideration rake packing.

By far, the only sure and satisfactory way, within the limits of economy, to protect rake ends from damage while a barge is under sea tow is to shore and brace internally with wood and wedges, and stiffen by welding additional clips and brackets. The spaces between longitudinal bottom rake frames (or floors) are packed using 2″ × 12″ timbers wedged and nailed in place to insure a tight fit. The packing usually extends from the rake after bulkhead forward and upward to the headlog. Wedges are driven in pairs from opposite fore and aft directions between transverse floors and plank packing. Additional vertical timbers are installed for stiffening as required. Frames and floors are tied together by welding short pieces (clips) of angle iron. It is necessary only to tie (weld) together every other frame and floor in a checkerboard pattern.

It should be noted that wood packing is never wasted and may either be left installed for a future return trip, or it may be removed and put to good use at the delivery end of the voyage. The extra clips welded to floors and frames are better left in place.

In conclusion, we should, by all means, let experience be the guide when packing a rake end. It may be found for some barges that the foregoing described method of packing a rake end is too light or too heavy; in either case, alter the packing to suit the job. The above description is meant only to point up the necessity for taking special precautions and to illustrate one method of accomplishing the required

ends. The sizes of timbers, planks, clips, etc., will vary from one job
to the next, according to the dictates of good judgment.

6. *Deck cargo.* Any cargo mounted on a barge or loaded on the
weather deck of a towed vessel must be lashed down or secured prior
to departure of the tow.

Wires, chains and turnbuckles are liberally put to use to adequately
secure cargo of any type. Boats, as cargo, are cradled in a wood or
steel frame first, then secured by attaching wire or chain straps. The
cradle is welded to the deck and additional bracing is installed by
welding lengths of pipe or angle iron between gunwale bar of the boat

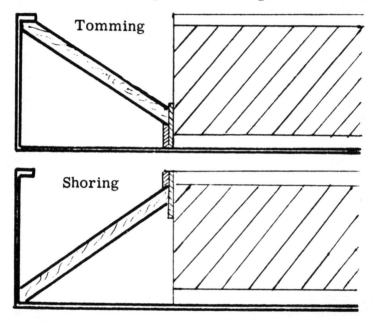

Fig. 118. Tomming is preferable to shoring because it resists the lifting effect
of any buoyant cargo when decks are awash. Shoring tends to allow the cargo to
lift as the vessel rolls.

and deck of the barge. Figure 118 illustrates a typical method of securing general cargo. Cargoes that may be damaged by water spray
should be covered with canvas tarpaulins that are doubled or trebled
if necessary. The purpose of any tow is to deliver tow and cargo in
good condition; damage to either spells a tow failure. Therefore,
adequate preparation and securing of any cargo is mandatory prior
to tow departure and it is essential to towing success.

Ballasting. Note that the ballasting to be discussed here is not the
rake ballasting previously described.

Vessels and barges are ballasted to improve stability and to increase
displacement. Ballasting may be accomplished by the use of sand,

gravel, stone, rock, water, or oil. The choice of a particular ballast will depend to some extent on the following: Ease in loading and discharging; free surface effect; comparative stability and freedom from shifting; safety; minimum damage to tow while being transported; minimum preparation of tow to receive the ballast.

When seagoing tows of long voyage and extended duration pass through areas of known heavy weather, ballasting is of prime importance. Under these circumstances light vessels and barges are ballasted to obtain greater stability.

1. *Ease in loading and discharging.* Any ballast carried should possess the attribute of being easily loaded and unloaded. One that requires the expenditure of considerable time and money in loading aboard or discharging ashore is not considered to be a satisfactory ballast. Liquids are perhaps the easiest to handle since all that is required is a pump with adequate suction lift and total head pressure to pump out ballast. The tow need not have internal piping; however, where installed, piping should by all means be used to transfer liquids. Oil ballasts, while perhaps paying for the cost of a tow, either in whole or in part, possess an inherent disadvantage in that they usually contaminate internal surfaces of a barge and consequently require an additional expense for cleaning, and in the case of a volatile liquid—gas-freeing.

Water is by far the handiest of all liquid ballasts; it is clean, cheap, plentiful, and easy to pump.

2. *Free-surface effect.* By free-surface effect is meant the effect on stability of a vessel or barge by free movement of the surface of a liquid that is constantly shifting (sloshing from side to side) as a result of rolling and pitching. Generally speaking, free-surface effect will be experienced only with liquid ballasts and then only if a compartment is not completely filled with liquid. In a full tank or compartment free-surface effect is nil. On the other hand, bulk cargoes such as grain, sand, gravel, stone, or rock cannot produce a free-surface effect. But they do require the installation of shoring and shifting boards to prevent any movement and shifting.

3. *Comparative stability.* The purpose of any ballast is to increase stability of a vessel and if the ballast itself is not stable it stands to reason that the total effect produced on stability will be adverse. In line with stability, ballast must be confined to prevent shifting. This is accomplished by the use of shifting boards and bulkheads. The shifting boards and bulkheads are constructed of wood in such a manner as to prevent the ballast from assuming a new position resulting from a shift of the center of gravity of the mass during periods of rolling and pitching in heavy weather.

4. *Safety.* A ballast must be safe to handle. Volatile liquids that are susceptible to fire and explosion should be avoided. By its very nature a tow is usually a hazardous operation and the use of a volatile ballast would serve only to compound any risk involved.

5. *Minimum damage to tow.* A necessary requisite of any ballast is that it should not cause damage to a tow. Some ballasts, such as heavy rock and stone, when carelessly loaded and stowed result in damage and cause indents and distortions to internals. There is the possibility that a hull may be punctured during loading operations without showing visible damage. However, while under way, the ballast may shift due to the tow working in a seaway causing the hole to be exposed—a condition that results in flooding of the compartment. Should filling of the compartment result in negative buoyancy, the tow, as the Arab of the poem, will "silently steal away"— in this case, to the deeps.

6. *Minimum preparation of tow to receive ballast.* Needless to say, any extensive preparation of a tow to receive ballast, such as building shifting boards and bulkheads, will increase total cost of the tow, so that the type of ballast to be employed should be selected with this in mind. Some liquid cargoes require tanks or compartments sufficiently clean to prevent contamination of the cargo.

Through an overall study of the factors involved in the selection of a ballast the reader may develop his own pros and cons which should result in choosing a ballast suitable to his particular needs.

By far, the most commonly employed ballast, as stated above, is water because it is clean, easily transferred, safe and stable when a compartment is full. Ballasting with water is usually accomplished with the thought in mind to try and minimize any stresses that might be set up in a hull by the addition of weight. Concentrations of ballast either forward or aft should be avoided. Checkerboard ballasting is perhaps the most practical method. Checkerboarding has an advantage in that the ballast plan can be easily remembered. All bulkheads must be watertight, whereas, in other methods such as centerline tank ballasting, transverse bulkheads between wing tanks need not be watertight. However, all bulkheads should be watertight regardless of ballasting plan in order to improve the safety factor in the event of shell damage.

Bilge Pump. In conjunction with carrying ballast either in bulk or liquid form, a very necessary piece of equipment is the bilge pump. For it is the job of a bilge pump to maintain reserve buoyancy of a tow. Compartments that are not loaded with ballast must be kept pumped dry at all times to maintain stability and preserve positive buoyancy. Reserve buoyancy is absolutely necessary because without it a tow will not float. For small tows a hand bilge pump should prove satisfactory provided the hull is tight. On larger tows the practice is to provide one or more gasoline- or diesel-engine driven pumps that are test-operated prior to departure of the tow.

Sounding Pipes. On large vessels each compartment and tank is fitted with a sounding pipe as a means of gauging the tank to determine the presence of water. Soundings are taken by the use of a flexible steel tape with a weighted bob on its end. The tape is blue-chalked while lowering and, upon reeling in after the tape has struck bottom, the level of any water present may be quickly ascertained by discoloration of the wet chalk as compared to the adjacent dry chalk.

Many barges are not fitted with built-in sounding pipes and, therefore, some provision must be made for taking soundings at frequent intervals during the course of the tow without opening up a compartment or tank. Perhaps the simplest method is to cut a small hole in the deck over the compartment to be sounded. A vertical length of pipe threaded and capped on the upper end is welded to the deck over the hole. The compartment is sounded simply by removing the cap to provide access for the tape. The cap is replaced after taking a sounding. Sounding pipes are absolutely necessary and no amount of rationalizing should forestall their installation.

A doubler is usually installed on the bottom in way of the end of a sounding line. This doubler is known as a *striking plate*. A striking plate is not usually fitted on a barge where the sounding line has been installed temporarily. The purpose of a striking plate is to prevent excessive wear of the bottom plating that is struck constantly by the plumb bob upon lowering the tape.

Refueling. At some point in the preparations for an offshore tow the problem of refueling tug(s) must be taken into account in the event that the tow will exceed the cruising radius of tug(s). Ports of call must be decided upon and lacking these along the proposed route, some provision must be made to carry additional fuel required. Bunkers may be carried in tanks on the towed unit or a fuel barge can be included in the make-up of the tow.

OCEAN TOW HOOK-UP

The tow hook-up is a general term that identifies the total hawsers and connections that join a tug to its tow. Tow hook-up is comprised of some primary component parts which include the main tow hawser, intermediate spring hawser (when connected), bridle, back-up wires, towing strap and tow hook (when used), as well as secondary components that include shackles, fishplates, towing padeyes, pins, securing wires, retrieving lines and chafing gear.

Generally speaking, the tow hook-up should be weighty and sufficiently strong to withstand the combination of forces that come into play under the severest of weather conditions. However, an effort should be made to avoid making a hook-up too heavy, because of the general difficulty usually experienced in connecting up heavy component parts, but rather, have the gear too heavy than too light. A typical tow hook-up is shown in Fig. 119.

Tow Bridle. The bridle for ocean tows consists of two (2) legs of chain of equal length. For inland tows the bridle is usually wire rope for tandem tows and fiber rope for single tows. For towing numerous light barges inland it is a common practice to use fiber and synthetic ropes on other than integrated tows.

Bridles made of stud link anchor chain have proven most effective. The size and length of bridles vary considerably for different tows depending upon weight of tow, horsepower of tug, bollard pull and desired amount of spring in the tow hook-up. Refer to Chapter III.

The bridle is connected on the tow to towing padeyes or heavy towing bitts. The outboard ends of the bridle legs are connected to a fishplate by using anchor shackles or detachable links of anchor

Fig. 119. Typical tow hook-up showing chain bridle, fishplate and main tow wire hawser. Moran

chain. The inboard ends are figure-eighted on double bitts, as shown in Fig. 120, and the bitter ends are shackled to towing padeyes mounted on suitable deck doublers. A typical towing padeye is shown in Fig. 121.

Safety shackles or screw-pin shackles are used for all connections. The pins of screw-pin shackles are wired and tack-welded to prevent turning and inadvertent disconnecting. Where legs of the bridle pass through open chocks or between double bitts, it is a good practice to weld a length of flat bar stock across the top of the chock or bitt opening to prevent the bridle legs from jumping free of these fairleads.

Equal length of bridle legs. It is important that the legs of a bridle are of equal length so that any load and resultant tension will be distributed equally to both legs. One leg of longer length will cause an increase in towline loading on the shorter leg that may result in a failure of any of the component parts of that leg.

Sufficient length of bridle legs. The legs must also be of sufficient length in order to provide weight for spring, reduce yaw, and minimize the effects of a problem that is peculiar to a taut span. The taut span concerns the ratio of tension to weight or pull and the sines of the angles formed.

In Sketch A (Fig. 122) the short bridle legs result in a large bridle angle, theta ⊖. Sketch B illustrates a barge with long bridle legs and a small bridle angle, theta ⊖. Basically, the nearer **ABC** approaches a straight transverse line, the greater is the ratio of tension to force (pull). Conversely, the smaller the angle formed by **ABC** the lesser the tension, as in Sketch B.

Connection to Tow Hawser.

Refer to Fig. 123. A correct towing connection is illustrated in Sketch A. Do not tow on the bight of a cable as shown in Sketch B.

Fig. 120.   Securing chain bridles.

Wire. A wire tow bridle is seldom used for offshore towing. The make-up depends on the size of a tow. The following example typifies a possible wire bridle hook-up:

1. A wire bridle consisting of two (2) legs approximately 60 to 90 feet in length is connected on the tow.

2. 60 to 100 fathoms of 15″ circumference Manila hawser for an intermediate spring. A shorter length of nylon of equivalent strength is preferable because of its greater elasticity.

3. A main tow wire of 1¾″ to 2⅝″ connected to the intermediate spring.

The foregoing is a satisfactory hook-up for towing a vessel of 5,000 tons.

The tow end of the wire bridle is fitted with a large eye splice so that it can be laid conveniently over a bitt or bollard. The hawser end is fitted with a thimble to receive the pin of a shackle. Each leg of the bridle should be at least equal to the strength of the main tow hawser, although the pull on either leg will be considerably less than that on the main hawser.

Nylon. Nylon was not used for bridles until recently because of the expense of replacement due to heavy wear and tear and in no case is nylon used for bridles on deep-sea tows.

Tripping rope. A tripping rope or retrieving line of fiber or wire is used to retrieve the outboard legs of a bridle where they are connected to hawser at the fishplate.

A 3″ circumference fiber rope or small diameter wire rope is connected to the fishplate or connecting shackle to facilitate heaving in

Fig. 121. Chain bridle leg connected to towing padeye mounted on a suitable deck doubler.

and retrieving the bridle aboard the tow. After the fishplate is heaved aboard, the main tow hawser can then be disconnected and cast off, thereby releasing the tow.

The tripping rope on small tows is hauled in by hand or with the assistance of a handy billy (small tackle) and on a large tow it is retrieved with the aid of a winch, capstan, or windlass.

Conclusion:

1. Take all factors into consideration when selecting a suitable towing bridle.

2. When there is any doubt, remember to rig too heavy a bridle than one that is too light.

3. Ease in handling and rigging should not be a primary reason for rigging a particular tow bridle. Rigging can be accomplished

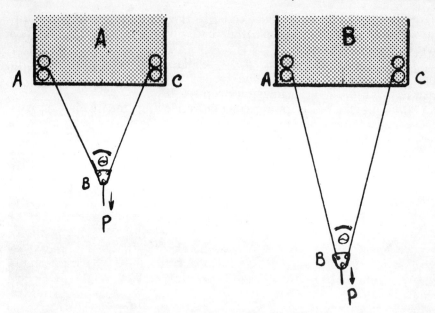

Fig. 122A. Short bridle legs, large bridle angle; B. Long bridle legs, small bridle angle.

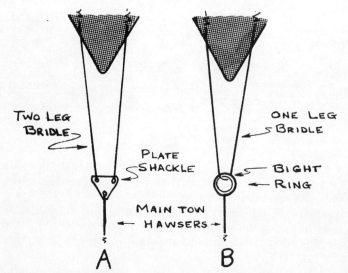

Fig. 123A. A correct towing connection. B. Incorrect towing connection.

more easily by employing the additional purchase power of tackle and winches.

Back-up Wires. Back-up wires are installed to hold a towing bridle in the event of failure of the towing padeye. The back-up wire is connected from the towing padeye to a bitt or cleat farther aft on the tow. It is usual to take several passes fore and aft between pad-eye and bitt before figure-eighting the remainder of the wire on the bitt. A turnbuckle is installed to take up all slack, but a steamboat rachet or come-along will serve the same purpose. Back-up wires are rarely spliced when secured and the ends are clamped with a minimum of three (3) clips.

A back-up wire provides: Factor of safety; additional strength; distribution of the towing load.

The back-up wire should be of sufficient strength to carry the towing load in the event that the main towing padeye or bitt fails and carries away.

Intermediate Spring Hawser. Intermediate spring is the term used to define the length of chain, wire, fiber, or synthetic rope used in the tow hook-up between the towing bridle and the main tow hawser.

Manila and fiber hemp lines are not generally employed as intermediate springs because they lack sufficient elasticity and weight to be of much use. The purpose of the intermediate spring, perhaps already deduced from the foregoing, is to provide weight and elasticity in the towing make-up and thus to act as a spring that will give under tension and provide some needed flexibility to the total tow make-up.

Flexibility of a spring is needed to prevent the tow wire parting when it is subjected to sudden loading shocks as a result of wave action, operating in a seaway, or sharp quick turns of the tug. The intermediate spring will also offset the tendency of the tow hawser to "jump on the line" (tow hawser coming up out of the water suddenly taut).

On ocean towing of any great distance the intermediate spring is made up of a length of chain. The size and length of the chain will vary according to the weight of the tow, horsepower of the tug and bollard pull. Refer also to Chapter III.

One shot of 2⅝" stud link chain in the make-up has proven satisfactory for towing vessels of approximately 9,000 tons displacement. For larger or smaller tows, vary the size proportionately.

Wire, once commonly used as an intermediate spring for inland and short coastwise towing, is being replaced to a great extent by synthetic fiber ropes. However, wire will better withstand wear and tear, due to chafing on the bottom in shallow water, than will fiber ropes that do not float.

The added weight of the wire or chain also reduces the effect on the tug of increased catenary when slowing down. The hawser will tend to lower more evenly along its length. This even lowering of the hawser will minimize the possibility of a tug getting "in irons." A tug is said to be "in irons" when it cannot make headway under its own power because of the weight of the tow wire extending vertically downward over the fantail, from the stern to the ground (bottom). The tug is in effect anchored to the ground from the stern. The deeper the water the greater will be the effect, although a large amount of wire stretched along the bottom in shallow water will anchor a tug just as effectively.

A tug "in irons" is in an extremely dangerous predicament and unless wire is immediately reeled in and shortened up, there is imminent danger that the tow will override the tug and result in a collision or sinking. The least that can happen is that forward progress of the tug will cease.

During recent years nylon and synthetic lines have come into more prominent use as intermediate springs on ocean tows because of their great elasticity and strength. However, their use should be limited to fair-weather ocean towing and short coastwise towing.

In conclusion, it is perhaps best to limit the tow hook-up to one intermediate spring whenever possible. Additional connections only serve to reduce the factor of safety in the total make-up, i.e., there are more connections that can possibly fail under strain when additional springs are included.

Bridle on tow. A tug can no more serve its purpose without bridles aboard of adequate strength and size than if it were to operate without a main tow hawser. All too often bridles have been considered of secondary importance, resulting in failure due to being undersized when for all practical purposes the bridle must be larger and stronger than the main tow hawser—formulas to prove otherwise notwithstanding.

A tug is not truly an effective towing plant unless it carries aboard a wide variety and assortment of wire and chain bridles of different lengths in good condition. The sizes of bridles should be chosen so as to effectively meet the requirements for all types of towing expected in the trade of a particular tug.

In many cases it has been the practice to prepare the tow prior to the arrival of a tug in order to save time and money. As a result, some tow hook-ups have been inadequate for the job. This, combined with an arriving tug carrying insufficient gear to effect the necessary changes, results in time-consuming and expensive last-minute searches to provide the required gear.

Before a tug is contracted to undertake a major towing job, the owner of the tow should assure himself, either through his representative or a surveyor, that the tug in question can actually undertake the intended tow with an effective towing plant.

Chafing Gear. Chafing gear is applied to protect working bridles and hawsers where they are subjected to heavy wear and tear due to rubbing or chafing on hard surfaces.

Wire bridles are fitted with chafing gear where they come into contact with gunwale bars, headlogs and decks. The chafing gear usually consists of numerous layers of heavy canvas or burlap tied to the wire at points of contact. The wire may be further protected with heavy coatings of grease. Then, too, chafing boards are sometimes secured to the wire so that any rubbing will tend to wear the wood rather than the wire. Canvas and split rubber hose are used on light tow hawsers.

Chain bridles must be secured to prevent movement and rubbing against adjacent steel decks, gunwales, etc. Chain is made of a

Fig. 124. Applying lubrication to the main tow wire.

harder material than the steel of deck plating and, therefore, it will wear the plating and result in damage. If the chain should wear completely through a headlog, there is a possibility that the rake compartment will fill with water. A water-filled rake may either cause distortion of the hull or result in a tortional fracture that may allow the barge to flood uncontrollably and sink. The fracture usually occurs at the rake transverse bulkhead separating the rake compartment from the adjacent watertight compartment.

A main tow hawser is particularly susceptible to wear in way of sections that pass over the fantail of the tug, or in way of a Dutch towing bar.

Chafing gear is not applied to a hawser on a tug equipped with automatic towing engine. The constant movement of the hawser as it reels in and out would soon break off any chafing gear applied. Instead, the hawser is heavily coated with grease, as shown in Fig. 124. The buffalo rail or gunwale against which the hawser rubs is

Fig. 125. Greased main tow hawser leading over the stern of tug. Moran

also coated, as shown in Fig. 125. The grease provides adequate lubrication that reduces heat produced from the friction of rubbing. The reduction of heat tends to minimize wear of the hawser.

When towing is done from the "H" bitts and the hawser is stationary, several methods are used to apply chafing gear to the main tow hawser. The wire may be wrapped in canvas or burlap to reduce chafing, or, as is the practice in Great Britain and Europe, the hawser may be fitted with hawser boards and split pipes. Two (2) split hawser half-boards, circular in shape, are covered by a split pipe and the whole mounted on the hawser. The halves are secured together by countersunk screws. The ends of the hawser boards are tapered so as not to snag on the gunwale or tow span.

The American practice depends upon the type of hawser—fiber or wire. Fiber hawsers are fitted with split hawser boards of 2″ × 3″ oak, approximately 6 to 8 feet in length. The board halves are grooved longitudinally to receive the towing hawser in a snug fit. The halves of the boards are secured together by straps or steel clamps.

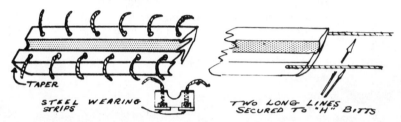

Fig. 126. Construction details of a typical hawser board.

Fig. 127. Hawser board on a fiber main tow hawser.

Figure 126 illustrates a typical American hawser board and Fig. 127 shows a hawser board installed. The tapered ends of the boards prevent jamming at the gunwale. The boards are not used where spans, towing arches or Dutch towing bars are installed. Instead, the hawser is paid out or taken in periodically to minimize wear.

A common practice and a good one is to shackle a length of chain into the tow hawser in way of the buffalo rail. A short length of tow strap connects the chain to the towing "H" bitts. The purpose of the chain is the same as that of a chafing board except that it is used for heavier tow-loading. Figure 128 shows this method of hook-up.

The American practice is to fit wire hawsers with the same type of hawser board as for fiber except that an effort is made to make the joints of the two halves watertight. A watertight joint will usually protect the wire from deterioration due to rust.

The inland and river practice is to secure a short piece of wire pendant into the end of the towline to protect the fiber from chafing in way of deck edges and in worn chocks. In docking practice this short wire pendant is passed to ships in rendering docking assistance.

Fig. 128. Chain inserted in main tow hawser for chafing purposes. Moran

There are some important points to be remembered concerning chafing gear:

1. It is used to protect lines where they pass over deck edges, through chocks, etc.

2. Chafing gear is homemade; that is, it is made aboard the tug from available material.

3. Chafing gear is classified in two categories—permanent and temporary. Permanent gear is expendable and temporary gear is consumable.

4. The use of chafing gear should never result from an arbitrary decision but, rather, it should be considered a mandatory requirement.

Spare Bridles and Hawsers. To operate satisfactorily as a tug, any vessel so-called must have aboard at least one spare towing hawser of wire or fiber and numerous assorted bridles of chain, wire and fiber composition.

The spares should be stored in an accessible and dry space. Hawser of fiber composition is usually stored in open boxes or in confining wood grates raised above the deck at least 6″ to allow for adequate circulation of air beneath the hawser.

The amount of spares that are carried aboard will depend upon the operating requirements of the tug. Another important consideration will be the total weight of the spares, because in many tugs, especially the seagoing types, draft is an important factor which tends to limit the range of the tug after fuel and stores are taken aboard. Table XI illustrates this by showing how much the weights of hawsers increase as the sizes increase.

Table XI. Coil Weight and Coil Length of Fiber Rope.

Circum. Ins.	Min. Lgth. Ft.	Approx. Wt. Lbs.	Circum. Ins.	Min. Lgth. Ft.	Approx. Wt. Lbs.
5/8	3,000	45	3-1/2	1,200	432
3/4	2,750	55	3-3/4	1,200	502
1	2,250	65	4	900	432
1-1/8	1,620	66	4-1/2	900	540
1-1/4	1,200	63	5	900	670
1-1/2	1,200	90	5-1/2	900	805
1-3/4	1,200	125	6	600	645
2	1,200	160	7	600	875
2-1/4	1,200	200	8	600	1,145
2-1/2	1,200	234	9	600	1,450
2-3/4	1,200	270	10	600	1,795
3	1,200	324	11	600	2,200
3-1/4	1,200	375	12	600	2,610

Towing Lights. Towing navigation lights are carried on a tug as standard equipment. The portable lights installed aboard towed units are powered by 30-day batteries.

Tow-riding Crew. A tow-riding crew is essential to the success of any long-distance towing venture. Without a riding crew on the tow, the tug must stop daily and send a boarding party by small boat back to the tow, for an inspection. Bilges must be pumped when necessary, deck cargo and lashings are inspected, navigation lights inspected and portable bilge and fire pump should be test-operated. Transferring an inspection party to the tow is a hazardous operation and it requires that the tug slow down during the transfer. Heavy weather precludes any transfer operation and if foul weather continues for a matter of days, the success of the venture may be placed in jeopardy; therefore, it is far better to have a riding crew aboard the tow than to hazard a voyage without one.

It is essential that signals be exchanged between the tug and tow, so that the tug is always aware of towing conditions aboard the tow. The two-way voice radio is acceptable and, in addition, at least two members of a riding crew should know semaphore or flag Morse code. The same applies to the tug. Many times a tow has been pulled too fast and there was no way to communicate this information to the tug because of a faulty radio tube, or weather conditions made reception impossible.

Rarely will personnel on a tug know when towing is too fast. This knowledge cannot be ascertained from a vantage point on a tug, for a tug with a heavy tow on a line will ride comparatively easy during heavy weather although towing hard. (The bhp or ihp compared with engine rpm is a fair indicator of the towing load.) The tow, on the other hand, may be accepting severe damage that cannot be known to the tug unless this information is passed on by a riding crew.

A riding crew is responsible to a tow captain. Watches are set up on a 4-hour-on, 8-hour-off basis around the clock. During a watch, rounds are made completely around the tow and into any accessible compartments every ½ hour, soundings are taken hourly, and at all other times the watch is maintained forward, constantly observing the towline and tow connections. It is the duty of the watch to start bilge pumps when necessary and to maintain a watertight hull. All bilges should be dry before a crew coming on duty accepts a watch. All suspect conditions, no matter how trivial they seem, must be reported immediately to the tow captain.

Searchlight. Tugs are fitted with powerful searchlights for use at night in general work:
1. To note the condition of the towline.
2. To check the condition of the tow.
3. To locate and observe maneuvers of vessels in the immediate vicinity.
4. To locate obstructions to tow navigation and maneuverability, such as bridge abutments, offshore oil rigs and towers, navigation buoys, jetties and breakwaters, to name a few.
5. To locate navigational aids, such as channel markers, buoys, etc.
6. To provide illumination while securing, casting off and adjusting the towlines.

COASTAL TOWING

A coastal tow is one that starts at one point along a coastline, proceeds usually within sight of land, and terminates at a point along the same coast.

The coastal tow is made up in a manner similar to intercoastal, trans-channel and offshore tows that proceed within sight of land. The fact that the tow must at times proceed beyond sight of land does not basically change it from a coastal tow.

The coastal tow, as shown in Fig. 129, is often a lighter tow than the ocean tow and the hook-up is also lighter.

Coal, lumber, oil and chemicals are transported in the coastal towing trade. A coastal tug is designed to serve dual functions—general towing and harbor docking work.

Towing is done on wire from an automatic towing winch, or from the "H" bitts on three-strand Manila or synthetic hawser.

Figure 130 illustrates a method of transferring the main tow hawser from the capstan to the towing bitts. First the tow is streamed to the desired towing distance, using the capstan. The end of the hawser is then figure-eighted over the "H" bitts and a stopper is

Fig. 129.   A light barge in a coastal tow.   Moran

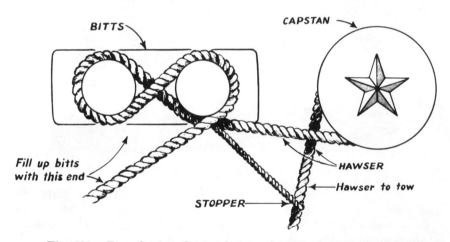

Fig. 130.   Transferring the tow hawser from capstan to tow bitts.

secured to the tension side of the hawser. The capstan is slacked off and the towing load is transferred to the stopper. The bitter end of the hawser is now taken off the bitts, removed from the capstan, all slack taken out, and the line again figure-eighted on the bitts. Finally, the stopper is released and the strain of towing is taken by the hawser on the bitts.

Coastal towing may be done on fiber, synthetic, or wire hawsers, depending on the size of the tow, tug and towing engine.

The make-up of the bridle on a tow is similar to that of an ocean tow, except that the size of the component parts will vary according to the strength required of the connections.

Many coastal tows run on tight schedules and unless heavy weather is encountered, the estimated time of arrival at destination is usually known at the time of departure. It has been said that on a coastal

Fig. 131.   Gob rope on a main tow hawser.

tow the cook can figure the noon position better than any mate. He just counts the quarts of milk and measures the salami and. . . .

Some special problems encountered in coastal towing, e.g., crossing the bar, streaming a tow, etc., are discussed in Chapter VI.

Gob Rope.   A gob rope of 2″ to 4″ circumference Manila is used to hold the main tow hawser on the centerline of a tug during rough weather to enable the tug to maintain better control over a tow. On larger tugs Norman pins and vertical rollers, where installed, serve the same purpose as the gob rope. Figure 131 shows a typical gob rope in use. Note the shackles that connect the rope to the deck and to the hawser. The top shackle encircling the hawser permits free movement necessary to pay out or shorten up quickly.

Lizard Stopper. A lizard stopper serves a purpose similar to that of the gob rope and it is illustrated hooked up in Fig. 132. The stopper is sometimes employed as a substitute for a Liverpool bridle and

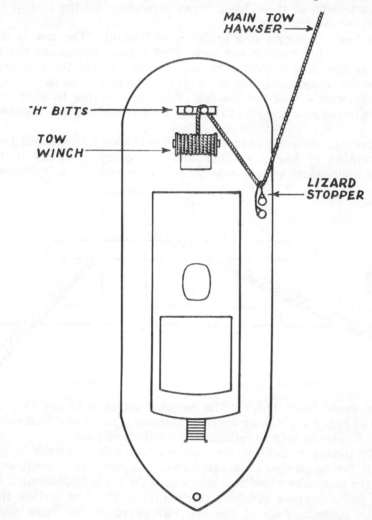

Fig. 132.   Lizard stopper hook-up.

standard tow bridle. The main towline is led from the tow winch (or tow hook), fairleaded to change direction and led forward to a point near the pivot point of the tug where it is clamped to a lizard stopper at the gunwale. The hawser may also be passed through a bight of the stopper. The lizard takes the strain of towing.

When fairleading the main towline around the "H" bitts, dip the hawser under the horn of the bitt as shown in Fig. 133.

OCEAN TOWING—AMERICAN

Figure 134 illustrates the basic types of offshore tows. There are many variations of these basic types depending on the size of tow and distance to be covered.

Single Tow. A single tow is the ideal hook-up. The tow is comprised of one tug pulling one tow. Under most conditions the tug maintains complete control over the tow and should the tow break loose for any reason, only the one unit need be recovered by the tug—not too difficult a task for the tug. But the breaking loose of more than one towed unit presents to the tug many problems to be discussed later.

The greatest difficulty encountered while towing a single unit (with the exception of heavy weather and emergency hazards) in fair weather under more or less ideal conditions, is yaw. Yaw is discussed

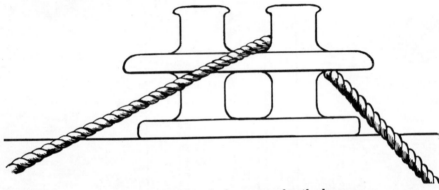

Fig. 133.   Dipping the hawser under the horn.

in more detail later, but for the moment suffice it to say that two lengths of heavy chain hung over the stern of a towed unit that cannot steer itself should help to minimize the effects of yaw.

Unlike towing in calm waters, wave action offshore tends to multiply the forces exerted on a tow hawser. A long ocean swell working on the unsynchronized tow may cause the tug's displacement and towing pull to oppose suddenly the weight of the tow so that these forces on opposite ends of the tow hawser reach maximum values simultaneously and may exceed the breaking strength of the hawser causing it to part.

Tandem tugs. The single ocean tow employing two tugs in tandem is shown in Fig. 135. The tow wire of the lead tug is shackled into a bridle on the bow of the second tug whose tow hawser in turn is shackled into the bridle of the towed unit—in this case, a dry dock. The larger of the two tugs towing in tandem would be placed between the lead tug and the tow, connected directly to the tow by a wire

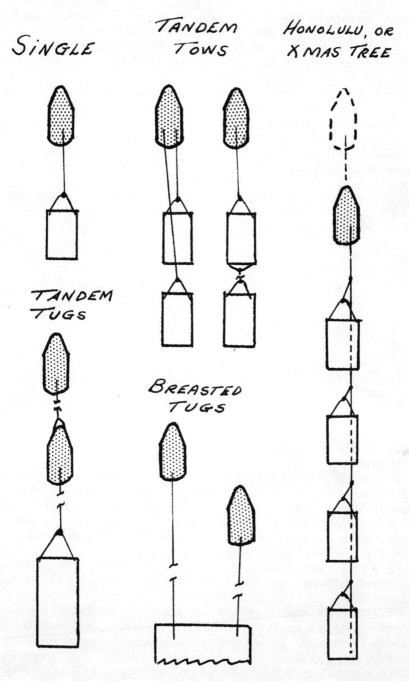

Fig. 134.   Some tow combinations.

hawser of approximately 150 fathoms in length. Consult the tables in Chapter III for the approximate size of hawser for the ihp of a tug.

Breasted tugs. The single tow utilizing two tugs in breasted formation is generally employed for towing unwieldy, cumbersome structures where towing speed is secondary in importance to maintaining towing control. By adjusting steering, horsepower output and speed, both tugs can better control yaw and surge.

Figure 136 shows this type of tow. The tug of greater pull is usually the lead tug on a slightly longer hawser.

Tandem Tow—One Tug. A tandem ocean tow employing one tug is not often resorted to for it is probably the most dangerous of all

Fig. 135.   Single tow—tandem tugs. Moran

tows, with the exception of the towing of outsized and unwieldy structures.

Figure 137 shows the arrangement of a tow of this type. The main tow wire is secured to a bridle on the first towed unit. A second hawser from the tug is passed over the deck of unit #1 and connected to a bridle on unit #2. Necessary fairleads and chafing gear are installed to complete the connection to unit #2. Both units are streamed directly from the tug.

As an alternate method to the above, a minimum of 600 feet of intermediate wire is secured between the units #1 and #2. The length of this hawser is important—the longer the better. When departing, both units are towed close-hauled until clear of the bar. Then a crew is sent to stream unit #2. After retrieving the crew, the main tow hawser is streamed and paid out slowly while steaming ahead at no more than ½ speed.

When main hawser is paid out to towing length, it is secured on the "H" bitts using stoppers. The tug may proceed at full speed after

Fig. 136. Bay-Houston Towing Co. tugs towing offshore drilling rig. Single tow—breasted tugs. Bay-Houston

the hawser is secured for towing. Do not tow on the drum of a non-automatic towing engine.

Arrival and Departure. No small part of an ocean tow operation are the arrangements made for the arrival and departure of the tow. One of the most hazardous tasks for tugs is the passage through crowded harbors and channels.

To facilitate the safe conduct of this operation, it is customary and often necessary for additional tugs to meet an incoming tow and to escort an outgoing tow. These extra tugs assist the ocean tugs in

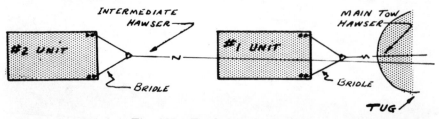

Fig. 137.   Tandem tow—one tug.

Fig. 138.   Single tow—breasted tugs with two tugs assisting the departure.
Moran

maneuvering their charge in the usually close confines of busy sheltered waters.

The assistance rendered is comparatively simple, e.g., the assist of pushing tug(s) as shown in Fig. 138, or the use of a tug on a short hawser astern of a heavy "dead" tow to assist in steering, as shown in Fig. 139. These are just two examples of the many uses whereby assisting tugs are employed to aid arrivals and departures.

Vessels to 5,000 tons displacement. Freighters, small coasters, auxiliary vessels and destroyers can be towed by one tug of 1,000 to 2,000 bhp using a minimum of 1⅛", 6 × 37 improved plow steel wire rope approximately 150 fathoms in length shackled to the legs of a chain bridle on most vessels, or to a length of chain passed through the bull nose in the bow of warships, as shown in Fig. 140.

Hardwood wedges are driven between chain and bull ring to prevent damage to the stem. Cork or wood hawser boards are fitted

under wire bridles to prevent rubbing damage when the hawser
slackens and tautens.

Vessels to 10,000 tons displacement.   Merchantmen, light cruisers
and frigates can be towed by one tug of 1,500 to 2,500 bhp using a
minimum of 1⅝″, 6 × 37 ips wire rope hawser approximately 150

Fig. 139.   Single tow—tandem tugs with one tug towed astern to assist with the
steering.   Moran

Fig. 140.   Tug *Marion Moran* towing an ARD close aboard.   Note the towing
connection is made through the bull nose of the tow.   Moran

to 200 fathoms in length shackled to a length of chain passed through
the bull nose of warships, or to the legs of a chain bridle on other
vessels. The same precautions are observed as for towing vessels to
5,000 tons displacement.

Vessels 15,000 to 20,000 tons displacement. Liners, tankers and naval vessels can be towed by two tugs of approximately 1,500 to 2,000 bhp each. The tugs tow abreast similar to those shown in Fig. 141. The usual practice is to disconnect both anchors and shackle their chains separately to the tow hawsers. The anchor chains are veered as necessary to the desired scope. An additional anchor is placed aboard and made ready for letting go for use in an emergency, or as a means of anchoring the tow.

One tug of greater horsepower may be substituted for the two tugs of lesser horsepower, provided it carries a tow hawser of sufficient strength.

When two tugs of equal bhp are employed, their wire tow hawsers are paid out to approximately 200 fathoms with the more powerful tug slightly in the lead by 100 to 400 feet. The anchor cables on the tow are veered to one or more shots. The diameter of wire will depend

Fig. 141.   Single tow—breasted tugs.   Moran

upon the type of wire rope employed. Consult Table I, Chapter III for the strength of different wire ropes.

Manila and synthetic rope is employed on occasion for tows of this type. A 50-foot length of 2″ to 2½″ diameter wire rope connects the tow "H" bitts, or tow hook to a 15″ to 18″ circumference Manila tow hawser approximately 120 fathoms in length that, in turn, is connected to another 2″ to 2½″ diameter wire pendant of from 10 fathoms to 60 fathoms in length, depending upon the size of the tow. The wire pendant is shackled to the anchor chain of the tow which is veered to one or more shots. It is not unusual to substitute chain in place of the 50-foot length of 2″ to 2½″ wire so that wear in way of the buffalo rail or tow span will be minimized. The chain when connected in the make-up is secured to a heavy tow strap, or to a tow hook.

During heavy weather, when additional spring is needed in the make-up, anchor chain on the tow is veered to additional length by the riding crew.

Should it be decided to connect a fiber tow hawser directly to a tow strap or tow hook, some extraordinary precautions must be taken to prevent excessive rubbing wear in way of rails and bulwarks. Split hose, as illustrated in Fig. 142, has been used on light tows with some success.

When synthetic ropes are employed, they are connected to a 50-foot length of $2\frac{1}{8}''$ to $2\frac{1}{2}''$ diameter wire rope, or chain of equal strength, which is connected to the tow strap on the "H" bitts or to a tow hook. The synthetic hawser is approximately 120 fathoms in length and is connected outboard to a 10- to 60-fathom length of $2\frac{1}{8}''$ to $2\frac{1}{2}''$ diameter wire rope that is shackled into the anchor chain veered to one or more shots.

Other details of connection were previously described, so that it remains only to determine the required strength of materials necessary and to locate the sizes on the appropriate tables in Chapter III.

Fig. 142.   Split hose chafing gear applied to a fiber tow hawser.

Vessels to 45,000 tons displacement.   Four (4) tugs of 1,500 bhp may be employed towing in two tandem hook-ups. The make-up is similar to that described above for 15,000 tons, except of course, that the strength of the connections is greater. Each lead tug is connected to the second tug with 150 fathoms of $2''$ to $2\frac{1}{8}''$ diameter wire rope. The second tug uses back-up wires to secure the bow bridle and to distribute the towing load.

Utilizing three (3) tugs of 2,000 bhp, the same tow would be connected, two (2) in tandem on one anchor chain and the remaining tug singled up on the other anchor chain.

Two (2) tugs of 3,000 bhp would tow abreast connected to two (2) separate hawsers of near equal length that, in turn, are connected to the anchor chains.

One tug of 6,000 bhp requires a minimum of 2,500 feet of $2\frac{5}{8}''$ high-grade plow-steel wire rope on an automatic towing winch. The tow hawser is connected to both anchor chains using a heavy plate shackle, or large heart-shaped anchor shackle. The anchor chains are veered as necessary by a riding crew to one or more shots.

Vessels over 45,000 tons displacement. Tows of over 45,000 tons displacement require special planning and handling, but it can be expected that tugs of, say, 9,000 ihp should be capable of handling the largest vessels afloat. The problem here lies in the strength of tow connections, i.e., towing padeyes, hawsers, hardware, etc. Employing several tugs reduces the strength-of-connections problem, but they necessarily increase the cost of the tow.

Heavy tows of great size should be given careful consideration and detailed planning, from strength of connections to weather conditions to be expected along the route. A tow should proceed along a proposed route during the most favorable time as predicted by a study of weather conditions.

The use of one tug for very large tows reduces the factor of safety considerably. It is far better and insures greater all-around safety to employ at least two tugs.

Fig. 143.   Tug towing dredge. Note bridle retrieving lines connected to the bridle and suspended from the gallows. Leon Trice

Dredges.   Dredges are designed to operate principally in protected waters and they are not usually constructed as seagoing vessels. Therefore, they require considerable preparation before they can be towed on an ocean. Towing a dredge can be a tricky and hazardous towing job under the best of circumstances.

The preparations necessary to make a dredge ready for tow are more extensive than for most other types of tows. Towing is done from the gallows (spud) end on chain bridles. The spud end is strengthened by the addition of internal bracing. The opposite (ladder) end of the dredge is secured by raising the ladder to a maximum height above the water. On some older dredges where the ladder will not raise sufficiently to prevent wave pounding damage to suction piping installed between the ladder legs, it is necessary to remove the suction piping. Occasionally the ladder is removed and shipped on a vessel as deck cargo or it is towed on another barge.

Figure 143 shows a typical dredge towing hook-up. Note the retrieving wires extending from the top of the gallows to about the middle of the chain bridles. These wires are used to facilitate connecting and disconnecting the bridle. The wires are wound on the drum of a winch. Operating the winch raises the bridle to prevent dragging the bottom in shallow water and to retrieve the bridle for disconnecting, or lowers the bridle after connecting for towing.

Floating Mining and Machinery Equipment. The towing of mining and machinery equipment requires that considerable time and energy

Fig. 144.   Single tow—one tug. Special equipment barge. Air Photos and Advertising

Fig. 145.   *Vertrek Midbody* 653 under tow of tug *Zwarte Zee III*, 10-5-61. L. Smit

be expended in the preparation of the tow. All machinery must be braced and secured to prevent movement or shifting.

It is the usual practice to tow with one tug of sufficient horsepower. A glance at Fig. 144 will show that the hook-up is basically the same as previously described for any other single tow. The amount and variety of machinery aboard generally presents special problems in securing for sea.

Other Special Tows.   Figure 145 shows an example of an application of specialized towing. A new midbody of a ship is being towed in a running sea.

The following will be noted in the photograph:

1. Yaw is indicated by one taut bridle leg. The tow is yawing because of turning or as a result of towing in a seaway.

2. Chafing plates on which the bridle legs ride extend forward and clear of the deck edge.

3. Chain bridle.

4. Navigational aids.

5. Bridle retrieving wire on tow.

6. Reinforced towing end of hull.

7. Chain intermediate spring.

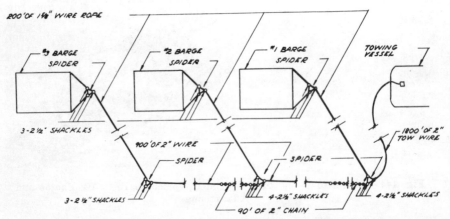

Fig. 146.   Honolulu, or Christmas tree tow.

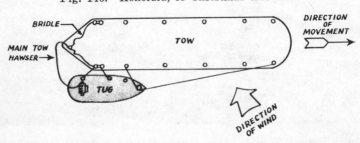

Fig. 147.   Departure of British and European tow.

Honolulu, or Christmas Tree Tow.   The Honolulu tow is a tandem tow made up of barges towed in column formation by one or more tugs. The main tow hawser of the tow illustrated in Fig. 146 passes over the fantail of tug downward and astern beneath each barge being towed. The Honolulu tow is a hook-up that fills a particular need of towing. On the Pacific coast the continental shelf drops off sharply some distance from shore. Ordinary multiple tow hook-ups permit a considerable catenary of tow hawser between barges. It is this catenary that at times fouls the shelf when passing from deep to coastal waters. As a result the Honolulu tow hook-up was devised as a means of keeping the catenary to a minimum. All barges are connected to a main tow wire that passes beneath the barges. The pull of each barge on the hawser keeps the catenary to a minimum. The sketch is schematic.

BRITISH AND EUROPEAN PRACTICE

Departure.   A tug ties up alongside the tow and proceeds towing the barge stern first. When tow is clear of the harbor and barge is ready for streaming, the tug's head is brought into the wind with the tow to leeward, as shown in Fig. 147. All lines are cast off and tug proceeds dead slow ahead and away from the tow. The force of wind will carry the barge downwind clear of the tug. The main tow hawser

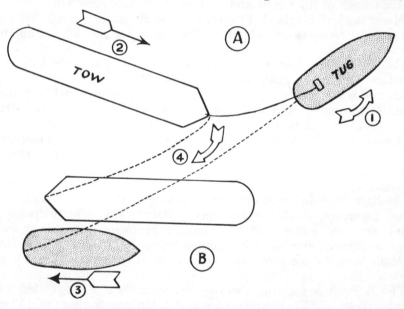

Fig. 148.   Arrival of British and European tow.

is paid out to about 40 fathoms of wire for short-stay towing and longer for heavy-weather towing. The tug is gradually speeded up until towing speed is reached.

Arrival.   Upon arrival at a pilot station the tug slows down gradually while heaving in (shortening up) on the main hawser to approximately 50 to 60 feet. Shortening up is done with the main tow hawser passing between stern rollers, stern chocks, or Norman pins.

The engine is stopped and the tug is sheered as in Sketch A to the approximate angle of (1) in Fig. 148. Meanwhile the tow continues

to move ahead as a result of momentum (2). A slow astern bell (3)
will back the tug down and draw the tow alongside the tug as in (3)
of Sketch B. The tug is then secured alongside in a manner similar
to Fig. 147.

Ocean Towing. A long tow hawser is essential for towing in heavy
weather. Great wave action can result in sudden shock loading that
can break a tow hawser. The scope and weight of a long hawser
tends to dampen surging and thereby reduces the effects of sudden
loading shocks.

In addition to a long scope of tow hawser it is usual to connect the
tow hawser to a heavy chain bridle on the tow in a manner similar
to the Amercan practice. A length of Manila—and more recently
synthetic rope—connects the bitter end of the hawser to the "H" bitts
or spring tow hook. The fiber rope acts as an additional damper on
sudden strains. The automatic towing engine serves the same purpose
as the length of fiber rope and, in fact, it does a better job.

Many tugs of England, France, Greece, Holland, Ireland and Italy
carry long hawsers of cable-laid fiber rope for use as a main tow
hawser.

Cable-laid fiber rope is stiff and heavy and requires the largest of
capstans and gypsy heads to heave it in. Other tugs use towing engines and wire depending on the size of the tug and its primary function. Ocean-going tugs of these nations range in horsepower from
1,000 to 4,000 and there are a few of even greater horsepower.

A spring tension towing hook, described in Chapter II, is employed
that will absorb up to one-half of the maximum breaking strain of
the hawser for which it is designed.

The main tow hawser on some European tugs, notably those of
L. Smit & Co.'s International Tug Service of the Netherlands, is of
large diameter, double nylon rope construction. The increase of
diameter alone means difficult handling problems, but this is overcome to some degree by using double lines. Doubling the lines theoretically doubles the strength and it enables easier handling aboard
the tug.

The L. Smit & Co. tug, *Zwarte Zee*, of 9,000 ihp is outfitted with
Manila ropes of 25″ circumference and nylon double ropes of 15″ circumference each, five steel wire ropes, a few over 2¼″ diameter, and
each approximately 3,280 feet in length. (note 1)

It is expected that these tow hawsers will be capable of pulling
giant tows of 130,000 tons deadweight.

Vessels to 5,000 tons displacement. For towing small coasters,
auxiliary vessels, etc., a short pendant of 15″ Manila connects the
tow hook to 150 fathoms of 3½″ (1⅛″ dia.) wire rope that is shackled
in turn to the two legs of a chain bridle.

Vessels to 10,000 tons displacement. For towing merchantmen, light cruisers, large frigates and heavy destroyers, etc., a short pendant of 18″ Manila connects the tow hook to 150 fathoms of 4½″ circumference wire rope that is shackled to two legs of a chain bridle, or to a length of anchor chain extending out through the bull ring in the bow of a warship.

Note: Hardwood wedges are driven under the chain in the bull ring to prevent damage to the stem. Fenders or chafing gear are placed under a cable on deck to prevent thumping damage while cable slackens and tautens.

Vessels to 15,000 tons displacement; tugs to 1,900 bhp. The European method of connecting a tow provides for considerable flexibility in the hook-up.

A 4½″ wire pendant of approximately 9 fathoms is connected to a tow hook. 120 fathoms of 15″ circumference Manila rope is shackled to the pendant.

A length of 4½″ wire rope from 9 fathoms to 60 fathoms (for a heavy tow) is shackled to a chain bridle or to the anchor chain veered to one or more shots as found necessary.

Note: The first wire pendant is sometimes omitted and a short strap or a short length of chain is substituted that extends just beyond the rail of the tug similar to Fig. 128.

Vessels to 15,000 tons displacement; tugs 2,000 bhp and more. The same hook-up as the foregoing is required except that 5″ wire rope is substituted for the 4½″ and 18″ Manila is substituted for the 15″.

TOWING CONNECTIONS

In recent years efforts have been made to overcome the problem of fabricating a towing connection on a tow whenever the necessity arises. Owners, designers and builders have been made aware of the importance of installing a heavy tow connection of sufficient strength when a vessel is being built.

The problem has been overcome in the past by utilizing the anchor cables as towing bridles. However, this is not altogether a satisfactory solution because it deprives the vessel of a most important factor of safety, i.e., the ability to be anchored in the event it breaks free of the tug during heavy weather near a lee shore. A riding crew lowers the anchors to near maximum length on a drifting vessel (one that has parted a tow connection). The anchors may snag bottom and retard vessel's shoreward progress until such time as the tug can reconnect its tow hawser. Hence, the desirability of a towing bridle separate from the anchor chain and this requires padeyes or brackets to which the bridle can be connected on the tow.

The padeye was previously discussed; we now turn to one of the most successful towing brackets designed.

A special problem developed in recent years, that of safely towing the large supertankers of great size and displacement. One important aspect of the problem was how to install a connection of adequate strength on the tow.

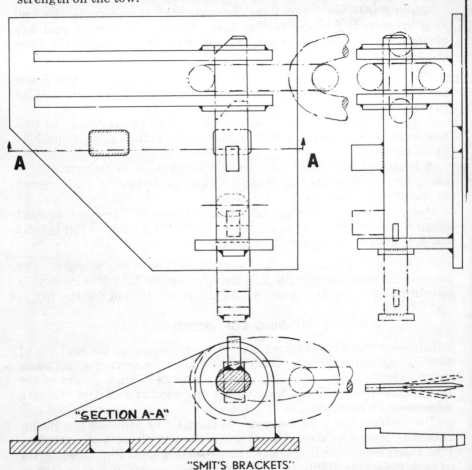

"SECTION A-A"

"SMIT'S BRACKETS"

Fig. 149. Plan of "Smit's Bracket."

Quick-Action Smit's Bracket. One solution to the problem is the "Smit's Bracket" developed by Ir. G. Langelaar Gzn, M.R.I.N.A., M.S.N.A.M.E., Technical General Manager of L. Smit & Co.'s International Tug Service operation.

The bracket is illustrated in Fig. 149. In order to facilitate towing operations of a casual or emergency order L. Smit & Co. ". . . suggest fitting such a 'Smit's Bracket' on the forecastle of all super-class vessels." (note 2)

The complete bracket is mounted on a suitable deck doubler and the whole is strengthened by stiffeners carried down within the hull and tied into structurals. The complete installation is shown in Fig. 150.

A sliding bolt facilitates inserting and securing the end link of a chain between the brackets. The sliding bolt in turn is secured by the split wedge inserted in the opposite end of the bolt body. The split wedge is secured by spreading the leafs of the wedge.

Fig. 150. View of installed "Smit's Bracket." L. Smit

Fairleads. A fairlead, as the name implies, is a fabricated shape used to change the direction of a flexible member of the hook-up of a tow.

At times existing chocks, rollers and double bitts installed aboard a tow are used as fairleads. Often, however, a satisfactory fairlead of sufficient strength and size is not conveniently located and, therefore, one must be fabricated and installed. Figure 151 shows a fairlead of this type. Note that one leg of the chain bridle extends forward through the small opening of the fairlead over the bow end of the tow. A piece of steel flat bar is welded across the top opening to prevent the bridle from jumping the confines of the fairlead while the tow is pitching heavily. Both sides are stiffened with steel brackets and the whole is mounted on a doubler of suitable size, to insure a satisfactory connection to the deck and to distribute the load over a large area of deck.

It will also be noted that the forward deck edge over which the chain will rub and chafe is strengthened and fitted with a steel wearing piece that extends transversely for approximately three feet beyond the width of the fairlead. This is to insure that a sufficient

Fig. 151. Bridle fairlead on a tow. L. Smit

breadth of deck edge is protected during times when the bridle leg leads at oblique angles from the fairlead during turning maneuvers, yaw, or heavy weather.

The practice of installing a fairlead, commonly known as the *bull nose*, in the bow of a vessel usually has been limited to warship construction. This type of fairlead is illustrated in Fig. 152. The bulbous bow of large vessels permits the use of this centerline fairlead because the entrance of the streamlined stem and modeled forebody facilitates direct forward movement and reduces tendency to yaw. However, during heavy weather most tows will yaw, including those being towed through a bull nose, so that one of the main problems of a tug during periods of heavy weather, especially with following wind or sea, is to keep the tow from coming abreast of the tug at any time. As a result, the tug must employ stern rollers, Norman pins, gob ropes, lizard stoppers, or maneuvering bridles in order to keep the towline leading aft. These devices should keep the towing force aft

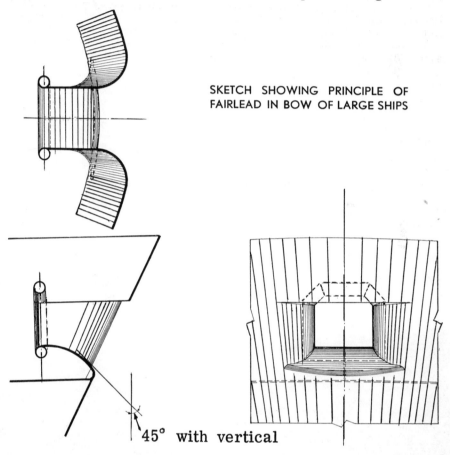

SKETCH SHOWING PRINCIPLE OF
FAIRLEAD IN BOW OF LARGE SHIPS

45° with vertical

Fig. 152.   Fairlead in bow of large ships. L. Smit

and aid in altering course and they also reduce the possibility of girding the tug.

The three curved surfaces of the fairlead shown are formed by radiused plates. Sides and bottom are curved because these are the surfaces of greatest chafing contact. A sharp corner could snag and cause damage to the chain, or more likely, damage to plating and possible fractures with detrimental effects to the watertight integrity of the tow. Consequently, the bottom and sides of a fairlead must be shaped to a gentle curve at least five times the thickness of the chain bridle leg. The fairlead must be strong and securely mounted; structures in way must be reinforced and chafing areas must be protected.

NOTES: CHAPTER V

1. ". . . each to be one kilometre long with circumferences of 7¼″ and 6½″ (58 mm. resp. 52 mm. dia.)." "Tugs and towing gear keep up with Supertankers," *Tug, Towage and Salvage Review*, n. 17, Autumn 1962, p. 11.

2. "Quick-Action Smit's Brackets," *Tug, Towage and Salvage Review*, n. 17, Autumn 1962, p. 7.

CHAPTER VI

MISCELLANEOUS TOWING OPERATIONS, TECHNIQUES AND HAZARDS

RESCUE TOWING

Rescue towing involves the rendering of assistance by a tug to a vessel in distress. To be effective the assistance must be rendered quickly. The distressed vessel must be located somewhere within steaming radius for a tug to render assistance quickly. The cause of distress in many cases results from heavy weather; therefore, the tug must be of ocean-going design capable of proceeding through heavy seas at a maximum speed.

A vessel may become disabled and in need of assistance through any one of a number of causes, or a combination thereof:

Storms and heavy seas	Loss of propeller
Collision	Loss of rudder
Fire	Striking a submerged object
Machinery breakdown	Foundering
Shift of cargo and resultant damage	Grounding or stranding
Fractured tailshaft	Barratry, mutiny, sabotage or other unlawful act

The tug must locate a casualty quickly, connect a towline and reach a safe harbor for rescue towing to be successful. Accurate navigation necessary to locate the casualty, expert seamanship to effectively connect a towline and maneuverability of the tug with power to apply to towline pull are requisite to the trade.

Salvage and rescue tugs are maintained on stations accessible to the major shipping lanes of the world. The tugs are owned and operated by private companies, e.g., Merritt-Chapman & Scott of the U.S.A., L. Smit & Co.'s Internationale Sleepdienst of The Netherlands and Alexandra Towing Co., of Great Britain.

In some oceans, particularly the North Atlantic and North Sea, the prevalent heavy weather conditions during winter cause many ships to experience difficulty in what might be called a normal passage and a steaming vessel is sometimes within a hair's breadth of distress. A tug called upon to render assistance proceeds into a literal "hell of angry seas" that often threatens its own survival. The fact that many successful rescues under those conditions are a matter of record proves the extraordinary skill and dedication of the men who man the gallant rescue tug. (note 1)

Agreement and Contracts. The master or authorized company representative will usually agree to a daily hire rate, or a *Lloyd's Open Form* will be signed. The following are the general terms of agreement concerning remuneration for the salvage (rescue) costs.

After a casualty is towed into port, the salvors cable Lloyd's in London, or the American underwriters, requesting the Owners or Underwriters to post a security bond equal to the amount that the salvors expect to collect under the *Lloyd's Open Form*. The Owners or Underwriters then have approximately two weeks to comply. A failure to comply allows the salvors to "slap a plaster" through court order, on the house of the casualty. The casualty is then under arrest of a U.S. marshal or a sheriff until a settlement is reached.

In most cases a bond is posted by the principals for the vessel so that the vessel may proceed on her normal business.

The salvors then prepare a salvage brief. The brief, in itself, is a "tale of woe" for it contains a description of the salvage, hazards encountered, perils overcome, gear expended, etc. In most cases the brief makes excellent reading in melodrama and it is usually prepared by professionals in such matters.

In Britain the brief is sent to the salvage company's legal advisors who request Lloyd's Committee to appoint an arbitrator and set a date for the hearing.

Meanwhile, back at the Owner's office, a counter brief is being prepared, containing their arguments to show that the whole salvage operation was really "a piece of cake." It is their contention that, in fact, the operation was quite simple.

Both sides usually exchange briefs prior to submitting them to an arbitrator. Opposing attorneys argue the briefs presented to the arbitrator who finally decides the amount of the award. The decision may be appealed. The ground rules are similar in United States practice.

Vessel Assisting Another Vessel. In some instances of rescue towing the first vessel to arrive on the scene of a casualty is another ship. Rather than await the arrival of a rescue tug, the ship will attempt to connect a towline. Waiting for a rescue tug may take several days that can spell the difference between life or death for the casualty.

An emergency tow wire is carried aboard most vessels. The hawser is commonly known as the *insurance cable*. This tow hawser is employed to make a connection to the casualty.

Refer to Fig. 153 and proceed as follows:

1. Rig the bridle legs around the stern quarter bitts through the after fairleads outboard and then back aboard to the after deck (fantail). Both outboard ends of the bridle are then connected to one

large pear-shaped shackle to which the tow hawser (insurance cable) will be attached. The bitter ends of the bridle legs are led forward and secured to other deck fittings, e.g., bitts, cleats, etc.

2. Meanwhile, aboard the casualty the inboard end of the tow wire (insurance cable) is shackled to one of the anchor chains. (One anchor is stopped off and disconnected from this chain.) The anchor shackle is attached to the outboard end of the tow wire. A plate shackle, or shackle with forelock, may be substituted for the anchor shackle.

A messenger is secured to the outboard anchor shackle of the wire and, in turn, the messenger is bent onto a heaving line and made ready for passing to the rescue vessel.

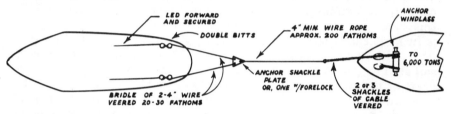

Fig. 153. Rescue towing—ship towing ship.

3. The rescue ship makes its approach to the casualty and the heaving line is caught. The messenger is hauled aboard using the heaving line and it is then led to the gypsy head of a winch and the tow wire is heaved aboard and shackled to the bridle. The messenger is untied and stowed away. Any stoppers holding the tow bridle aboard the rescue vessel are severed, allowing the bridle to fall outboard. The anchor chain is veered to the required scope while the rescue vessel steams slow ahead. Speed is increased slowly and the anchor chain is veered to longer scope as found necessary to keep the towline submerged with sufficient catenary to prevent "jumping on the line."

4. In heavy weather a rescue vessel approaches the bow of a casualty at a large angle from the lee side and passes across its bow. A buoyed line is dropped from the stern of the rescue vessel and allowed to drift down on the casualty. This line is retrieved by the casualty and secured to a messenger. The messenger, of course, is secured to the tow wire as described above. A note of caution—heaving lines that have seen considerable service will usually part under a moderate to heavy strain. The forces generated by heavy weather will place an added strain on a heaving line, so that only the best available lines should be used.

It is possible for a vessel to tow a casualty of perhaps twice her own tonnage, but during heavy weather she may only be capable of

maintaining her heading to keep from broaching in heavy seas. This
is usually sufficient to avert a disaster and after the passage of hours
or days the storm will finally abate and headway will be resumed.
Abundant chafing gear must be applied and reapplied as it wears off.

Connecting a Towline To a Casualty.   A tug will usually stop in line
with a casualty in order to determine the amount of drift. Depending upon sea conditions, the tug should be positioned so that the distance to the casualty will remain fairly constant with a minimum of
maneuvering while lines are being run to connect up for towing.

The casualty, if a large steamer, will usually drift downwind at a
faster rate than a tug because of the greater area of hull that is subjected to the force of winds. The tug should lie off the lee bow of a
casualty at a sufficient distance to enable a transfer of lines. During
this time the casualty will drift close to the stern of the tug.

In most cases, the stern of a casualty will head into the wind and
drift with her bow headed downwind. This is because of the larger
sail area of the bow as compared with the stern, as well as the deeper
draft at the stern offering greater resistance to drift than the lighter
bow. In this condition it is comparatively easy for a tug to maintain
a satisfactory distance between both vessels while lines are being run
simply by "kicking" the engine ahead when necessary.

One method of connecting up for rescue towing follows (refer to
Fig. 154):

(1) A casualty throws a heaving line to the tug. (2) Tug's messenger is bent onto the heaving line and hauled aboard the casualty.
The inboard end of the messenger is connected to a length of wire
pendant (3) approximately 150 to 200 feet of 2″ diameter wire rope.
(3) The wire pendant with towing shackle connected is heaved
aboard using messenger (2). (4) A double nylon spring approximately 50 to 100 fathoms is shackled to the bitter end of wire pendant
(3). The nylon spring is stopped off on the deck of the tug. The wire
pendant (3) aboard vessel is connected to anchor chain (anchor disconnected) using the towing shackle. (5) The bitter end of nylon
spring is connected to the main tow wire on the drum of towing
engine. (6) Anchor cable is payed out. When veered to satisfactory
length, brake is set, pall engaged and stopper connected. (7) Tug
proceeds slowly ahead. Stopper of nylon spring is severed and spring
allowed to pay out. Main tow wire is payed out to desired scope (5).
Anchor chain is veered as found necessary (6).

Stern-first Tow Connection.   It is advisable to tow stern-first when a
casualty has broken in two and the stern half is recovered. The stern-
first method of towing is also employed where there is serious bow
damage to a disabled vessel. Figure 155 illustrates this method of
towing. The lead tug is not visible in the photograph, although its
towline can be seen. This particular casualty is shown arriving after
completing a successful voyage under tow. Note also the two tugs

Fig. 154.   One method of connecting a towline to a casualty.

secured aft to facilitate navigation and maneuvering in the busy harbor.

For a vessel of this size, a satisfactory hook-up would be:

Approximately 150 feet of 2″ diameter wire rope secured to the stern bitts and fairleaded through the stern chock, shackled to approximately 100 fathoms of 15″ circumference Manila rope, or 50 to 100 fathoms of 2¼″ diameter nylon, shackled to main tow hawser of 2″ diameter wire rope a minimum of 1,500 feet.

It is advisable to secure a back-up wire completely around the after house. A bridle is not used. The Manila or nylon intermediate spring is included to provide stretch and flexibility in the make-up.

Fig. 155. Stern section of S.S. *Fort Mercer* being towed into New York, February, 1952. Official U.S. Coast Guard photograph

Of course, this hook-up is for a tug of up to 3,000 bhp and should a larger tug be employed, the make-up should be proportionately heavier, or the tug's engine output should be limited.

The need for occasionally attaching a towline to the stern of a vessel should be given consideration in the design of a vessel. A ship need not be a casualty to find a use for heavy tow brackets and fairleads on the stern. These could be used for: Stern towing connection when damaged; tug connection, or tackle connection to assist the vessel when grounded; as an emergency towing connection to assist other vessels.

Two tugs. Two tugs are often employed to tow a casualty stern-first, as illustrated in Fig. 156.

One tug is secured ahead and pulls with a tow hook-up to the stern of the casualty. The second tug is secured aft of the tow with a hook-up to the sheered-off end of the casualty. The second tug steams at a slightly slower rate of speed than the lead tug, thereby acting as a floating rudder to improve steering and reduce yaw.

Passing a bridle to the casualty. A description of an earlier method used to connect a towline (that may prove a satisfactory operation on special occasions) follows:

1. Wire bridles are passed to the casualty and connected in a manner similar to that described above for ocean towing.

2. A length of Manila approximately 100 fathoms, or a 50- to 100-fathom length of nylon, intermediate spring is connected to the bridle. A length of chain will do, provided that the weather is favorable to facilitate the handling of heavy chain. However, in an emergency situation it is usually not desirable to expend precious time in trying to rig chain that is difficult to handle at normal times and practically impossible to rig during heavy weather.

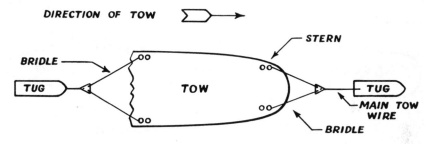

Fig. 156. Towing a casualty stern-first using two tugs.

3. The intermediate spring is connected to the main tow wire. The sizes of all of the foregoing will, of course, depend upon other factors, such as tonnage and tug power.

Submarine Rescue Towing. Rescue towing of submarines is rarely called for; however, whenever assistance is to be rendered in an emergency, the following factors should be kept in mind:

1. Even when surfaced, there are portions of a submarine extending longitudinally and transversely under water that are not easily discernible from a vantage point aboard the tug. These protuberances can cause damage to a tug, therefore extreme caution should be exercised in making an approach, passing close aboard, and while tying up.

2. Weighted tire or wood fenders should be hung over the sides of both tug and submarine. The fenders should be positioned opposite each other and lowered to a depth under water sufficient to protect the sub's protruding bilge.

3. Tow connections are made after a conference between the tug captain and submarine commander resolves method, sizes of lines, towing connections and speed of tow. In addition, communications or emergency signals must be established between both vessels so that information concerning intentions and difficulties encountered

may be freely exchanged between both vessels to avoid any misunderstanding.

Aircraft Rescue Towing.   In the event that an aircraft requires assistance it may circle and fire a Very pistol. A tug should immediately ready a boat for launching to pick up survivors. Hospital areas must be designated, medical supplies broken out including extra bedding, blankets, sheets and warm dry clothing.

Occasionally an aircraft will attempt to signal the exact location of a distressed vessel to an assisting tug proceeding to the scene. The aircraft will circle above the tug, fire a Very pistol or rocket, and fly off in the direction of the required aid (toward the casualty). The tug then sets its course in the direction taken by the aircraft.

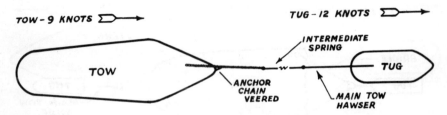

Fig. 157.   Towing a casualty that has lost rudder.

Towing a Vessel That Has Lost Its Rudder.   In the case of a vessel that has lost its rudder and requires assistance in order to proceed into port, it is not necessary for a tug to actually take the casualty under tow. The vessel is still capable of making good headway under its own power and requires only the needed directional pull to steer and maintain a fairly steady course.

There are two basic tactics exercised for assisting a vessel that has lost its rudder.

1. The tug connects to the bow of a casualty in the usual manner for a rescue tow, as shown in Fig. 157—anchor chain connected to intermediate spring that is connected to main tow hawser. Tug then proceeds at a rate of power to develop a speed of, say, 12 knots. The casualty then steams at a power output sufficient to develop and maintain a speed of 10 knots. In other words, the tug applies more power to the towline pull than the casualty applies to its propulsion. The casualty steams at a speed sufficient to increase towing speed while the tug steers the required course. Under these circumstances the tug tows a weight considerably less than the deadweight of the casualty.

2. The tug connects a tow hawser to its bow towing bitt or bollard. The outboard end is passed to the casualty and it is shackled into a fishplate on a bridle rigged on the stern of the tow. The vessel gets under way and proceeds ahead at full speed towing the tug. The required course is maintained by the tug applying right or left rudder

which, in turn, veers the stern of the casualty to port or starboard, see Fig. 158.

Assisting a Stranded Vessel. Occasionally a tug is called upon to render assistance to a vessel that has gone aground or one that has stranded. Upon arrival at the scene the direction of any set must first be determined. No attempt should be made to pass a line to a casualty without at least one of the tug's anchors down. The tug should anchor at a safe distance offshore and back down inshore toward the stranded vessel. A messenger line is passed to the casualty using a line-throwing gun, or workboat. The main tow hawser is secured to the messenger and, in turn, it is also passed to the casualty. Upon coming aboard the casualty, the messenger may be taken to

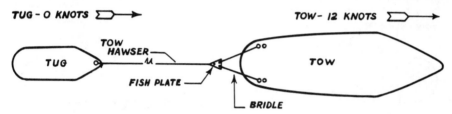

Fig. 158.   Steering a casualty that has lost its rudder.

the drum of a winch or capstan to heave aboard the main tow hawser. Lacking power on the casualty (dead ship) a bight of the messenger is inserted into the snatch block on board the casualty and the tug hauls on the messenger to heave aboard the towline.

The main tow hawser, upon coming aboard, is secured to a suitable connection on the casualty, or to a bridle. Because only a slight force can be applied by pulling with the tug alone, the stranded vessel's anchors should be hauled offshore, using workboats or the vessel's lifeboats. The anchors should be dropped offshore at a sufficient distance to provide adequate scope and length to insure satisfactory holding power. Where beach gear is available, it should be rigged. By heaving in on the vessel's anchor windlasses and proceeding full ahead on the main engines of tug while simultaneously hauling in on the tug's anchor cables, a sufficient force may be exerted to free the stranded vessel. Heaving and pulling should begin so that a maximum force will be applied at a maximum high tide. It is advisable to determine the amount of the ground reaction, i.e., the amount (tons) that the casualty is aground. A study of ground reaction and the means used to ascertain the amount of ground reaction has been covered in another work by the author. (note 2)

Usually there is a *set* that tends to veer a tug, that is pulling without an anchor down, toward the opposite side with the possibility that the tug may also ground unless some action is taken to overcome the effects of any set. The use of an anchor from the tug may at times limit the maneuverability and wrenching effect that the tug is capable

of exerting on a casualty. Consequently, a Liverpool bridle is rigged
on the tow hawser of the tug so that the tug is free to shift the direction of its pull in order to offset a change in direction of set or to
facilitate wrenching operations. Figure 159 illustrates this type of
operation. Note that beach gear is secured to the stranded vessel;
lacking beach gear the bower anchors of the casualty are substituted.

A word of caution—take adequate precautions to control the vessel
when it comes free. In most grounding cases, locked-in potential
energy in the tow hawser is converted into kinetic energy of motion
in the vessel immediately upon the vessel coming free of the ground,
causing the casualty to move rapidly to deep water. The tug risks
being overridden by the freed vessel unless some precautions are

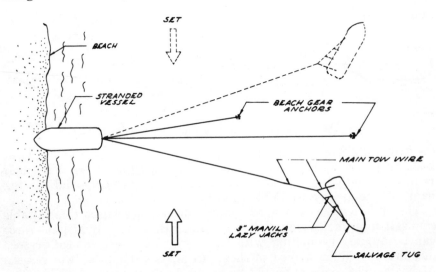

Fig. 159.   Tug assisting a stranded vessel.

taken to move it quickly from the path of the moving vessel. The tug
must maneuver swiftly. In some cases it is necessary to cast off the
towline. If the tug tries to maneuver without first casting off the
towline, it may find itself "in irons" and unable to move to avoid a
collision.

Preparations to cast off a towline under these circumstances must
be made beforehand, that is, before any heaving operations are com-
menced. A buoy should be tied to the bitter end to facilitate recovery.

Another method of rigging cables and towlines to assist a stranded
vessel is illustrated in Fig. 160. The tug pulls alternately from side
to side while beach gear rigged on the casualty is alternately hauled
and overhauled in a wrenching effect. The idea is to pull the vessel
from side to side. Any movement of this nature is of great value in
freeing the vessel. The movement may be minimal at first, but with
repeated efforts the movement will gradually increase until finally

the vessel is freed. The operation should commence on a flooding tide.
Trimming the casualty by the stern or offshore end can also aid in
reducing ground reaction.

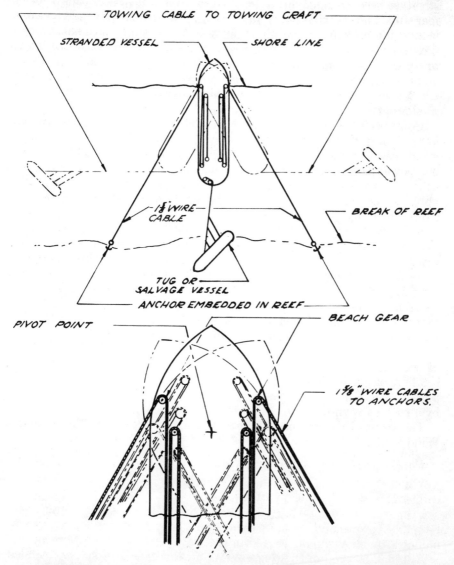

Fig. 160. Wrenching a stranded vessel using tug and beach gear.

Heavy Weather. Perhaps the single most important uncontrolled
factor that can spell success or failure of any offshore tow is weather.
Heavy weather is probably responsible for more tow disasters than
any other single cause.

A long tow hawser is essential in heavy weather. Sudden shock-loading caused by tumultous seas may part a shortened towline. This sudden shock-loading is reduced by spring in the make-up. Spring effect is accomplished by a long scope and catenary, weight of the make-up, and by stretch of the towline. A length of chain is added to provide weight and a length of Manila or nylon provides stretch. Catenary, weight and stretch may be applied to the make-up singly or in combination. All are acceptable and each has its advantages and disadvantages. One important factor in favor of the use of chain for weight, either in the intermediate connection or for a bridle, is its strength.

Conversely, a long scope of wire and heavy chain increases the weight and drag opposing the forward motion of a tug which, if great, can put the tug "in irons." Therefore, a tug of sufficient towing power is essential. On tugs of insufficient horsepower it is sometimes desirable to tow using double nylon hawsers that are considerably lighter than equal lengths of wire, thereby minimizing the possibility of a tug getting "in irons."

Another means employed to reduce sudden shock-loading of a main towline during heavy weather is the automatic towing engine. The tow engine is actually a winch that automatically maintains a predetermined setting for hawser strain and length. At times of heavy loading, the hawser pays out and when excess load is reduced, the hawser is shortened up to the set length. The result is that the automatic towing engine reduces sudden strains and dampens surging between tug and tow better than any other method devised.

Sea conditions are the direct result of wind that, in turn, is a result of weather conditions. In many instances a sea will make up in a locale at a great distance from the center of the atmospheric disturbance in a manner analogous to the distant spreading of ripples caused by a rock thrown in a body of water.

The general conditions of weather are determined by the Beaufort Wind Scale.

Force	Condition	MPH
4	Moderate breeze	13-18
5	Fresh breeze	19-24
6	Strong breeze	25-31
7	Moderate gale	32-38
8	Fresh gale	39-46
9	Strong gale	47-54
10	Whole gale	55-63
11	Storm	64-75
12	Hurricane	above 75

The Beaufort Scale Force 12 wind is a revolving storm that rotates counterclockwise in the northern hemisphere and clockwise in the southern hemisphere. The hurricane of the Caribbean and North Atlantic, the typhoon of the China Seas and the cyclone of the Indian Ocean and Arabian Seas are the same storm types.

The *dangerous semicircle* of a storm is that part of the cyclonic circle that combines with the track of the storm's course. In the northern hemisphere it is the right-hand side of the storm track.

In order to obtain good pull and maneuverability in a storm, a steady flow of water to the propeller and rudder is required. Pitching in turbulent seas reduces the effectiveness of the propeller, particularly if it leaves the water intermittently. The stern of a tug must be kept down in the water. This may be accomplished by judicious ballasting and by the weight of a long scope of tow wire. Hence, we see another advantage of a tow hawser that sinks rather than one that floats.

Vigilance and expert seamanship during storms are two very important factors necessary to the survival of tug and tow. Constant observation of wind and sea conditions and corrective maneuvers are necessary to maintain heading and prevent broaching, girding or capsizing. Tug personnel must be prepared at all times to cast off a sinking tow.

When towing in heavy seas, the length of the towline is adjusted so that both the tug and tow reach the crest and trough of their waves simultaneously, thereby reducing the effects of shock-loading and lessening the chances that the tow will "jump on the line."

Girding, or Tripping. Girding is a British term. A tug is said to be girding when she is towed sideways by an opposing force on her own towline. There is imminent danger that a tug will capsize when she is girded.

Figure 161 illustrates a typical docking maneuver that may result in girding of a tug.

1. The tug pulls vessel broadside to clear a pier.
2. The vessel when clear moves ahead quickly and out of the slip at full speed, changing the angle of the towline pull to the side thus tripping (an American term for girding) the tug.

At the time of an imminent girding situation, the tug captain must trip the tow hook by lanyard from the bridge releasing the tow hawser, thereby disconnecting the capsizing moments. An axe should be mounted on a bulkhead near the tow hook to be used in an emergency for severing the hawser in the event that a tow hook fails to release, or at times when a tow hook is not used.

A tug will more readily gird or trip the closer that the tow connection or hook is to amidship. And, too, as illustrated in Fig. 162, the height of the tow hook is an important factor in the magnitude of the force produced and calculated as capsizing moments. The greater the height above the center of flotation, the greater will be the moments developed tending to capsize a tug.

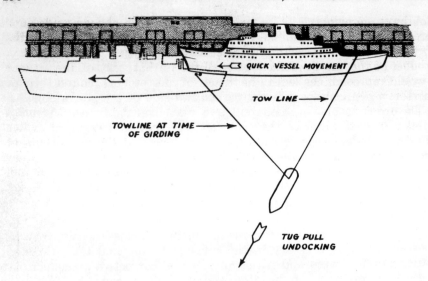

Figure 161.

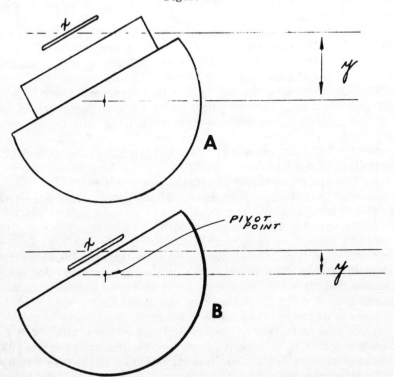

Fig. 162.   Effect on tripping moment of tow hook height.

A leverage principle is involved. Simply stated, using Fig. 162 for reference, a force x applied to distance y will produce a greater list of vessel A than vessel B because the total force of leverage is a product of the length of the lever and the force applied. The distance y would represent the length of the lever and the tons pull on the tow hawser would represent the force applied.

The total problem is slightly more complicated because the pivot point is rarely stationary but does shift as the location of the center of gravity and the metacenter move during various conditions of loading and degree of tug list. It is sufficient for the tugman to know the basic facts involved because in a girding situation he will not

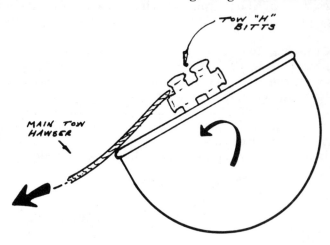

Fig. 163.   Tripping or girding.

have time to start any calculations should he care to and, unless practical steps are immediately taken by him to correct the girding situation, he may need a waterproof pen to complete any calculations started.

Suffice it to say that a tug may gird during an ocean tow when the towline leads as illustrated in Fig. 163.

The British use a "gogeye" to prevent girding. The gogeye is a line connected to the towline from a capstan on the after deck that enables the tug to be drawn under the towline by heaving in on the gogeye.

American tugs often use gob ropes to secure their towlines aft and prevent tripping. When a towline is not secured aft, the tow when running abreast of the tug as a result of following sea, wind, current, tide or any set will change the towline pull to a direction transverse to forward progress. The moments created by the pull act in a couple tending to decrease transverse stability of tug.

The towline may be placed between vertical roller chocks where fitted at the stern rail, a procedure that will minimize the effects of any moments tending to capsize the tug, but at the same time it will hamper maneuverability of the tug. Norman pins are fitted along the rail to allow the towline to lead slightly off to either side thereby moving the pivot point slightly forward, improving maneuverability.

If a tug should find itself in the situation illustrated in Fig. 163, it must immediately make every effort to bring the stern under the towline. One method is to secure a stopper on a short pendant to the towline from a point on the deck aft of the towline and near the centerline of the tug. After the stopper is clamped to the towline, the tow hawser is payed out from the winch, placing the strain of towing on the pendant and shifting the vessel's heading by pulling the stern around.

Tow Overriding Tug. One of the most dangerous hazards encountered in marine towing is one that finds a tow overtaking and bearing down on the tug. The condition is dangerous because the overtaking tow can collide with the stern of the tug resulting in damage that may open up the hull and sink the tug. Barges that have large rake ends and exaggerated rake flair may actually override and set down on the after deck of the tug immediately submerging it, as shown in Fig. 164. Serious damage to house and hull can result in

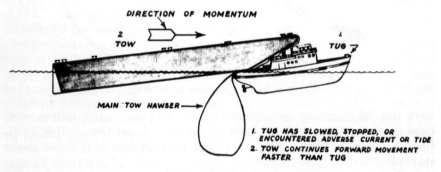

Fig. 164. Tow overriding tug.

progressive flooding (uncontrolled) and the tug may sink quickly. It is absolutely mandatory for the safety of tug and crew that all main deck watertight doors and ports be closed while towing on a short hawser, so that in the event of an overriding situation the tug stands a chance of remaining afloat. If door and ports are left open, progressive flooding will result, quickly causing the tug to lose positive buoyancy and sink.

An overriding situation may arise from any one of a number of causes.

Current. Adverse currents can work to cause a tug to slow down and the tow to continue its forward movement. Unless some corrective action is taken, the tow may override and sink the tug. In this connection it is considered of utmost importance for a tug not to tow fast on a short hawser wherever changes in currents or tides are expected.

Speed reduction. A sudden reduction in speed of the tug's engines may find the tow continuing forward at a faster rate of speed than the tug. In other words, a tow may not slow down as quickly as a tug. The result is an overriding situation. Speed reduction by a tug must be in small increments and it should be done with extreme caution when a tow is on a short hawser.

Watch the wind carefully during speed reduction. The sail areas of tug and tow will react to the force of wind to a greater or lesser degree, depending upon the speed of tow. The wind will influence the course of a light draft, high-sided tow to a greater extent than a deep-draft, low silhouette tug when slowing down.

Engine breakdown. Some emergency procedure should be established on a tug for engine breakdown. This is a serious dilemma! The general alarm should be sounded so that steps may immediately be taken to counteract an overriding situation.

On a very short hawser, pray if you have time.

On a medium length hawser of, say, 300 to 600 feet, veer the steering wheel, prepare to sever the hawser, but do not unless the danger is imminent. Remember the increasing catenary of a nonbuoyant hawser will tend to draw the tug and tow closer together.

On a long hawser 600 feet and over, veer the steering wheel and prepare to sever the hawser, but do not unless danger is imminent. Install the Norman pins and lead the towline aft of the pins to prevent a girding situation. If unable to do this, clamp a short tow pendant to the main tow hawser using a carpenter stopper and pay out the towline until it is drawn inboard and lies in a fore-and-aft direction with the pendant taking some of the strain. Any wind will tend to keep the tow from closing, but this will be offset to some extent by the catenary of the tow hawser which will increase as the tow slows, thereby drawing the tug and tow closer together. Keep these factors in mind; they will affect different tows in various degrees.

A tow on a long wire hawser in shallow water may become effectively anchored to the bottom as catenary is increased after engine breakdown. The increased catenary will drag first and then hold the bottom as more wire comes into contact with the ground. As a result, both tug and tow may stop at a considerable distance from each other.

Yaw. A tow that veers to the side on a tow hawser is said to yaw. The yaw may take one of several forms:

1. The tow may sheer to one side of the tug and hold there in a diagonal line to forward movement.

2. The tow may snake a tortuous path, scribing a sinuous track at a constant speed.

3. A towed unit may oscillate easily or violently around its center of gravity.

4. The tow may sheer quickly in lateral movement and upon reaching maximum limit of side travel the tow will snap-turn, pivoting on its bow. This turn can result in capsizing the barge or broaching and is known as "popping the whip."

A vessel with a damaged and jammed rudder will yaw and drive a sheering course parallel to that of the tug.

At times during rough weather there is much yaw, particularly on tows that cannot be steered to maintain a course behind the tug. Even at times when a tow is steered, there can be yaw.

A tow (exclusive of swim-ended barges) will usually yaw uncontrollably on one short towline hauled close aboard the tug.

Light draft barges generally will be more affected by winds and, therefore, yaw is reduced.

Yaw is hazardous for the following reasons:

1. A wildly yawing vessel in tow may present its beam to the seas in a broaching situation and capsize.

2. The weight of towline and directional pull leading across the quarter of a tug calls for "hard-over" rudder to bring a tug back on course. The combined effort of heeling due to rudder position and list due to weight and pull of the towline can capsize the tug.

A tow subjected initially to adverse wind, sea, or current will sheer in a direction with the force and upon reaching maximum transverse travel, the unit may sheer in the opposite direction and thus commence yawing in a pendulous motion. Should this type of yaw become excessive, it may gird the tug or sink the barge.

Yaw may also be brought on by towing within a critical range of towline length wherein a tow may tend to yaw.

Many methods have been devised to prevent or reduce yaw and each has been used with varying degrees of success. A few of the more practical methods follow:

1. *Skegs*. Twin skegs located as far outboard as possible on the stern are the best arrangement. Adjustable skegs are excellent. One immovable centerline skeg is not satisfactory. On multiple towed units the skegged barges should be placed last in the tow.

2. *Rudders*. On towed vessels place the helm over 15 to 20 degrees and hold it there. The tow may yaw for awhile, but eventually it will steady up on a following course, though not always directly behind the tug.

3. *Bridles*. a) Shortening one leg of a bridle on long ocean voyages where prevailing winds and seas are known. On a chain bridle, removing two or more links from one leg should be enough.

b) Rigging one leg of the bridle through the hawse pipe and one leg up and over the gunwale to bitts on deck, as shown in Fig. 165.

c) The point of connection should be above the center of gravity.

4. *Drogues*. Drogues are sometimes placed aboard unwieldy, cumbersome tows, e.g., dredges, drill rigs, mining equipment, and

they are put over the stern during heavy weather by a riding crew to increase stern drag and to reduce yaw. Two lengths of heavy chain are hung, one from each stern corner. The chain is usually 100 to 200

Fig. 165. Tug *Edward Moran* hooked up to chain bridle of S.S. *Astrid Naess.*
Moran

feet in length. Although they prove effective, their use should be limited to emergency situations (heavy weather, high seas, etc), because the resistance of the tow is increased from 250% to 300%, thereby decreasing towing efficiency and increasing fuel costs.

5. *Towline*. Lengthening or shortening the towline will affect yaw. There is a critical range of hawser length, when a tow is running in a seaway, wherein yaw increases.

6. *Trim*. Trim by the stern of a tow has been found to be absolutely necessary to reduce yaw. One (1) or two (2) foot drag by the stern should prove satisfactory. A tow that is down by the head may prove uncontrollable.

7. *Loading*. Deck loads that are placed too far aft will increase yaw. Whenever possible, locate deck cargoes as near amidship as is feasible and trim by ballasting. A ballast without free-surface effect is essential.

Inland towing. Yawing of inland tows is dangerous because of the many narrow waterways and channels. It is also extremely dangerous because of the hazard to passing vessels and other tows, particularly at night and at other times of reduced visibility.

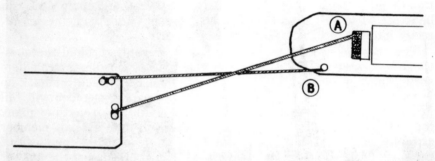

Fig. 166.   Crossed towlines.

Referring to Fig. 166, a common practice for inland tows is to connect the main tow hawser **A** to the tow and to connect a secondary steady line **B** from the tug quarter to the opposite bow corner of the tow.

The crossed towlines shown in Fig. 166 are better than the twin towlines shown in Fig. 88. However, twin towlines are excellent for towing on short towlines where a tow must follow directly behind a tug. Both methods are better than a single line connected to a bridle.

Fouled Propeller of Tug.   A diesel-powered tug can be dangerously overloaded when the propeller becomes fouled for any reason. As the engine slows down, the governor automatically opens admitting more fuel which results in overloading in a pyramiding effect and eventually engine damage will occur unless safeguards are installed.

On the other hand, the engines of steam tugs will gradually stop as soon as the boiler pressure equals the power output, hence a fouled propeller will not overload the steam engine.

Fiber hawsers may be cleared from a propeller by the use of axes or underwater cutting torches. Wire hawsers may be cleared by the use of wire cutters, hacksaws, underwater cutting torches, or small explosive charges.

In order to work on a fouled propeller it is necessary to raise the stern so that the propeller is as clear of the water as possible. This may be accomplished by ballasting bow tanks and pumping out stern water tanks.

Sinking Tow.   A sinking tow can sink a tug. Upon taking its final plunge, a sinking tow can pull the stern of a tug under water, or capsize the tug through girding, in the event that the main tow hawser does not part, or before the hawser parts.

When connected to a sinking tow by a main towline fairleaded through stern roller chocks, or otherwise limited in transverse travel by gob rope, lizard, gogeye or Norman pin, the increasing weight of the sinking tow will be transmitted to the tug connection and it will be partially imparted to any structural fairlead that changes the direction of pull. On wooden tugs, the stern bulwark and main deck can be expected to suffer serious damage probably admitting the sea directly into the hull, as illustrated in Fig. 167.

The problem of a sinking tow generally revolves around the question of what will fail first—the main tow hawser, bridle, intermediate spring, make-up connections, or the hull fitting to which the hook-up is made fast. It can be expected that the weakest member will fail first, but the weakest member may have a breaking strength of many tons. First calculate the breaking strength of the weakest member (usually the hawser) in pounds and add this weight at the stern of the tug. Then calculate for a change of trim problem and the answer should indicate the probable draft to which the stern of the tug will sink before the hawser parts. Having prior knowledge of how deep your stern will submerge may instill some confidence in a given towing situation, but it should be remembered that this particular calculation will not provide an answer as to what structural failures might take place before the break occurs. Possibly bulwarks and stern plating may fail, thereby flooding the tug, or water may enter over door coamings and into deck openings, flooding uncontrollably.

Try to ascertain beforehand what a particular tow and its tow connections will do to your tug when a tow sinks. The knowledge will help you to establish and maintain a satisfactory degree of watertight integrity throughout the tug during a long voyage.

There are several methods employed to overcome the dangers inherent in a sinking tow; all of them require the immediate disconnection of the tow hook-up. Few sinking tows will allow time to disconnect any accessible connection and, at any rate, a tow should not be cast off until it is actually submerging. A fiber tow hawser may be severed by axe or cutting torch. A wire hawser may be severed by torch or by the use of explosive charge; an axe may also prove effective in an emergency. Failing all else, the main towline must be slipped and allowed to run off the drum.

Explosive charges should never be connected or used by inexperienced persons. Foul weather conditions may cause static electricity, and stray hull currents are produced that can set off an electrical detonator prematurely.

If at all possible, try not to sever your tow connection to a sinking tow when operating in water shallow enough for the hawser to reach bottom. Simply pay out the towline until the sunken tow reaches

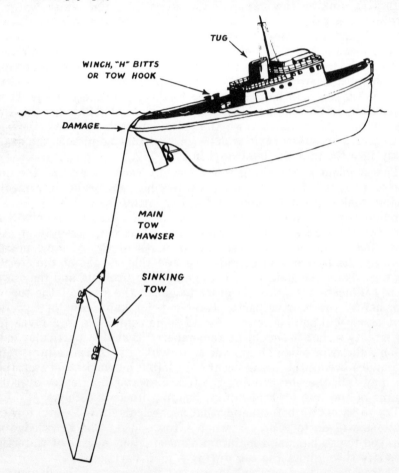

Fig. 167. Perilous situation before tow hawser breaks.

bottom. The hawser may be used later as a means of locating the tow for any salvage venture planned. The hawser is buoyed off so that it will be visible on the surface of the water and the tug is free to proceed to other employment.

Any number of incidents may cause a tow to sink, e.g., heavy weather hull damage, deteriorated hull-plating failures, striking submerged objects, collisions with other vessels, heavy rains or seas entering deck openings, excessive towing speed that pulls the tow under or damages the rake end.

Usually a riding crew is provided with portable pumps and patch materials to overcome many of the problems that lead to a sinking tow situation.

When a riding crew is not provided for any reason, the tug usually sends a boarding party daily to inspect the condition of the tow. In addition, a continuous watch should be maintained aft on the tug observing the tow continuously for the telltale signs of an impending sinking. They include an increase in draft of tow, change of trim, and increasing list. When any of these conditions is noted a boarding party must be put on the tow to investigate. When necessary they must start portable pumps already on board and apply patches as found necessary. The term "pumps already on board" means just that. Pumps must be placed aboard before the start of all offshore tows and some inland tows. Pumps often mean the difference between saving and losing a tow and they cannot be readily transferred from tug to tow at sea.

A final word—the stern deck of a tug is a most dangerous location during a sinking tow situation. Only those personnel needed to cast off the tow should be present.

The decision to cast off a sinking tow rests with the tug captain, who should include in his night orders a procedure to follow in the event a sudden sinking situation occurs during his absence.

Fire On Tow Or Tug.   Fire at sea is considered a rare hazard for offshore towing, but not so for inland tows.

Fire, when it does occur on a tow, can be expected to result from spontaneous combustion, for unless a riding crew is aboard, there is little else to cause a fire beside lightning. Hand fire extinguishers are placed aboard in strategic locations. It is advisable to have aboard a length of fire hose with fittings that can be connected to the portable pump, for if all else fails, the pump suction hose can be lowered overboard into the sea and the pump started, thereby fighting fire with sea water.

On the other hand, a tug or towboat is equipped to fight fires, as are any other self-propelled vessels. Fire on a tug or towboat may result from any one of a number of causes:

1. Ropes, chafing gear, etc., exposed to sparks or open flames.
2. Welding or burning on bulkheads adjacent to tanks or compartments containing oil, grease, or other combustible material.
3. Inadequate ventilation of stowage spaces.
4. Paints and thinners forming a combustible atmosphere.
5. Electrical shorts and failures.
6. Dirty gaseous bilges.
7. Galley fires in the Charley Noble or in grease collections.

Parted Lines. When the towline to a *single tow* parts there is little else to do than reel in the remainder of the hawser, circle around, approach and retrieve the tow. Upon heaving aboard the bridle and hawser, the parted end is spliced to the tow hawser aboard the tug and towing again commences. The cause of the break should be reasoned out to the best of one's ability and towing practice modified to eliminate or negate that particular cause.

A break in the towline of a *tandem tow* presents quite another problem. On offshore tows, the lighter of the two tows is connected last, so that when drifting down-wind the tows should remain well spaced. Retrieve the hawser and resplice.

When the intermediate hawser connected between the tows breaks, the problem becomes slightly more complicated. The lead tow is shortened up and a chase begins down-wind to intercept the drifting tow. A boarding crew must then reconnect the intermediate hawser to the lead tow, or connect to another tow hawser directly from the tug, depending on how the hook-up was made. In this connection, it is far better to tow two or more barges (or whatever) from separate tow hawsers directly to the tug than to connect the barges together. One of the reasons for this is that if any one tow sinks, it will not jeopardize the remaining tow(s). For instance, a lead barge sinks and tows under and sinks the second barge to which it is connected. Another reason is that a break in one towline from the tug releases control of only the connected unit. Additionally, a sinking tow on a separate towline to the tug will not jeopardize the remaining unit(s).

On the other hand, for coastwise and shallow water towing there is the possibility that the long towlines, required for units other than the lead tow, may drag the bottom due to scope and large catenary; therefore, it is often more practical to make intermediate connections between units, thereby reducing the amount of uncontrolled catenary.

A drifting tow should not be abandoned for the following reasons:

1. It is a hazard to navigation.
2. It usually represents a large investment.
3. It may become lost, necessitating a long expensive search.
4. Salvage operations may be costly for a stranded unit on a distant shore.

Parting of nylon hawsers usually occurs between 40% and 50% stretch. The snap-back force is terrific and a parted line under tension can maim, or kill. Stand clear!

Nylon lines, with the exception of new cable-laid nylon lines will not give audible warning of an impending break, as will some other types of lines. Because of its great elasticity, caution should be exercised in handling nylon lines. All personnel should stand clear when surging on a nylon tow hawser.

Collision. There is always the danger of collision with other vessels on offshore tows. Navigation lights are shown by tug and tow according to law indicating the length and number of towed units. Even so, the danger of collision is great. Of all collisions only slightly more than one-fourth occur at times of less than two miles visibility, so it can be seen that low visibility is not the primary cause of collisions. What then are some of the causes and when do collisions occur?

1. Mistaken signals are frequently the cause.
2. Simultaneous signal sounds are sometimes lost.
3. Excessive speed in meeting and passing situations.
4. Failure to reduce speed in fog.
5. Failure to stop engines in fog when the location of a fog signal heard from another vessel forward of the beam is not ascertained. A reduction in speed is a must in order to allow time for all vessels to clarify maneuvering intentions.
6. Signals are sometimes not exchanged although this is mandatory.
7. Inexperienced lookout.
8. Failure to identify and interpret navigation lights properly due to confusion with shore background lights.
9. Improper radar plot. The relative motion and CPA (closest point of approach) need to be determined by properly plotting positions of several ranges and bearings of target (vessel).

Collisions occur frequently in narrow channels and congested waters. Navigating in narrow channels approaches an art, for the pilot must allow the water-pressure patterns set up by his vessel in motion to work for him. In an approaching situation with another vessel in a narrow channel, he must also anticipate the effect of the approaching vessel's bow pressure patterns on his own vessel as well as the passing vessel's negative pressure at the stern. The water falling off his near bank also must be taken into account. In many instances experienced pilots use direct-opposite rudder to what would normally be expected in order to offset the anticipated effects of passing situations.

A collision with a tow may involve the tug, towline, or the tow itself.

A collision with a towline will often sever the hawser, but rarely will it damage the tug and tow.

A collision with a tug or tow, however, can result in a sinking or hull damage. If the tow is struck, the main tow hawser should be shortened to bring the tow close aboard the tug for an inspection and to make necessary repairs.

In some instances it may be seen that a vessel will pass between tug and tow. Slow down the main engines and immediately pay out the main tow hawser quickly. The increased catenary resulting from both actions may allow the vessel to pass over without severing the towline. Take care during these maneuvers and be ready to apply full power and shorten up as soon as the danger is past. The initial lengthening of the hawser and slowing of the engine can put a low-powered tug "in irons." If the tug cannot quickly retrieve sufficient weight of wire and his engine is not of sufficient power to overcome the added weight to stop the barge from closing, there is a grave possibility that the tow will collide with the tug in an overriding situation.

Miscellaneous Hazards. There are numerous occasions when a tow will encounter dangerous situations, often only momentarily. A few are listed here.

Striking submerged objects. There is not a place that a tow is reasonably safe from striking submerged objects, except perhaps in dry dock. The damage done may range from minor indents to large holes. In any event, a riding crew must sound all buoyancy tanks and watertight compartments every watch in order to find out as soon as possible any damage resulting from striking a submerged object. Usually the striking will be heard or felt, but sometimes it is not; therefore, soundings are necessary. One telltale sign of damage will be the escape of air under pressure when an attempt is made to open a sounding line or manhole cover. The cover should be dogged down immediately because the pressure will retard the ingress of water into the compartment. If left open, the trapped air will escape and the compartment will fill rapidly to the waterline, causing the unit to list to that side.

Several courses of action are possible:

1. Patch the hole by drawing a collision mat outside the hull over the hole, using hogging lines and then pump out the compartment, using a portable pump installed aboard for the voyage. As the compartment is pumped down, the patch will seat more firmly. Be careful not to allow the mat to be forced completely through the hole.

2. Allow the compartment to fill and counterballast an opposite compartment to bring the unit to an even keel. This decision cannot be made until it is determined that there is, in fact, sufficient reserve buoyancy to continue the voyage. It is important that the unit be brought back to an even keel before continuing the trip, so that any additional damages can be detected immediately by a new list.

3. Occasionally a struck object will lodge itself in a hole it has made. It should be dislodged if possible; otherwise, its working and movement resulting from towing in a seaway can cause additional damage.

On river towboats the striking of submerged objects is a rather common occurrence. A towboat may exceed 100 strikings during her lifetime so that vulnerable appendages are designed and constructed sufficiently strong to withstand most of these accidents; consequently, this hazard on the rivers should be considered operational rather than accidental.

Crossing a bar. The bar referred to is the one usually found at the entrance to harbors. With a tow proceeding at full speed there usually follows a stern wave behind tug and tow. As the tug scrapes the sand bar with engines still turning full ahead, it will fetch up and stop momentarily until the stern wave overtakes and passes the tug. The additional depth of wave water passing the tug will lift the tug and carry it on over the bar. This procedure is termed "jumping the bar." It will not, however, take all tugs over all bars. Local conditions and practice must be known beforehand as well as drafts, tides, depths of water, etc.

Shallow water. When operating in shallow water or when going from deep water to shallow water, extreme caution should be exercised to prevent the towline from dragging along the bottom. A rough rocky, coral or gravelly bottom may snag, chafe and part the tow hawser.

Buoyant lines are best suited for shallow-water towing, or a wire hawser fitted with an intermediate length of chain. The chain is connected where the greatest amount of chafing is expected. A short length of chain dragging the bottom will not chafe. However, the chain should not be too long because it may stop and anchor the tow.

Low bridges. On inland waters low bridges can be a hazard to other than local tugs. Generally tugs are designed for the waters wherein they will operate and nonopening bridge clearances are taken into account. Occasionally, however, tugs alien to the locale or maverick tugs will find themselves navigating waters flowing under these bridges. Extreme caution must be exercised during an approach. Some conditions may be present that can reduce clearance unexpectedly—decreased draft of tug, or exceptionally high waters resulting from floods, rain, or winds, to name a few.

Tides and currents. Probably one of the least understood hazards in towing, as evidenced by the number of overriding casualties, is the adverse effect of tides and currents on tug and tow.

A tug proceeding from a favorable current into an eddy current or turning into a strong crosscurrent will slow down considerably. The towed unit meanwhile, still in fair water, will continue its forward progress at a rate faster than the tug. Result? An overriding situation!

Some adverse currents are met at bends of rivers and canals, approaches to locks and bridges, harbor entrances, mouths of rivers, footings of bridges and submerged boulders.

Strong tides are hazardous. In Europe a large range of tide is normal. In parts of Asia the tides range in excess of 30 feet. A running tide in these areas is equivalent to a strong current.

Underwater currents may adversely affect a deep-draft towed unit but have little or no effect on the tug. Here again, *caution* is the watchword and any unexplained strange behavior of a tow may be caused by these little-known currents.

Large vessels are usually docked at the peak of a flood tide while the water is still, but since the introduction of tugs of greater horsepower this is not always the case.

Heavy tows lying alongside out-of-the-way piers and docks preparing to hook-up may suddenly start listing. This is not uncommon and sometimes the blame can be attributed to the inshore side of the tow landing on accumulated silt at the footings of pier piles during an ebb tide.

A *hollow sea* can often be met when entering harbors. The hollow sea is caused by a current set against waves resulting in a sharp angle from trough to crest. Tugs entering harbors should be watchful for the hollow sea as it presents a potential danger to tug and tow.

Other hazardous areas may sometimes be detected by *broken water*.

The Bore, Eagre and Pororoca are regional names for a tidal wave, or two or more successive waves of above average height and force that are generated by a flood tide held back temporarily by the flow of river water.

Another hazard is the whirlpool. When it occurs in the Strait of Messina it is called a *Galofaro*.

Local Storms. We will now take under consideration some storms that occur around the world and give their local names. Knowing their local names can sometimes be important so that when word is passed that a *Chubasco* is on the way, preparations will not be made for a gourmet Mexican repast. And if you don't think *Chubasco* sounds appetizing, try *Chocolate Gale, Pampero, Papagayos* and *Gregale*.

Baguio.   A tropical wind of hurricane force occurring at the change of the monsoon season in the Philippines.

Bayamo.   A violent squall with lightning and thunder that blows along the south coast of Cuba. The squall originates in the Bight of Bayamo and dissipates in rain.

Belat.   A strong north to north-northwest wind that blows along the south coast of Arabia between December and March.

Bora.   A cold wind, strong to hurricane force, that blows from one day to a week and longer along the coasts of Dalmatia and Albania.

Bull's-eye Squall.   A squall along the South African coasts identified by a small isolated cloud marking the center of the squall.

Buster.   A heavy southerly squall that lasts from one to three hours along the south and southeast Australian coasts.

Caldereta.   A brisk hot wind blowing from the mountains along the northern coast of Venezuela.

Chocolate Gale.   A sharp northwest wind in the West Indies.

Chubasco.   A violent squall along the west coast of Mexico, often originating in the vicinity of the Gulf of Tehuantepec.

Coronazo.   A strong southerly wind along the west coast of Mexico.

Cyclone.   A revolving storm in the Indian Ocean that rotates counterclockwise above the Equator and clockwise below it.

Elephanta. A south to southeasterly gale that blows along the Malabar coast during September and October.

Gregale. The Maltese name for northeasterly strong winter winds that blow in the central Mediterranean in the vicinity of the Ionian Sea.

Hurricane. A wind of Force 12 or greater in a revolving counterclockwise storm that ranges from the Atlantic and Caribbean to the Gulf of Mexico and North Atlantic.

Levanter. A strong northeast wind in the Mediterranean, also called *meltem* or *euroclydon*.

Line Squalls. Line squalls occur at the head of a cold polar front of dense air mass advancing into warm humid air. Identified by an advancing line of cumulo-nimbus clouds, the squalls are violent and brief with winds often accompanied by hail and heavy rain.

Pampero. A violent storm of cold winds emanating from the southeast Andes mountains that sweeps across the Pampas of Argentina onto coastal waters.

Papagayos. A violent gale force northeast wind off the west coast of Central America, especially near the Gulf of Papagayo, that may occur from December to April.

Santa Ana. A strong hot easterly wind blowing from the desert through Santa Ana Canyon in Southern California to the coastal regions of Santa Barbara Channel and San Pedro.

Selatan. A strong southerly wind of the North Celebes blowing during the monsoon season.

Sharki. A strong southerly wind of the Persian Gulf blowing to Force 7 during winter months; also called *Kaus*.

Simoon. A brief, violent hot sandy wind along the coasts of the Arabian peninsula; also called *Samiel* or *Samum*.

Southerly Burster. A sudden shift of wind from the northwest to a violent southerly wind along southeast Australia. The storms occur from October to March and they are marked by a sharp fall in temperature.

Southwest Monsoon. A wind of the Indian Ocean, Mozambique Channel, South China Sea and the Southwest Pacific that can blow from April to October.

Storm. A wind of Force 11 or greater with velocity from 56 to 65 knots.

Sumatra. A strong southwesterly wind in the Strait of Malacca that occurs during the monsoon season.

Tehuantepecer. A violent northern wind blowing from the Gulf of Tehuantepec, Mexico.

Vendaval. A strong southwest gusty wind in the vicinity of the Gulf of Gibraltar during winter. Also a squall accompanied by thunder and lightning that occurs along the coast of Central America.

Williwaw. A violent sudden wind whistling down from the mountains in the Aleutian Island chain that occurs near the shore.

Willy-Willy. A violent wind- and rainstorm that occurs off the northwest coast of Australia.

NOTES: CHAPTER VI

1. Some idea of the difficulty of a rescue operation may be had from reading of the efforts of Tug *Turmoil* in the much-publicized ordeal of the freighter S.S. *Flying Enterprise,* and of the account of the assistance rendered to torpedoed merchant ships by Tug *Foundation Franklin* during World War II.

2. Edward M. Brady, *Marine Salvage Operations,* Cornell Maritime Press, 1960.

GLOSSARY

Abaft. Aft; toward the stern of; to the rear.

Abeam. At right angles to the keel; abreast.

Aces. Lengths of steel rod shaped at the end into hooks that are used to pile and stow anchor chain in a chain locker.

After perpendicular. The vertical line intersecting the load waterline at the after end of the sternpost.

Air holes. Small holes cut into longitudinals and floors of confined compartments to permit venting while pumping the compartment.

Amidships. A term used to define the center section of a vessel as opposed to its bow and stern ends.

Anchor. A cast steel or heavy iron shaped implement fitted with tapered flukes that engage the ground. The vessel is connected to the anchor with a length of chain cable or wire rope and, as a result, the vessel remains stationary in the water.

Aperture. The space provided for the propeller between the stern frame and the sternpost, bounded at the bottom by the skeg and at the top by the oxter plates.

Appendages. Those fittings and structures that extend beyond the outline of the hull; that is, bilge keels, rudder, rudderpost, strainers, struts, skeg, etc.

Arch piece. The upper curved section of stern frame in way of the aperture oxter plates at the junction of rudder post and sternpost.

Astern. 1. To the rear or abaft of an imaginary transverse line drawn at the stern of a vessel. 2. The movement of a vessel backwards. 3. The direction the main engine is turning as opposed to ahead.

Auxiliary line—Lyle gun. A 3″ circumference line on which a breeches buoy is suspended.

Backhaul rope. Used to haul back a block after it is overhauled.

Barge. A craft of steel or wood construction used to transport cargo over water.

Bar keel. A solid, heavy wrought iron bar of rectangular cross section used in older ships.

Bearding. The line of intersection at the junction of the butts of plates and the stem or sternpost.

Belay. To secure a rope; make fast.

Bight. The middle part of a rope forming a loop.

Bilge. The lowest portion of a vessel within the hull.

Bilge keel. Longitudinal narrow steel plates attached externally at right angle to the bilge strake in way of the curve of the bilge to decrease rolling of a vessel; sometimes called the *rolling chocks.*

Bitter end. The inboard end of any line, cable, anchor chain, or pendant. The end opposite to the anchor end.

Bitt. A heavy steel casting used to fairlead and secure mooring and towing hawsers to a dock, vessel, or tug. Usually constructed of two short vertical cylindrical capped hollow posts fitted to a base plate that distributes any load to deck plating.

Black Sea mooring. A 10″ Manila mooring line approximately 180 feet in length spliced to a 1¾″ wire rope approximately 60 feet in length with a five-foot eye spliced in one end.

213

Block. The combination of frame and pulley, or sheave, bounded and secured by a strap and pins, and mounted with a hook and becket that is used to gain advantage or fairlead in the make-up of lines attached to a load.

Bollard. A single post used for tying lines.

Bottom, outer. The outer shell bottom plating of a double-bottom vessel, the inner bottom being the tank tops.

Bower. An anchor carried in the hawse pipe in the bow of a vessel.

Bow line. A mooring line leading to a dock at an angle of less than 45 degrees through a bow chock.

Brace. A diagonal transverse or longitudinal shape, or structural member used to strengthen, stiffen and distribute any load between structures.

Brackets. Small pieces of plate, usually rectangular in shape, used to join beams to frames, frames to floors, etc.

Breasthooks. Horizontal steel plates installed internally at the bow to stiffen bow plating against *panting*.

Breast line. A mooring line leading at nearly right angle to keel and dock.

Broach. To veer with the set; a stranded vessel lying broadside to the shore as a result of the effects of winds, seas, or currents; a vessel presenting its beam to the seas.

Broken water. Small waves breaking as a result of conflict of opposing currents on an otherwise calm surface of water; also, choppy small waves along shoals and shallows.

Buffalo. Bulwarks at the bow above the forecastle deck.

Buffalo rail. A low wooden rail on the forecastle of schooners; a term sometimes applied to the bulwark around the stern of a tug.

Buoy. A stationary floating object moored to the bottom with anchor and cable.

Cable-laid rope. Three, 3-strand ropes twisted into a cable; a nine-strand rope.

Callao rope. A mooring line for tying up lighters working cargo alongside a vessel anchored in an open roadstead; 15 feet of 12″ fiber rope spliced to a wire pendant on each end.

Camber. The transverse curvature of any deck.

Camel. A wood float used to fend a ship off a dock.

Canal line. A 3″ circumference and larger rope used in towing canal boats.

Capstan. A revolving drum used to heave in lines.

Centers. Fiber core of wire rope that cushions and lubricates the center strands under load; heart rope.

Chafing gear. Material such as canvas, wood, or soft metal installed on wire or fiber rope in way of sharp corners and contact with harder surfaces in order to minimize the effects of rubbing and wearing.

Chock. A heavy shaped fitting through which lines and hawsers are led to reduce chafing.

Clear for running. Rope coiled down and clear for running through leading blocks without fouling.

Coaming. The vertical plating fitted around the periphery of a hatch opening.

Coir rope. A line of great resiliency made of coconut husk.

Collar. A plate doubler fitted around a pipe at its penetration through a bulkhead or deck in order to make a watertight joint.

Counter. The section of a ship that extends abaft the sternpost and overhangs the aperture and rudder.

Dead rise. The amount of vertical rise of the bottom from the keel to the turn of the bilge; also called *rise of floor*.

Deadwood. That portion of the hull in way of sternpost and keel without internal space.

Deck beam. A horizontal transverse shape connecting the port and starboard shell frames to which deck plating is attached.

Deck stringer plate. A heavy outboard strake of main deck plating that is attached to the gunwale bar and sheer strake.

Devil's claw. A hook-shaped clamp, forked to engage a link of anchor chain that is used to hold the anchor and chain while the wildcat of the anchor windlass is disengaged.

Dip rope. A rope used to clear a fouled anchor, approximately 7" circumference.

Dolphin. A cluster of numerous piles driven adjacent to each other and bound together with wire rope, clamps and through bolts that is used to fend and warp docking vessels.

Doubler. A steel plate of small dimensions used to reinforce, as a foundation, patch, or for additional strength.

Drag. A vessel is said to have drag when it is trimmed by the stern.

Drag rope. A rope attached to a grappling hook used to snag and recover lost objects when dragged along the bottom.

Drain holes. Small holes in bottom longitudinals and floors to allow draining of liquids when pumping.

End-for-end. To reverse a rope.

Fake. One turn of a rope in a coil forms a fake. Several fakes make a layer, tier, or sheave; several layers, one on top of another, form a coil.

Falls. The rope which makes up the tackle rove through sheaves of a block.

Falls, anchor. Tackle used with a davit for hoisting an anchor to the deck.

Falls, cargo. A 3- or 4-strand rope used for handling cargo.

Fathom. Six feet linear.

Flat plate keel. A fabricated steel keel built up from three members: the flat plate or dished keel, the center vertical keel or keelson, and the rider plate.

Floor plates. Usually diamond plate, fitted above floors to facilitate traversing internal bottom areas.

Fluke. The tapered prong of an anchor at the palm, which holds the ground.

Foot valve. A clapper valve installed on the lower end of a vertical suction pipe in order to permit flow of liquid in one direction only. It prevents liquid from flowing downward and thus aids a pump in maintaining suction.

Forefoot. That part of the lower end of the stem which is connected to the keel.

Frames. Vertical structural shapes, extending from floors in way of margin plate to the junction of deck stringer plate and sheer strake. Frames determine the shape of the hull. Shell plating is attached to the frames.

Freeboard. The distance between the surface of the water and the main deck. It is a measure of the reserve buoyancy of a vessel.

Freeing ports. Openings in lower ends of bulwarks at the deck to allow for quick drainage of water and thus freeing the deck of the weight of seas. Sometimes fitted with swing check gates and gaskets to allow for the passage of water in one direction only—overboard.

Garboard strake. The first longitudinal strake of plating secured to the dished keel. It is usually heavier plate than adjacent bottom plating and is identified as "A" strake.

Gross tonnage. A volumetric measurement of the internal capacity of a vessel, assuming 100 cu. ft. to equal one ton.

Grounding. A vessel's bottom touching ground voluntarily or involuntarily, or a vessel resting on the bottom as a result of tide changes, currents, etc.

Ground tackle. The combination of planted anchor and cable.

Gudgeon. A projection of the rudder post fitted with a bushing to receive the pintle of a rudder blade.

Gunwale bar. A structural shape, often angle bar, used to tie together the deck stringer plate and sheer strake.

Guy lines. Ropes used to steady a mast, kingpost or pole.

Handiness. The maneuvering qualities of a vessel.

Handsomely. Carefully, slowly ease the strain on a hawser or rope.

Handy billy. A tackle consisting of one single and one double block used to gain advantage on the hauling part of heavy tackle.

Hauling part. The part to which a force is applied.

Hawse. The anchor chain passes from deck through a hull opening called a hawse. Often the hawse is made of large diameter pipe and termed *hawse pipe.*

Hawser. A 3- or 4-strand plain laid rope of 4½" circumference and larger, used for towing.

Head line. A line from the bow bitt of a tug to a tow.

Hold on. To stop pulling on a line. Hold what you have!

Hook rope. A rope used in mooring a vessel to a buoy, or in weighing anchor.

Jacob's ladder. A rope ladder with wooden rungs hung over the side for use by a pilot.

Jumping on the line. A tugboat coming up suddenly taut on a slack tow hawser.

Lanyard, fender. A regular lay rope of 3"–3½" circumference used for lashing fenders to rail on tugboats.

Lanyard, whistle. The rope used to blow the whistle.

Lashing ropes. Ropes used to secure cargo in transit.

Lay. The angle of strands in a rope—varied by the amount of turn put in the strands of a rope, e.g., soft lay, medium lay, hard lay.

Lizzard. A rope fitted with a thimble and used as a leader for running rigging.

Lizzard stopper. A short rope fitted with thimbles on both ends used as a stopper and fairlead for a towline.

Lug ropes. Short heavy ropes used to tie together canal barges.

Main deck. The principal strength deck in a vessel and upper flange of the hull girder.

Man ropes. Lines hung over a vessel's side to assist in boarding.

Medium lay. The standard lay in ropes, neither soft nor hard.

Messenger. A convenient line of small diameter used to haul a line of larger diameter.

Mooring line. Line used to tie up a vessel to a dock or mooring.

Norman pin. 1. A horizontal pin inserted in a towing bitt or bollard to prevent the hawser from slipping out. 2. A vertical portable pin inserted in a bulwark rail to limit lateral movement of a towline.

Nose plate. The vertical shaped and furnaced rounded plate fitted around the forward face of the stem which joins the forward edges of port and starboard strakes and provides a stem fairwater to permit easy entrance of the bow.

Padeye. The combination of a circle of steel stock secured to a doubler plate that is attached to a deck, bulkhead, overhead, or structural. It is used to secure blocks, stoppers, rigging, deck cargo, straps, etc. The doubler serves to distribute any load over a greater area.

Panting. The tendency of bow plating to move in and out as a result of water pressure differential caused by a vessel pitching in a seaway.

Parcelling. After a rope has been wormed, it is parcelled, i.e., wrapped with long canvas strips with the lay in a spiral, overlapping fashion. The finished parcelling sheds water and resists absorption of moisture.

Pay out. Slacken a line made fast on board.

Peak tanks, fore and after. Large compartments located at the bow and stern of a vessel for the storage of water or ballast. Peak tanks are fitted with piping for the transfer of water. The trim of a vessel can be changed by transferring water from one tank to the other.

Pelican hook. A quick-release hinged hook used where speed in disconnecting is important.

Pintles. Vertical pins attached to rudders that fit into gudgeons on the rudderpost around which the rudder pivots.

Pitch, propeller. The distance the blade of a propeller will advance during one complete revolution.

Plain laid. A three-strand medium lay rope.

Preventer. A rope used for added support and safety.

Raft ropes. A three-strand rope used to tie logs together into rafts for floating to a sawmill.

Rake. An inclination from the vertical of a mast, stem, stack, etc., usually in a fore and aft direction. A term also applied to bow and/or stern compartments of certain barges.

Ram plates. Vertical plates installed in way of inside bow spaces to prevent "panting" of bow plating. Usually fitted in conjunction with breasthooks.

Running line. A messenger coiled in a small boat and payed out between ship and dock, used for running out mooring lines.

Scantlings. The dimensions of shapes, plating, etc., used in construction of vessels.

Sea chest. A structure fitted to internal shell plating below the waterline to which valves and pipes are attached for supplying sea water to condensers and machinery, sanitary water, etc. The structure is usually box-shaped and fitted with external strainers.

Set. The direction in motion of a current, wind, or sea, or combination thereof.

Sheer strake. The uppermost side shell row of plates secured longitudinally to the gunwale bar.

Shot line. A soft lay projectile rope used with Lyle guns in rescue work.

Shroud lay. A four-strand, extra-hard lay rope.

Skeg. A lower extension of the stern frame on some vessels that extends aft of the sternpost to support the rudderpost. It confines the lower limit of the aperture.

Slip rope. A rope bent onto anchor chain and led to a vessel's quarter for use in slipping anchor cable.

Snatch block. A single-sheave block that can be opened at one end to receive the bight of a rope.

Snubbing rope. A rope used to retard progress of a load or another rope.

Sound. The practice of measuring depth with a line and weight.

Splice. A method of joining two ropes together or of forming a loop in a line by bending the line back onto itself. The splice is made by unlaying the strands and interweaving to form a permanent connection.

Spring line. A mooring line leading 45 degrees to the keel used to check forward or astern movement of a docking vessel.

Standing part. The end of a rope that is secured or fixed.

Stay. A rope used to brace a mast.

Stem. The bow frame casting at the extreme forward end of a ship to which the #1 plates of all strakes are attached. Nose plating is fitted around forward end of the stem.

Stern line. A mooring line leading to a dock at less than 45 degrees to the keel used to check forward movement of a docking vessel.

Strand. Two or more yarns twisted together in opposite direction to the twist of the yarns. Strands are twisted together to form rope.

Strap. A short rope spliced onto itself; an endless grommet.

Strap, belly. A rope used to suspend a kedge anchor from a boat while the anchor is being carried out. The belly strap is passed around the boat.

Superstructure. A bridge, pilothouse, cabin, mast, or structure built above the main deck.

Tackle. A term applied to the combination of falls and blocks used to gain advantage in power, or for fairlead.

Tank top. The plating, sometimes called the *inner bottom*, that confines the upper limits of a double-bottom tank.

Taut. Rope that is tightly stretched and under strain.

Tiller rope. Line connecting the steering wheel or windlass to the quadrant or tiller.

Towline. A rope used in towing that connects a tug to its tow.

Towline, stern. A line that holds a tug's stern to a breasted tow.

Trim. To adjust the fore and aft drafts by transferring cargo or ballast longitudinally within a vessel.

Tripping bracket. Small plates or flat bars attached at right angles to floors, keelsons, girders and beams at intervals along their length as a reinforcement to prevent racking.

Tripping line. A lanyard used to release a tow hook, pelican hook, etc.

Tumble home. The gradual narrowing of a vessel's beam from waterline to top of sheer strake.

Visor. The small inclined canvas or metal awning over portholes or windows that extends around a pilothouse to reduce sun glare.

Warps. A light rope used to pull a vessel toward a pier.

Winch. A small hoist engine used to pull lines, or for handling cargo.

Wrenching. To alternately pull in opposite directions on the outshore end of a stranded vessel in an attempt to wrench vessel free of the ground.

BIBLIOGRAPHY

Argyriadis, D. A. "Modern Tug Design with Particular Emphasis on Propeller Design, Maneuverability, and Endurance," *Society of Naval Architects and Marine Engineers*, Paper n. 7 for meeting of Nov. 14–15, 1957, 48 p.

Baier, L. A. "The Resistance of Barges and Flotillas," *Society of Naval Architects and Marine Engineers*, Transactions v. 55, 1947.

Beattie, R. "Tug Design and Development," *Motor Ship*, v. 40, n. 475 (February 1960), pp. 446–448.

Benford, H. "Control of Yaw in Towed Barges," *International Shipbuilding Progress*, v. 2, n. 11, 1955, pp. 296–319.

Burke, R. E. "Nomogram for Determining Endurance of Naval Vessels," *American Society of Naval Engineers—J*, v. 67, n. 3 (August 1955), pp. 605–610.

Caldwell, A. *Screw Tug Design*, Hutchinson's Scientific and Technical Press, London, 1946, 154 p.

Dimitryevic, M. "Factors Affecting Design of River Tug," *American Society of Naval Engineers—J*, v. 66, n. 3 (August 1954), pp. 651–658.

Dyer, H. B. "Modern Towboat and Barge Design," *American Society of Civil Engineers—Proceedings*, v. 82 (J Waterways and Harbors Division), n. WW5 (December 1956), Paper 1122, 9 p.

Glosten, Lawrence R. and Heyrman, Jacques S. "Offshore Barge Transportation on the Pacific Coast," *Society of Naval Architects and Marine Engineers*, Paper n. 10 for meeting of November 11–12, 1965, 21 p.

Hardy, A. C. "Pushboats and Integrated Tows," *Shipbuilding and Shipping Record*, v. 90, n. 17 (October 24, 1957), pp. 541–543.

Horton, C. R., Jr. "Power for Pushing," *S.A.E.*, Paper 378B for meeting of June 5–9, 1961, 3 p.

Horton, C. R., Jr. "Push Versus Pull," *Motor Ship*, v. 39, n. 5 (May 1954), pp. 20–23.

Jacobs, R. D. "Diesel Engine Development and Towboat Applications," *S.A.E.*, Paper 529A for meeting of May 8–9, 1962, 4 p.

Knight, G. R., Jr. "Look at Hydroconic Design . . . Will this Development Improve Tugs?" *Marine Eng/Log*, v. 63, n. 3 (March 1958), pp. 84–86.

McMullen, J. J. "Stagnation in Harbor Tug Design?" *Marine Eng/Log*, v. 63, n. 6 (June 1958), pp. 64, 131–132.

Moor, D. I. "Investigation of Tug Propulsion," *Roy. Instn. Naval Archs.—Quarterly Trans.*, v. 105, n. 1, January 1963, pp. 107–152.

Moran, E. F., Jr. "Long Distance Towing and Tug Design," *Society of Naval Architects and Marine Engineers*, New York Metropolitan Section meeting of September 21, 1950.

Munro-Smith, R. "Tug Design," *Shipbuilder and Marine Engine Builder*, v. 69, n. 650 (January 1962), pp. 47–53.

Prince, W. *Seamanship As Applied to Towing*, J. D. Potter, London, 1934, 62 p.

Roach, C. D. "Tugboat Design," *Society of Naval Architects and Marine Engineers*, Paper for meeting January 1954, 41 p.

Strandhagen, Adolf G., Schoenherr, Karl E. and Kobayashi, Francis M. "Dynamic Stability on Course of Towed Ships," *Society of Naval Architects and Marine Engineers*, Transactions v. 58, 1950.

PERIODICALS

Marine News, "Demonstrates Hydroconic-hull Tug" (January 1961), p. 50.
Shipbuilding and Shipping Record, "Barges in USA and Europe," v. 84, n. 27 (December 30, 1954), pp. 869–871, 873.

INDEX

INDEX

More CMP Books Of Interest

$8.50

MARINE SALVAGE OPERATIONS

By Edward M. Brady

Surveyor, United States Salvage Association, Inc.

Marine Salvage Operations is concerned with actual ship salvage operations as distinct from the preservation and saving of material. It is a practical "basic" handbook covering the techniques, equipment, and problems of general ship salvage. In most cases, large ship salvage is described throughout; however, for small salvage operations, it is only necessary to scale down the size and scope of the required operations and apply the principles described.

Primarily written for ship salvage men, commercial and naval divers, merchant marine and naval officers, *Marine Salvage Operations* is full of information that will appeal to SCUBA divers professionally interested in salvage.

In marine salvage, there are three general types of salvage operations:

Strandings—Sinkings—Rescue Towing

The principles and practice of each type of operation are fully covered along with preliminary background material. The preliminary material covers the methods of salvage diving, and discusses the pros and cons of each type of dress for a particular salvage dive . . . Deep Sea Dress—Diving Mask with Air Hose and Life Line and SCUBA. In addition, full coverage is given to equipment and gear, diving boats, and safety precautions for all divers. The background material referred to is a section on The Fundamental Hull Structure of a Vessel and Naval Architecture as related to buoyancy and stability, paying particular attention to the effects of changing and shifting weights aboard a vessel, and their effect on buoyancy and stability.

Among the practical aspects of *Marine Salvage Operations* discussed are:

Equipment and Structures Used in Salvage—Salvage Practice—Miscellaneous Salvage Operations, Techniques and Hazards—Cutting and Welding—Preliminary Reports—Sounding Record—Weather Recording—Strandings, Top-Side Survey—Salvage Plan—Diving Record—Closure Log—Glossary.

Throughout *Marine Salvage Operations*, emphasis is placed on a most important, though sometimes overlooked, element in ship salvage . . . *man*. The man who knows the principles of the subject and is able to apply them will do the best job in a given situation. A pump and a method are only as effective as the man who uses them.

256 pages   Illustrated   Indexed

SHIP MANAGEMENT

A STUDY IN
DEFINITION & MEASUREMENT

By
Rodney M. Elden

There are few subjects that do not touch the lives of those who manage ocean shipping. Labor and world affairs, meteorology and maintenance, finance and insurance are only a few of the daily companions of the ship manager. Numerous texts have been written on the antiseptic facets of ship management, yet only a few isolated papers and editorials have dared tackle the total subject with all its delicate interplay.

This study does not contend that ship management is essentially difficult but does show that it is so complex and varied that almost any generalization can be shown by illustration and example to be right in some situations and wrong in others. Treading with a philosophical and sometimes humorous step, Ship Management winds its way through this foggy jungle of sacred cows, conflicting interests and modern marine mythology.

This study has the basic objective of identifying and depicting the many problems of ship management and, through analysis and synthesis, to measure the degree of controllability inherent in each problem and thereby identify those key aspects which should have real import and significance to the owners and managers of ships. Among the "key findings" of this study are:

> Maintenance is by far the most controllable expense in the operation of ships and its magnitude remains camouflaged to a large degree because of the absence of functional cost breakdown in current industry's accounting procedures.

> "Automation by Gadgetry" will possibly introduce more problems than it solves and quicker and better results will be obtained by investment in better ships having a lower "built-in maintenance load."

After reviewing those operating costs which are internal and discriminatory in nature, Ship Management explores the nature of "definition and measurement" processes and proposes that they are the key to and common denominator of successful evaluation of ship operation and management.

Mr. Elden, who is Operating Manager of the Joshua Hendy Corporation, operators of seven different types of merchant ships, presents this study in such a manner that the less experienced as well as the more knowledgeable will find it can be viewed as a whole in a single evening. **$4.00**

NUCLEAR SHIP PROPULSION

By Holmes F. Crouch

A new technology, already a fact in naval operations, is rapidly coming to the merchant shipping industry. It is at present a technology of incomplete understanding. There are several reasons for this. First, once a reactor is buttoned up and in operation, it cannot be seen, felt or heard. Second, much of the published technical information is accompanied by scientific theory and mathematical rigor which seldom are converted to shipboard environment, and third, there is an unavoidable amount of technical complexity which is not readily self-evident to the busy, practical reader.

This book is written to advance the understanding of nuclear ship technology. It is intended for those who design, build, operate, manage, maintain, pay for, and travel on nuclear ships. Here, under one cover, two major technologies are coupled in the composite language of "nuclear-ship" by a man with wide experience in the conventional ship field as well as the ever-expanding field of nucleonics.

The approach to the subject in *Nuclear Ship Propulsion* is such that the reader with some maritime background and an active interest in nuclear potentials can gain a systematic understanding of this vital subject. The primary concern is with merchant nuclear ships, though many of the technical concepts and safety principles apply equally well to naval nuclear ships.

It is the purpose of *Nuclear Ship Propulsion* to serve as an interpretive link between the more highly technical literature and the needs of the professional reader who seeks appreciation of nuclear technology, rather than a mastery of it.

400 Pages   132 Line Drawings   63 Tables   (Oct. '59) $10.00

MERCHANT SHIPS: A Pictorial Study

By John H. La Dage and Associates

This *greatest collection* of organized information about ships in book form has been described as a work on which superlatives can be bestowed without hesitation. By the use of 1,160 illustrations and 150,000 well chosen words of text, the factual story of merchant ships is unfolded in a most instructive and interesting manner. From the forecastle head to the tail shaft and propeller, all types of *Merchant Ships* are dissected, as by a skilled surgeon, with their innermost parts laid bare with camera and pen.

512 Pages   8½ x 11 Format   Illustrated $15.00

ENCYCLOPEDIA OF NAUTICAL KNOWLEDGE

By W. A. McEwen and A. H. Lewis

Here, unique in the current field of maritime references, is a true *Encyclopedia of Nautical Knowledge*. The exhaustive coverage contained in this volume cannot be found in any other single volume source. Presents and interprets the language of all things maritime, the ancient, the old, and the modern.

640 Pages   7 x 10 Format   Double Column   Thumb Indexed $12.50

MODERN SHIPS

Elements of Their Design, Construction and Operation

By Lt. Comdr. John H. La Dage
Chief, Section Applied Naval Architecture, U.S.M.M.A.

Modern Ships, a reference text, presents to ship's officers, cadets and students of marine transportation, shipping personnel, students of naval architecture and anyone interested in the efficient operation of ships, information from the general fields of Naval Architecture and Ship Construction, those theories and practices which apply to everyday ship operation and maintenance. This information is presented in a style readily understandable by all engaged in ship operation.

Among the many subjects covered and questions answered are the following:

How much, for example, is known about bending stresses on the welded ship in these days of ship crackings?

How is a ship's motion in waves affected by loading?

Why does a ship "smell" shoal water? And why are ships passing close aboard "sucked" together?

The answers to these and many hundreds of other interesting practical questions are covered in the following chapters:

Principal dimensions and characteristics	Tanks, bilges and piping systems
Modern types of ships	Turning and steering
Tonnage measurement	Launching
Classification	Drydocking
Freeboard and load lines	Ship's calculations
Strength of materials and ships	The ship in waves
Lines, offsets and the mold loft	Resistance and powering
Riveting and welding	Propellers and propulsion
	Ship trials

A definitive table of contents breaks down the above chapter headings into 102 subheadings covering a wide field of subjects heretofore found only by searching through many volumes.

Throughout the text, emphasis is placed on those phases of ship design, construction and operation which, in the opinion of the author, have not been accorded the importance they deserve in the education of students in the marine field. Each chapter of Modern Ships is followed by a section of review questions and a bibliography.

The student of Naval Architecture, Naval Architects and Marine Surveyors will find much information of value on the relationship of design to use and operation.

The text is illustrated with 99 photographs and 117 line drawings, graphs and schematic diagrams by Lt. Frank X. Schuler, U.S.M.S.

392 Pages.   Indexed $7.00

Fourth Edition—Revised & Enlarged

MERCHANT MARINE
OFFICERS' HANDBOOK

By E. A. Turpin and W. A. MacEwen

This new Fourth Edition (1965) of the *Merchant Marine Officers' Handbook* has been revised and corrected to serve as a modern, well indexed, practical reference book for everyday use on shipboard, and to give the essential information required for Masters' and Mates' examinations.

Following an Introduction on the day-by-day work of ship's officers, which is guaranteed good reading, the *Handbook* covers Instruments and Accessories Used in Navigation, Radar and Loran, Piloting, Tides & Currents, Sailings, Celestial Navigation, Meteorology, Cargo, Shiphandling, Cargo Gear, Ground Tackle, Signals, Rules of the Road, Radar and the Rules of the Road, Ship Construction, Maintenance and Repair, Tonnage and Stability, Fire, Emergencies, U. S. Marine Laws, Engineering for Deck Officers, First Aid and Ship Sanitation.

The large Appendices include Rules and Regulations for Deck Officers' Licenses, Commissions in the U. S. Navy Reserve, Mathematics, Tables and Useful Information.

A complete index makes quickly available, in this *Handbook,* more needed information for Deck Officers than ever compiled in any single volume.

The *Merchant Marine Officers' Handbook* is in fact a collection of important facts, half-forgotten, mislaid, left behind—you'll find them all stowed in this handy volume. It is a rich condensation of two veteran seamen's experience and research.

896 Pages   Fully Illustrated $10.00

AMERICAN MERCHANT
SEAMAN'S MANUAL

By

Felix M. Cornell and Allan C. Hoffman

With this revised and enlarged fifth edition, the Seaman's Manual remains alone in its field as the complete handbook for the merchant seaman, and an invaluable guide for the thousands of men who are sailing our merchant fleet.

By using it the "deepwater" sailor can prepare himself for his A.B. and Lifeboat Certificates, and also continue with study of Navigation, Stability, First Aid, etc., until he has enough time to sit for a Mate's License. A guarantee of the book's teaching value lies in the fact that it is being used as a standard text in all Maritime Service Training Schools.

It is chock full of the information you want, arranged so that you can find it when you need it. The book covers Seamanship, Navigation, First Aid and Ship Sanitation, Laws Concerning Merchant Seamen, Ship Construction and Stability, Handling Inflammable Liquids, Fire Prevention, Tankerman's Guide, new Rules of the Road, Handling Small Boats under Sail and Oars, an entirely new chapter on Safety—plus a bangup section of general information for all who "go down to the sea in ships."

Fully Illustrated and Indexed

880 Pages   **With 1960 Corrections**

$8.50

CMP Marine Engineering Books

RED BOOK OF MARINE ENGINEERING QUESTIONS AND ANSWERS:
Steam and Motor*

William B. Paterson

    Vol. I. Third & Second Assistant Engineer

    Vol. II. First Assistant & Chief Engineer

Both volumes of the famous "Cornell Red Book" have been completely revised in the light of current requirements. They answer representative questions in the manner required by inspectors. Numerous sample sketches are included when sketches are required as part of an answer. All problems are fully worked out.

    *Diesel— Over 2000 H.P., and Under 2000 H.P.

Vol. I.	288 Pages	Illus.	2nd Edition	1964	$5.00
Vol. II.	352 Pages	Illus.	2nd Edition	1965	$5.00

MODERN MARINE ENGINEER'S MANUAL

Alan Osbourne, Editor

Volume I. *Revised and Enlarged, 1965*   *A. B. Neild, Jr., Revision Editor*

This second edition of the modern operating "Bible" for marine engineers is a complete revision in every way and contains comprehensive coverage of all propulsion machinery aboard turbine and reciprocating-engine vessels. A team of qualified contributing editors has revised each section of the volume. Updating and rewriting where necessary, they have also retained all material from the first edition that is still in general use. *Contents:* Safety and First Aid—Engineering Materials—Pipe, Fittings and Packing—Lubrication—Bearings and Shafting—Pumps—Thermodynamics—Combustion—Marine Gas Turbines—Boilers—Boiler Operation and Maintenance—Condensers, Feedwater Systems and Evaporators—Marine Steam Turbines—Reciprocating Engines—Mathematics and Mechanics.

1184 Pages	*Illustrated*	*Indexed*	*$15.00*

Volume II.   *Alan Osbourne, Editor*

The second of the two volumes comprising the best practical handbook of marine engineering published. *Contents:* Diesel Engines—Refrigeration—Heating—Ventilation Insulation—Deck Machinery—Electricity—Instruments—Propellers—Tests and Trials —Tables.

1190 Pages	*Illustrated*	*Indexed*	*$8.50*

NUCLEAR SHIP PROPULSION

Holmes F. Crouch

Written by a nuclear specialist with broad practical marine engineering experience, this book is an interpretive link between the highly technical literature of nuclear theory and the needs of the professional who seeks an appreciative understanding of nuclear ship technology rather than a mastery of it. Footnote references are provided to guide those interested in nuclear-marine theory to the proper sources. *Contents:* Similarities and Differences—Commercial Advantages—Diversity of Fuel Forms—Fuel Calculations —Removal of Heat—*Savannah* Reactor Features—Other Ship Reactors—Gas Reactor Turbines—Areas for Break-Through—Shielding Considerations—Refueling Procedures —Design Safety—Regulatory Safety—Health Physics—The Course Ahead—Bibliography.

386 Pages	*Illustrated*	*Bibliography*	*Indexed*	*$10.00*

MARINE RADIO AND ELECTRONICS

Allan Lytel

Gives extensive coverage of the equipment and its operation in the field of marine radio and electronics. *Contents:* Introduction—Small Boat Radio—Two-Way Radiotelephone (Installation and Maintenance)—Citizen's Band Radiotelephone—Deep Water Radiotelephone—Radiotelegraph at Sea—Radar and Loran—Radio Direction Finders —Depth Finders—Other Marine Electronics—Appendices.

256 Pages	*Illustrated*	*Indexed*	*$7.00*

MODERN MARINE ELECTRICITY AND ELECTRONICS

by PERCY DE WILLARD SMITH

More than two decades have passed since the last revision of *Modern Marine Electricity*. During this time the electrical plants of merchant ships have changed extensively. This book is intended to meet the obvious need for an up-to-date manual of modern marine electrical practice. It is in fact a new book rather than a revision, since the material of the last edition has been reexamined and rewritten where necessary and wholly new textual and illustrative material comprises a major part of the work.

Subjects covered include, by chapter: basic introductory information, A-C and D-C light and power systems, voltage regulation, generators, motors, motor starting and control equipment, the group control, deck machinery, electrical propulsion, interior communication, gyrocompass, Gyro-Pilot®, maintenance, hull corrosion and cathodic protection, and a highly useful miscellany of tables, symbols, formulas and conversion factors.

The latest equipment and methods in each of these areas are discussed, illustrated, diagrammed, and thoroughly indexed. The treatment of electrical propulsion and interior communication systems is almost a book in itself, and particularly detailed coverage is given to depth sounding principles and equipment. Throughout, Mr. Smith writes with an awareness of the fundamental shift from the direct current system to alternating current with its inherent flexibility.

Another special feature of the volume is Part II, a slipcase containing 20 large schematic and wiring diagrams to further amplify an already comprehensive text.

This book has been prepared for the marine electrician and the marine engineer, but it will be of great value to shipbuilders, electrical draftsmen, engineers and electricians employed in any phase of installation, operation or maintenance of shipboard electrical equipment.

704 Pages   Illustrated   Indexed $12.75

BOOKS FOR THE MAN IN THE
ENGINE ROOM

MARINE ENGINE ROOM BLUE BOOK OF QUESTIONS AND ANSWERS—W. B. Paterson, Editor

For firemen, watertenders, oilers, junior engineers, electricians, refrigerating engineers, deck engineers, deck engine mechanics, machinists, pumpmen. *Contents:* Introduction—The Wiper—Station Bill—Fireman and Watertender Take the Watch—Questions for Fireman and Watertender—Oiler Takes His Watch—Questions for Oiler, Electrician, Refrigerating Engineer, Deck Engineer, and Deck Mechanic—Refrigeration—Tools and Their Uses. This new (1966) third edition contains 1300 multiple-choice questions and answers on the following subjects: fireman and watertender, oiler, junior engineer, refrigerating engineer, electrician, machinist, pumpman and general, emergency, fire fighting, etc.

320 Pages   *Illustrated*   *$5.00*

MARINE POWER PLANT GUIDE—W. B. Paterson

A volume of practical know-how for all duties of the unlicensed engine-room personnel. Included are questions and answers for fireman, watertender, oiler, electrician, "reefer engineer." *Contents:* Ship's Power Plants — Mechanics — Tools — Steam and Water Cycle—Piping—Valves and Traps—Packings and Insulation—Boilers—Draft—Fuel Oil—Plant Operation—Reciprocating Steam Engines—Steam Turbines—Main Condenser—Air Pumps—Pumping Systems —Friction and Lubrication—Evaporators—Electricity — Refrigeration — Safety — Useful Information—Questions and Answers.

368 Pages   *Illustrated*   *Indexed*   *$5.00*